THE ART OF
COMPUTER
PROGRAMMING

BY DONALD WILLIAM DRURY

TAB BOOKS Inc.
BLUE RIDGE SUMMIT, PA. 17214

The INKEY routine in Figs. 5-6 and 5-7 is from the May, 1979, issue of the *Radio Shack TRS-80 Newsletter*. Reprinted by permission of Tandy Corporation.

Excerpts from "A Bug in Basic" by W. D. Mauer in Chapter 5; "An Interview of Lisp" by John Allen in Chapter 8; "The Evolution of FORTH, An Unusual Language," by Charles H. Moore in Chapter 8; and the article "Whose Basic Does What" by Terri Li in the Appendix are Copyright August 1979; August 1980; and January 1981 by BYTE Publications, Inc. Reprinted by Permission.

The print formatting statement in Chapter 5 is from "The Electronic Librarian," *Kilobaud Microcomputing*, p. 53. Copyright 1979 by Kilobaud Microcomputing. All rights reserved. Used by permission.

FIRST EDITION

FIRST PRINTING

Library of Congress Cataloging in Publication Data

Drury, Donald William.
    The art of computer programming.

    Includes index.
    1. Electronic digital computers—Programming.
I. Title.
QA76.6.D78   1983   001.64'2   82-5960
ISBN 0-8306-0455-3   AACR2
ISBN 0-8306-1455-9 (pbk.)

Contents

Acknowledgments

I would like to take this opportunity to thank several companies and individuals without whose help this book might not have been written.

First I would like to thank the following publications for generously granting me permission to use copyrighted material in this book: The Tandy Corporation for permission to reprint the INKEY subroutine from the May, 1979, issue of the *TRS-80 Newsletter;* *Microcomputing* for permission to use code sequences from their November, 1979, issue; and especially *BYTE* magazine for permission to quote from several articles.

Also, let me thank Frank Atkinson and Gary Anagnostis of Datatrack Inc. Information Service of Columbus, Ohio, who deserve special recognition for their help in constructing the Index and the Glossary. Gary also resurrected over 100 pages of manuscript from a disk we thought was ruined. Bill Schwartz of the Radio Shack Computer Center deserves thanks for providing use of the equipment on which the final manuscript was printed.

Finally I would like to thank Bev Straw for a critique of the first five chapters; and last, but not least, my wife Barbara for bearing with me under the ardors of authorship.

Introduction

Many books have been written on programming in the last twenty years. During this time computers and programming have made giant strides in both power and sophistication. Many tasks once impossible to implement are now performed routinely.

One of the most important technological events of the last decade was the introduction and marketing of the microcomputer. It brings the power of computing affordably to many. The number of computers in offices, schools, and homes has increased dramatically. This exposure and the need to understand the capabilities of these machines has led to increased emphasis on "computer literacy" at all levels of education and in the general public.

With so many books published, why write another? My answer has several facets. First, in writing a book every author hopes to treat the material in a fresh new way—explain it clearly to those who perhaps had trouble with other explanations.

Second, many of the books on programming are either written for beginners who know nothing at all about computers or programming, or for professionals in computer fields. Few books address the person who has had some introduction to programming and is looking for ways to increase his skill and decrease wasted time. This person will find many practical hints in this book to help him increase his programming skills.

Third, many books are oriented toward users of large computer systems. The owner of a microcomputer is not interested in reading about Hollerith cards or card readers. He will probably never use them. In this book I concentrate on topics that are directly applicable to the microcomputer and use languages common to them in my examples.

Finally, I hope that if you are just getting acquainted with computers, you will find this book helpful in beginning on the right foot in programming. So many people develop poor programming habits that they find it difficult to change even when they know it might improve their programs. Simply by developing correct programmable habits the task will become easier and more enjoyable.

The book is organized into three main sections with a development of concepts and ideas throughout. The first two chapters cover the basics of computer languages and introduce basic computer terms and ideas.

Chapters 3 through 8 outline the sequence of program de velopment and discuss alternatives in program design. (If you are already fairly familiar with both high-level and assembly-language programming you might wish to skip Chapters 3 and 4.) This material is designed to be studied in sequence. It introduces subjects that are discussed more fully in later chapters. For this reason I discourage skipping around until after you have gone through them in order.

The applications programs in three differen computer languages given in Chapters 9, 10, and 11 illustrate many of the concepts discussed in Chapters 3 through 7. Careful study of these programs will help solidify many earlier points. In addition, you will have these programs as a starting point if you wish to expand or modify them.

The art of programming, though requiring clear thinking and meticulous attention to detail, can offer you the thrill of victory when it is completed and performing as expected. With the aid of my book you will find success more often and with less effort than before.

Chapter 1
Introduction to Programming

Computers have had such an impact on everyday life that terms such as *computer programmers, programming* the computer, *programming language*, and just plain programming are now familiar to you. For some people, however they conjure up visions of supersophisticated individuals who deal in a highly complex field. To them, just the thought of becoming a programmer seems beyond the realm of possibility at least without a great deal of training.

Fortunately this is not true. It is true that some programs are complex, and some programs do require a good deal of specialized knowledge in a particular subject matter. By following these guidelines, however, you *can* learn to program whatever task you wish the computer to perform.

Programming is logical thinking. In simplest terms, a program is a set of instructions telling a machine or a person how to do something. A *computer program*, therefore, tells the computer how to do something; in particular, it gives the computer the specific steps to perform the task you desire. When you want your computer to do a job, all you need to do is tell it exactly what you want done and how you want it done. A program is a precise set of instructions in a specific order to be executed faithfully in a literal way.

A *programming language* is merely the means by which you can communicate with your computer. There is even a language to communicate with the simplest four-function calculator. Applied to programming, a language is a necessary means to communicate your program to your computer.

Any computer performs, with literal faithfulness, those and only those instructions you give it. This characteristic makes working with computers a mixed experience. The result is that you must be careful what you tell the computer to do. A computer does exactly what you instruct it to do, regardless of how you want it done. The techniques discussed here will allow you to start realizing the potential of your computer and make you a part of the era of personal computing.

In any field or profession if you have a problem, the first step you would take is to devise a solution. In programming this solution is called an *algorithm* when it is expressed as a step-by-step procedure. You are already familiar with this type of procedure though perhaps not by this name. A simple example of an algorithm for starting your car is:

1. Open your car door.
2. Place yourself in the driver's seat.
3. Fasten the seat belt.
4. Place the key in the ignition.
5. Turn the key.
6. Depress the accelerator pedal.

At this point, if the algorithm is correct for the automobile involved, the engine should start and you will be able to drive it away.

Entering any algorithm in this form into a computer will only produce an error message. It is well known that human languages are ambiguous and cannot be used "as is" in a computer. That is, the same word or phrase can have a number of different meanings depending on usage. A computer language, on the other hand, must be precisely defined and its meanings must be completely specified.

Converting an algorithm into a form that can be used by the computer by means of one of the computer languages is called programming.

Programming is very definitely a personal thing. Two people programming the same problem do not necessarily develop the same sequence of program instructions even though they may get the same result. We are all individuals and often approach a problem in different ways depending on our background, previous experiences, and ways of thinking about problems. An engineer with a great deal of training in mathematics may use an approach requiring complex equations while someone with less background in mathematics may devise an equally satisfactory approach using only high-school algebra. One person may be satisfied to use a set of instructions that take a great deal of program memory while another may wish to look for ways to condense his program into the minimum amount of space. Each of us will want to choose a familiar approach.

Your style should grow and develop as you get into the process of programming. Your competence—and confidence—should also grow as you practice the techniques and skills explained in the following chapters.

The best way to learn to program is by practicing programming. You should find this learning period adventurous and best of all, fun! Don't be afraid to make mistakes through exploration. Your computer won't mind. Try out alternative ways of doing whatever it is you want to do with your computer.

The following chapters are a set of guidelines which many programmers, both professional and hobbyist, have found useful in creating programs in the least amount of time and effort. They are, however, only guidelines. You must decide when a particular technique or procedure will be more useful than another in helping you develop programs you wish to write.

Chapter 2
Basic Concepts

COMPUTER ORGANIZATION

Computer technology has its own unique language, which we must familiarize ourselves with in order for more effective and enjoyable programming. In this chapter, I'd like to introduce and define some of the fundamental computer terms, which you may or may not be familiar with.

Information within the computer is stored as groups of "bits." A *bit*, which stands for Binary digIT, can only be either a 1 or a 0. This "two-state logic" is the only practical way to represent information in present day computers. The two states of the circuits (1 or 0) are referred to as either "on" or "off" and represented by the symbols "1" and "0" respectively. Virtually all information processing today is done in this binary format. In most microprocessors these bits are structured in groups of eight. A group of eight bits is called a *byte*. And one byte is equal to one *word*. A group of four bits, or half a byte, is called a *nibble*.

Computer instructions are represented internally as one or more bytes. The binary code used to represent instructions is dictated by the manufacturer and is an important factor in determining the speed and power of any individual microprocessor.

NUMBER SYSTEMS

To the user, binary format is extremely difficult to use and methods to avoid your having to use it are readily available in most

4

computers on the market today. Of all the ways in which information may be entered into the computer, it is the least understandable. Ultimately, however, all other languages must be translated or converted to binary format before the computer can execute the instructions it is given.

For example, the number we call "nine" is represented by the following combination of binary digits.

00001001

Each digit represents a power of two. The bit or symbol on the extreme right represents two to the zero power. The next one to the left represents two to the first power and so on. The digit farthest to the left represents two to the seventh power (see Fig. 2-1).

Therefore, in evaluating the number above we have from right to left:

$1 \times 1 \quad = 1$ (2 power 0)
$0 \times 2 \quad = 0$ (2 power 1)
$0 \times 4 \quad = 0$ (2 power 2)
$1 \times 8 \quad = 8$ (2 power 3)
$0 \times 16 \quad = 0$ (2 power 4)
$0 \times 32 \quad = 0$ (2 power 5)
$0 \times 64 \quad = 0$ (2 power 6)
$0 \times 128 = 0$ (2 power 7)

Total $\quad = 9$

Such a system is obviously impractical to use on a continuing basis. It is much easier to remember the number "9" than "00001001."

Power of 2	Value
0	1
1	2
2	4
3	8
4	16
5	32
6	64
7	128

Fig. 2-1. Powers of two.

Binary Code	Purpose
10101111	Clear accumulator and carry
00111010	Get first number
01100000	
00000000	
01000111	Put in B Register
00111010	Get Second Number
01000001	
00000000	
10010001	Subtract B from A
00110010	Store Result
01000011	
00000000	

Fig. 2-2. Subtraction program in binary.

The difficulty in programming in binary is illustrated by the program in Fig. 2-2. This program obtains two whole numbers from memory locations, subtracts the second from the first, and stores the result in a third memory location. There are two coding errors in this program. If you are familiar with Z-80 assembly language, you might try to find the errors. Obviously the potential for mistakes is very great, and the time necessary to find and correct errors is prohibitive for programs of any complexity or length. The correct version is shown in Fig. 2-3.

More convenient representations have been devised, however, which improve the person-machine interface (Fig. 2-4).

The octal numbering system encodes three binary bits into a unique symbol. In this system any combination of three bits is represented by a numeral between 0 and 7. Octal has been traditionally used on older computers which were using various numbers of bits ranging from eight to perhaps sixty-four. This eight-bit format has become standard.

In a more practical scheme—the hexadecimal numbering system—a group of four bits is encoded as one hexadecimal digit. Hexadecimal digits are represented by the symbols from zero to nine and by the letters A, B, C, D, E, and F. For example, the four bits 0000 equals the hexadecimal "0," 0011 equals three, and 1111 equals the letter "F."

Our subtraction program now becomes much easier to read (Fig. 2-5). It is somewhat of an improvement since there are only

Binary Code	Purpose
10101111	Clear accumulator
00111010	Get first number
01000000	
00000000	
01000111	Store in B Register
00111010	Get Next Number
01000001	
00000000	
10010000	Subtract B from A
00110010	Store Result
01000011	
00000000	

Fig. 2-3. Corrected version of subtraction program.

Decimal	Binary	Hex	Octal
0	0000	0	0
1	0001	1	1
2	0010	2	2
3	0011	3	3
4	0100	4	4
5	0101	5	5
6	0110	6	6
7	0111	7	7
8	1000	8	10
9	1001	9	11
10	1010	A	12
11	1011	B	13
12	1100	C	14
13	1101	D	15
14	1110	E	16
15	1111	F	17

Fig. 2-4. Equivalent values in four number systems.

two symbols for each byte instead of eight. It makes errors much easier to detect.

Earlier I stated that the computer only understands binary instruction codes, and so these hexadecimal codes have to be converted to binary before they can be executed. This is a tiresome, boring task in which all sorts of petty mistakes can be made such as the transposition of a bit or digit or the omission of a bit.

Hexadecimal Code	Purpose
AF	Clear accumulator and carry
3A	Get first number from
40	Memory location 0040
00	
47	Put in B Register
3A	Get Second Number from
41	Memory Location 0041
00	
90	Subtract B from A
32	Store Result in
43	Memory Location 0043
00	

Fig. 2-5. Subtraction program in hexadecimal.

Conversion however, from one system to another, is a perfect job for the computer since a computer never gets tired or bored and never makes silly mistakes. Most microcomputers today come equipped with a program that will do this all for you. It is usually completely automatic and many users do not realize that it even exists.

Even with two symbols instead of eight for each byte, there are still problems in understanding what the code really does. There is also no easy way, in the hexadecimal version, of distinguishing instructions from data.

ASSEMBLY LANGUAGE

One answer to this problem is to assign a name to each instruction code. The code name is called a *mnemonic* or memory jogger and describes what the instruction does. Every microprocessor manufacturer provides such a list for the microprocessor instruction set. There is nothing sacred about them, and you can use your own if you wish. They are standard, however, and so are most easily understood in this form by other users.

A second reason for using the standard mnemonics of the manufacturer is the fact that all commercially produced assembler programs, i.e., programs which input assembler mnemonics and produce binary object code which can be loaded directly into the computer, will recognize only the standard mnemonics as valid inputs.

Once you have chosen labels for each instruction, you still need to find a way to program this format into the computer. The program still must be translated either into hexadecimal or directly into binary before it can be used by the computer.

This can be done manually. That is, you can translate the labels into instructions one by one. This is called *hand assembly*. It is another of those tasks that you let the computer handle. Like hexadecimal-to-binary conversion, hand assembly is an uninteresting rote task which can be plagued with numerous minor errors. Most microprocessors complicate the process even more by having instructions with various byte (word) lengths. Some instructions have one byte, some two, some three bytes, or even more. Some instructions require data in the second and third bytes; others require memory addresses, register numbers, or other types of information.

A computer program that does all this automatically is called an *assembler*. The assembler program translates your program written

Assembler	Mnemonics	Purpose
XOR	A	Zero accumulator and carry
LD	A, (0040)	Get first number
LD	B, A	Store in B
LD	A, (0041)	Get Second Number
SUB	B	Subtract the two
LD	(0043), A	Store result

Fig. 2-6. Subtraction program in assembler mnemonics.

in mnemonics (called the *source* program) into a machine language or *object* program which the computer can execute. Figure 2-6 is an example of the output of such a program.

Most assemblers, in addition to translating the instructions into their binary equivalents, provide such additional conveniences as:

1. Allowing the user to assign names to memory locations, input and output devices, and even sequences of instructions.

2. Converting data or addresses from various number systems to binary and converting characters into their ASCII or EBCDIC binary codes.

3. Performing some arithmetic as part of the assembly process.

4. Telling the loader where to put the instructions and data.

5. Allowing you to assign areas of memory for temporary data storage and to place fixed data in program memory.

6. Allowing you to control the format of the program listing and the input and output devices used.

7. In some cases you can provide information required to include standard programs from program libraries or programs written at some other time in the current program.

Naturally the size of the assembler program increases as more features are added and more memory is required to use it. The important point is not how many features it has but how easy it is to work with in normal use.

Assembler programs have their own rules, by which you have to learn to abide. These typically include the use of certain markers (such as spaces, commas, semicolons, or colons) in the proper places, correct spelling, the proper control information, and with some the correct placement of names and numbers. These, however, are minor inconveniences, which are easily tolerated and overcome compared to the alternatives.

THE MONITOR

Even with the use of an assembler and careful checking of the program logic, your machine-language program may not operate as you intend. It then becomes necessary to determine what is happening to the data during program execution.

To facilitate this task most microcomputers have *monitor* programs available, either within the operating system or as separate programs. These enable examination of register contents and memory addresses at specified points during execution.

Most monitor programs allow you to alter the contents of specific memory locations and registers, change the address at which program execution will start or continue, move blocks of memory from one location to another, find specific sequences of code within the program, and designate a series of program addresses at which execution will halt and the various registers and memory locations can be checked.

Programs such as this have as their sole function the ability to permit you to determine whether or not your machine-language program is executing as you intended. If it is not, the program helps you find out what errors are causing the false results and permits you to correct them.

HIGH-LEVEL LANGUAGES

Many of these assembly-level problems can be solved by using *high-level* or *procedure-oriented languages*. Such languages allow you to describe tasks in forms that are problem oriented rather than computer oriented. Each statement in a high-level language performs a recognizable function. It will generally correspond to many assembly-language instructions.

A program called a *compiler* translates the high-level source program into object code or machine-language instructions.

A number of high-level languages exist for different purposes. If you can tell the computer what to do in algebraic notation more easily than in some other form, you can write your program in FORTRAN (FORmula TRANslation language), the oldest and one of the most widely used of the high-level languages. If you want to add two numbers using FORTRAN, just tell the computer:

$$SUM = NUM1 + NUM2$$

This is much simpler (and shorter) than the equivalent machine- or assembly-language program.

Other high-level languages available for microcomputers include COBOL (for business applications), PASCAL (another algebraic language), BASIC (the most commonly supplied microcomputer language), and LISP (a language used for symbolic manipulation and language simulation).

I am not suggesting here that such usage is exclusive. You can write programs using algebraic notation, for example, in any of the languages. I merely make note that certain languages were created originally for certain types of application, and that using a language designed primarily for your type of problem will result in easier, more efficient coding.

Obviously high-level languages make programs easier and faster to write. It is estimated that a programmer can write a program about ten times faster in a high-level language as compared with assembly language. This is not to mention all the other steps in the programming process, which also become simpler and faster.

THE INTERPRETER

Even with the compiler, however, you still have the problem of verifying program operation. In examining object code produced by a compiler, it is often difficult to equate a specific section of code with its corresponding high-level instruction. In addition you are concerning yourself with registers, addresses, etc., which are necessary, but not pertinent to, your particular problem.

What is needed is a way to execute the source program statements directly, so you can check their operation and modify them, if necessary, before compiling. To accomplish this you use a program called an *interpreter*.

An interpreter allows you to write your program in a high-level language, execute it directly to verify operation, and modify or reexecute any portion of the program until it is correct. This is all done before compilation so that when you compile your program, you know it is operating correctly. You might think of the interpreter program as an equivalent for high-level languages of the assembler monitor program.

SUMMARY

Figure 2-7 will help us review material treated in this chapter. As you look from the bottom to the top of the diagram, you find increasing complexity from source program to object program. At the same time it becomes easier to write the program. In essence,

High Level	PASCAL, FORTH
	APL, PL/1, LISP
	FORTRAN, BASIC, COBOL
Assembly Level	ASSEMBLY LANGUAGE
	OCTAL, HEXADECIMAL
Machine Code	BINARY

Fig. 2-7. Levels of complexity in programming languages.

as the computer assumes more of the translation you can write your programs in a simpler more "human"-oriented way. This has some disadvantages, which show up in slower execution and greater memory usage. This occurs because the programs required to translate high-level instructions have many compromises made necessary to take care of different situations which could arise.

At the bottom there is the binary object code, the direct machine language of the computer. This requires no translation at all but is so error prone that it is almost never used except for special purposes.

Immediately above that you will see octal or hexadecimal machine code. There is a slight improvement in readability here but it is still very far from anything approaching a human problem format.

Next there is assembly language with mnemonics for the various instructions. At least you can begin having an idea of what these instructions do in the program without reference to a translation table. It still takes many assembly-language instructions to perform program functions such as adding or subtracting, or displaying a line of characters on the video display unit.

Finally there are the high-level procedure-oriented languages where instructions are closest in form to human languages. These are the easiest to write but tend to execute somewhat slower than programs written in assembler.

Useful programs for assembly-language programming are:

1. Hexadecimal loaders to put the object code into memory.

2. Assembler programs to automatically translate assembler mnemonics into object code.

3. Monitor programs to assist in testing and verifying correct program operation.

Programs useful for writing programs in high-level languages are:

1. Interpreter programs, the high level equivalent of the Monitor.

2. Compilers to translate the high level instructions into machine code.

Chapter 3

Problem Definition
and Program Design

One can approach programming in a number of ways. The inexperienced or naive programmer, might simply start writing the program. Very few people have this enviable ability. It has been said that about 10 percent of all programmers can sit down and write a workable program on the first try. Unfortunately the majority of the remaining programmers believe they are among this 10 percent. The result is that most programs need extensive modification and testing before they will perform as expected.

Writing workable programs "off the cuff" can only be done with the simplest programs. In most significant programs there are too many alternatives to keep track of, and too many things to consider for anyone without advance planning to program successfully.

For example, a simple program to get two numbers from the keyboard, add them together, and display the result, would be fairly easy to design. You have a simple sequence of instructions to code with no alternate paths. They can be listed in sequence and will execute with little problem.

If the program is made more complicated by adding conditions (such as, if the sum is greater than 10 then subtract 5 and divide the remainder by two, otherwise add the first number to the sum again. In either case display the result) you would have difficulty keeping track of things. This is still a fairly simple example, but such a task becomes impossible in a program of any size or complexity.

If programs are generally too complicated to write out "off the cuff," what other alternatives do you have for designing programs that will perform correctly and efficiently? The obvious answer is that you must determine in advance what logical structures will represent the operation of the program as you wish it to be. To do this you must be aware of some things that might affect either the operation of the program or the accuracy of the results. This is the total programming process and includes much, much more than merely writing program code in a programming language.

The steps in developing programs with minimum time and effort are:

1. Problem definition
2. Program design
3. Coding (writing the code)
4. Debugging and testing
5. Documentation
6. Redesign if necessary

This list, of course, is merely the tip of the iceberg. Simple programs, developed in later chapters, will aid your understanding and provide examples of the techniques and considerations necessary. Later we will also put these techniques together to analyze examples of programs in several computer languages.

PROBLEM DEFINITION

Chapter 1 stated that given a problem the first thing to do is devise a solution. At that stage of the problem-solving procedure, several important steps toward a solution have already been completed. If a problem is stated in a human language, the first thing you must do is define precisely the problem in all its ramifications.

You must consider the input and output of information. What forms will it take for your purposes, and what forms will the computer require for processing? What should be done if wrong information is entered? How will the computer know when the information is there?

Now consider the processing of information. What basic procedure will give the results you wish? How fast must they be produced? What are the memory requirements for the program code? The data? Any tables used by the program? What about special cases in processing? How accurate must the results be? How should the program handle processing errors?

What other errors could occur and which are most likely? Which errors might not immediately be recognized as errors? What methods can be used to recover from errors and proceed with normal execution? Are there ambiguities? How can the system or the program distinguish between similar errors? Are there errors which could require special system procedures or processing?

Finally, what about human factors? What procedures are most natural and customary? What instructions are needed for the inexperienced operator? How is the operator informed of errors? Are the displays easily read and understood? Is the program easy to use? Are there shortcuts for the experienced operator? Can the operator determine or reset the state of the system after distractions or interruptions?

To simplify the description a bit, let's assume that our programming language will be a high-level one such as BASIC, and that we have the use of an interactive interpreter program to enter and test our coding. This allows us to disregard all concern for the form of the input and output statements, except for the way they appear on the display. We should be aware that the interpreter automatically converts our ASCII coded input into binary before processing, and converts the result back again in to our display.

The first decision concerns the information to be input. Do we want this calculation performed on a single pair of numbers, or do we want the program to accept more than one set of numbers? The ability to vary the numbers to be processed will result in a more useful program and one which can be used in many situations.

What can be done if only one number is input from the keyboard? Do we want the computer to make sure two values are there, or to go ahead and attempt the calculation displaying some type of error message even if two values are not present at execution? A third option would be to insert some default value if nothing is input from the keyboard. If a default value is chosen, which input would receive it, or would it apply equally to either or both?

Answers to these questions clearly depend on what significance the calculation has. The numbers we begin with must be correct for the result to be correct. This implies checking the data to insure that it is there. If we plan on operating with one value but want the option of inserting a range of values for the second number, then a default scheme has merit as a time saver since only one value need be entered for each calculation.

Decisions such as these must be made at every stage of the programming process. You must decide which options will efficiently give the results.

In processing numbers there are three situations which must

be described. The basic addition is given by:

$$SUM = A + B$$

If the sum is greater than 10; the procedure is:

$$SUM = (SUM - 5)/2$$

If the sum is equal to or less than 10; the procedure is:

$$SUM = SUM + A$$

where A and B are the input variables and the usual algebraic conventions are assumed.

Computational speed is not important here, since these results are not being used elsewhere. Nor are memory requirements, unless this small program were to be incorporated as a part of a larger, more complex program. There are no special cases accounted for here. If any arise later, the design of the program may have to be reconsidered to take them into account.

The accuracy of the results will not be specified, though. This requirement will affect both the processing time and the data storage requirements of the program. In addition, special coding may be included if the results are displayed in a particular format. In the program it shall be assumed that accuracy to two decimal places is sufficient.

The most common error would be failure to insert a number for the program to process, or to insert a letter in place of the required number. In either case the program requires the operator to enter the correct information before proceeding. This is easily arranged. Most interpreters require information for input depending on the input variable specified.

Computational errors are unlikely in so simple a program. The possibility of negative results is precluded by the processing sequence, so long as the entries are positive.

Finally, it must be decided what prompt messages are most likely to be understood and interpretered correctly by the inexperienced user. He is not interested in anything but the result. Will he understand what do to if an error message appears? Will he understand what is displayed during processing, if errors occur, and when the results are displayed?

Let's stop here for a minute and summarize what has been decided about the problem solutions. First of all, the program accepts only numeric input from the operator. The operator is required to input two values before processing will start.

There are three mathematical algorithms which must be included. These are:

1. SUM = A + B
2. SUM = (SUM − 5)/2
3. SUM = SUM + A

Results will be displayed to two decimal places.

All prompts and error messages will clearly state what to do at that particular point.

The operator is able to repeat the computation with new values if desired.

PROGRAM DESIGN

We have now specified what our program is to accomplish. The next step is to design the program structure that will best accomplish this objective. There are several ways to approach this task. All of them have some obvious principles in common. Some of which are the same principles applied to any design.

1. Proceed in small steps. Do not try to do too much at one time.

2. Divide large jobs into smaller, logically separate tasks. Make the subtasks as independent as possible to ease the work involved in testing. This also allows you to make changes in one module without affecting the others.

3. Keep the program as simple as possible. This makes it easier to find mistakes.

4. Use pictorial or graphic descriptions where possible.

5. Make the program as clear and simple as possible. You can improve performance later once the system is working properly.

6. Proceed systematically. Use checklists and standard procedures.

7. Don't tempt fate. Use only methods you are sure of, or use them very carefully watching for situations that might cause confusion.

8. Plan for later testing and debugging.

9. Use simple and consistent terms and procedures.

10. Have the design complete before coding.

11. Be particularly careful of factors which may change. Make any changes in the program as simple as possible.

MODULAR PROGRAMMING

Similar to making an outline before writing a paper or article *modular programming* divides the program into sections according to function. Then each section is further subdivided until the final sections are small enough to easily program and understand.

With this example program the problem can be divided into three main sections: data input, processing, and display of results. Each of these can again be divided into smaller sections.

The program designer must decide how to divide the program into modules, and how to cut them together once coding has been completed.

This type of design has a number of advantages. It is easier to write, debug, and test a single module than an entire program. And it will be useful in more than the immediate program, particularly if it performs a reasonably common task.

Such division allows you to divide tasks, and to use previously written and tested programs to perform standard functions with only slight modification. Changes can be made to one module rather than the entire system. Errors can be isolated and then pinned down to a single module. Modular programming gives some idea of how much progress has been made in the program design and how much of the work is left.

There are such obvious advantages that sometimes the disadvantages are ignored. Modules may be difficult to fit together (especially if different people write them). They may require very careful documentation since they may affect other parts of the program. Difficulty in testing and debugging. Programs may be difficult to modularize or extra time and memory may be required to repeat functions in different modules.

In addition, separate programs (called *drivers*) might be written just to produce sample data to test the modules. These require extra programming efforts which add nothing to the program.

Finally, there are no systematic methods for modularizing programs. We must try to restrict the amount of information shared by modules and make them as independent of one another as possible.

The following principles provide some guidelines in the use of modular programming.

1. Modules that use the same data must be part of the same overall module.

2. Two modules in which the first uses or depends on the second (not the reverse) should be separate.

3. A module used by more than one other module must be part of an overall different module.

4. Two modules whose frequencies of usage are greatly different must be part of separate modules.

5. The structure or organization of related data must be contained within a single module.

Finding it difficult to modularize your program is a strong indication that the program is poorly defined. Too many cases requiring special handling or processing are problems which can easily be corrected by redefining the task of the program.

The program example we have been discussing appears in modular form as shown in Fig. 3-1. Each input variable is a separate module, each of the processing sections is a separate module, and the output is the final module.

THE FLOWCHART

The most familiar method of program design is the *flowchart*. Programming textbooks describe how to write complete flowcharts in order to begin writing the actual program. Since few programmers ever work this way, flowcharting has been more of a nuisance

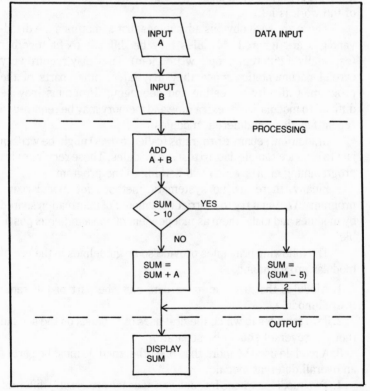

Fig. 3-1 Modular flowchart.

20

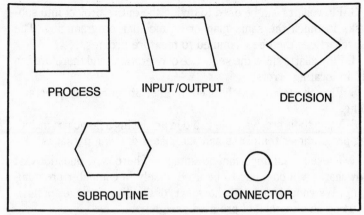

Fig. 3-2. Common flowchart symbols.

than a design method. The technique, however, does have a place in the arsenal of design tools. We shall attempt to show both the advantages and disadvantages of the flowchart in program design.

The basic advantage of the flowchart is that it provides a picture of the entire system being design. People find this picture more helpful than written descriptions. It is the classic example of a picture being worth a thousand words. Logical errors and inconsistencies are often clearly notable rather than hiding in a printed page. At its best the flowchart is a picture of the entire program showing the interrelations of each of the various parts.

Figure 3-2 shows us the most common flowchart symbols along with their meanings. The rectangle always represents some sequence or process which is carried out by the computer. The diamond shape is a decision symbol which signals a possible branching or alteration in the sequence of execution of the program instructions. The parallelogram is used to show the input of information, particularly operator input from the keyboard. Another common symbol is the small circle, which indicates connections between the various portions of a program when the flowchart is too large to fit on a single page. The other miscellaneous symbols are not widely used in microcomputer programming.

Flowcharts possess a number of other advantages for program design.

1. Standard symbols exist as described above. This makes flowcharts easy to recognize.

2. Flowcharts can be understood by people without a programming background.

3. Flowcharts can be used to divide the entire project into sub-tasks in much the same manner as modular programming. The flowchart can then be examined to measure progress.

4. Flowcharts show the sequence of operations and therefore can aid in locating errors.

5. Flowcharts are widely used in other areas besides programming.

6. Many tools are available to aid in producing a flowchart including programmer templates and automated drawing packages.

These are all important advantages. There is no question that flowcharts will continue to be used widely in computer programming. We should be aware, however, of the disadvantages of flowcharting as a method of program design.

1. Flowcharts are difficult to design, draw, and change in all but the simplest situations.

2. There is no way to debug or to test a flowchart.

3. Flowcharts tend to become cluttered so that important details are masked by detailed, unimportant information.

4. Flowcharts show only the program organization. They do not show how the data is organized or the structure of the input/output sections.

5. Flowcharts allow us to design in an unstructured and haphazard manner. This makes for more design errors which must later be corrected.

Flowcharting then, is a helpful technique which should not be carried too far. They are useful as documentation since they have standarized forms and are understandable to a nonprogrammer. However, as a design tool they cannot provide more than a starting outline. The programmer cannot debug a detailed flowchart and the flowchart is often more difficult to design than the program itself.

Sometimes several versions of a flowchart are useful. For example, one could be written in layman's language for nonprogrammers. A second in terms of the program variables might be useful to other programmers. A third, called a data flowchart, could show how particular types of data move through the system passing from one part of the program to the next.

Figure 3-3 illustrates an example of a flowchart. Because of the simplicity of the example, the modular form shown in Fig. 3-1, and the flowchart for the program are identical.

STRUCTURED PROGRAMMING

Another technique useful in writing logically clear and efficient

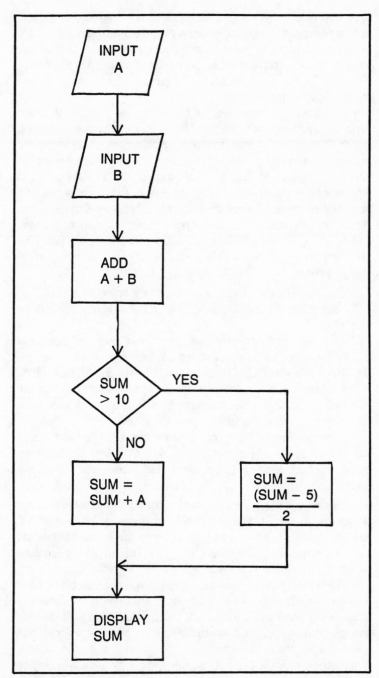

Fig. 3-3. Sample flowchart.

programs is *structured programming*. This is not a separate system or way of programming, but rather a way of organizing the program procedure in order to make it simple and trouble free. It does not exclude the other techniques mentioned here; rather it is a combination of them suited to the particular circumstances and problems involved in the programming task.

Structured programming is based on the premise that any programming task can be reduced to a collection of basic concepts, which fit together in very defined ways. There are only two basic structures in any programming language: *process,* where a specified action or sequence of actions are taken upon a certain data item, and a *branch* or *decision*, where program flow is altered on a test of a specified condition. I want to show that other well-defined structures are composed of the same basic structures mentioned above, and so are composite structures. Most textbooks or articles on structured programming will list some or all of the following structures as basic.

1. *Sequence*—a composite of two or more process blocks.

2. *If-then-else*—a combination of two process blocks and a decision block

3. *Loops*—a combination of a single process block and a decision block. These are usually subdivided according to whether the process block is executed before or after testing the condition involved in the decision. If the test is first, that is, if it is possible to skip the processing completely the structure is called a *do-while* structure. Otherwise it is designated as a *do-until* structure.

4. *Case structure*—this is a combination of several decision blocks and several process blocks arranged so that the first block is executed if the first decision is true, the second if the second is true, and so on.

Figure 3-4 illustrates the basic structures mentioned above drawn with flowchart symbols. These structures can be combined in any way desired. They can be nested, for example, one completely included within any of the others to any level of complexity required by the design of the program.

A few fundamental rules must be followed to insure correct and easily traceable logic. First, each structure must be limited to a single entry point and a single exit point. This extends all the way from the entire program, down to the smallest process or decision in a specific portion of the program.

Second, only the basic structures and their composites may be used in developing program logic.

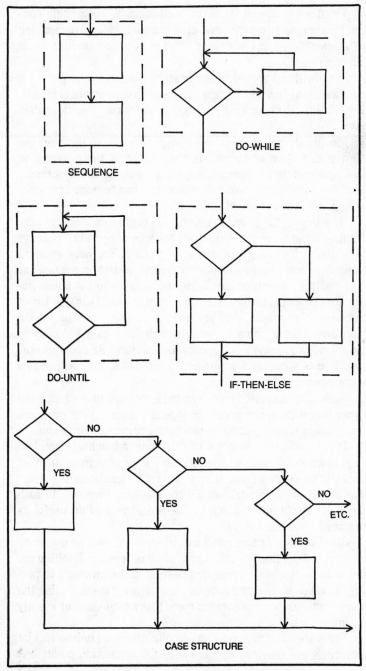

SEQUENCE

DO-WHILE

DO-UNTIL

IF-THEN-ELSE

NO

YES

NO

YES

NO

ETC.

YES

CASE STRUCTURE

Fig. 3-4. Basic program structures drawn with flowchart symbols.

25

Third, each nested structure used must be completely contained within the structure of which it is a part. Most programming languages require this with loops, but it is here extended to all structures.

Fourth, there should be no branching unless it is part of a structure. Branches which are not parts of structures are automatically eliminated by strict adherence to the structures described above.

Finally, do not attempt to optimize, that is, to increase the speed of operation or reduce memory usage of the program by violating any of the above rules. If it becomes necessary to optimize either memory usage or execution time this can be done later after the logic has been checked and verified.

By studying the above rules, you can begin to see some of the advantages and disadvantages. The sequence of operations is easy to trace allowing you to test and debug easily. You have standard terminology and a limited number of structures to become familiar with, and the structures can easily be made into modules. Researchers in computer programming have proved that this list of structures is complete. Any program can be written using these structures. The program is partly self documenting and easy to read. Structured programs are easy to describe with program outlines. Use of structured programming increases your output as a programmer.

Basically, structured programming forces you to be disciplined in your approach to laying out the logical design of your program. The result is more systematic and better organized programs.

Disadvantages include the fact that only a few high-level languages such as PASCAL will directly accept the structures. In other cases you will have to take the extra step of translating the structures into the appropriate code for the language involved. In such cases, the structured version of the program is often useful as program documentation.

Structured programs often execute more slowly or use more memory, or both than would otherwise be necessary. Limiting the structures to the basic forms makes some tasks awkward to perform. In other words, any program can be programmed using the basic structures, but this does not mean that we can do so efficiently or conveniently.

The standard structures can be quite confusing unless special precautions are taken to define where the separation points are between the basic units. This can be particularly confusing with nested loops and especially nested if-then-else structures.

Structured programs consider only the sequence of program operation, and this may at times make the handling of data awkward.

Many programmers are not familiar with structured programming and may find the method awkward and restrictive.

I am not trying to get you to become a structured programming "nut." Nor do I encourage you not to use it. It is merely one more tool in your programming kit which you can use, whenever appropriate, with any or all of the other techniques we will discuss. Whichever technique works best in a particular situation is the one for you.

Structured programming brings discipline to program design. It forces you to limit the types of structures and the sequence of operations used. It often reminds you of inconsistencies or possible combinations of inputs. It aids in debugging, testing, and documentation.

Structured programming, however, is not simple. You must define the problem with sufficient detail, and work through the logic carefully. This can be tedious and difficult, but it results in a clearly written, working program.

In applying structured programming to your programming tasks the following rules will be helpful.

1. Begin by writing a basic flowchart to help design the logic of the program.

2. Start with the basic structures. Any program can be written using only those structures.

3. Indent each level of structure a few spaces from the previous level so it is clear which statements belong where.

4. Emphasize simplicity and readability. Leave lots of spaces, use meaningful names and make expressions as clear as possible. Don't try to reduce the logic requirements at the expense of clarity.

5. Comment the program in an organized manner.

6. Check the logic. Try all special cases or extreme conditions and a few representative sample cases. Find as many errors as you can early in the programming process.

The structured version of our example is shown in Fig. 3-5. Only two of our structures are needed for this example, the sequence and if-then-else. Each structure is indented to its proper level in relation to the complete program.

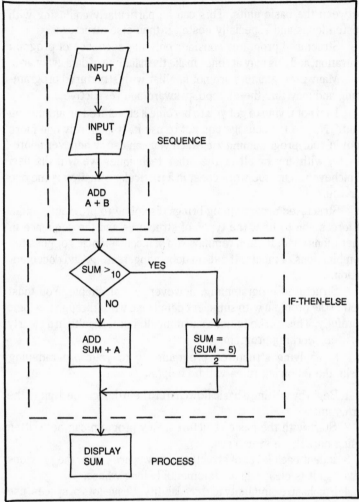

INPUT
A

INPUT
B

ADD
A + B

SEQUENCE

SUM >₁₀

YES

NO

IF-THEN-ELSE

ADD
SUM + A

$$SUM = \frac{(SUM - 5)}{2}$$

DISPLAY
SUM

PROCESS

Fig. 3-5. Structured flowchart.

TOP-DOWN DESIGN

Another popular method of program design is *top-down design*. Assuming that the program is modular, this method is also compatible with structured programming.

Top-down design addresses the problem of how to check and integrate the various program modules. While dividing the program into the subtasks, called program modules, we create the problem of how to check and organize them into an integrated program which works together.

In top-down design, begin by writing the overall supervisory program. Temporarily, the various subprogram modules are replaced with "stubs." These are short, temporary programs which record the entry and provide an answer to a selected program. This permits testing of the supervisory program.

Once assured that the overall logic is correct, begin expanding the stubs by replacing them with program modules. These may also contain stubs, which can be replaced later in the programming process when the current level of the module has been successfully debugged. This process is continued until all stubs have been replaced with working programs.

You can see here how testing and integration of the program modules takes place at each level of testing rather than all at the end as in flowcharting or strict modular programming. No special driver programs or data generators need to be written to test the operation of a program module. The program itself can perform this task. You also get a clear picture of where you are in the design process.

There are, however, occasional problems with this method. If errors occur at the top levels and escape detection until later, results can be catastrophic. In bottom-up or modular design, the effects of errors are usually limited to a single module.

Top-down design may not result in useful modules. A module may work well in the original program but may need extensive revision to perform in another program. In addition, the design of this method may not take full advantage of either hardware or software capabilities of the computer it is designed to run on.

A final problem may be the stubs themselves. If they do more than indicate that the jump has taken place, there may be problems in writing them. Again, this is design and coding of sequences which will never be used in the final version of the program.

Chapter 4
Data Structure

The process by which the input data becomes the result you desire, i.e., designing the program algorithm, is only a part of the total programming process. Of equal importance is the form or structure which the data must have in order for the program to work effectively. This design of data structures is the "other side of the coin" of effective program design. The two are equally important and necessary in the process of program development.

The form of the data when it is arranged for processing and storage will often determine how effective the program will be when processed, and how quickly and easily the results can be produced. It will also be a major influence on the design of the program algorithm since most algorithms assume a predefined data structure.

Deciding how the data will be presented to the algorithm becomes a major design decision. It should be made before, or concurrent with, the design of the algorithm itself since any changes in the data structure might possibly require a complete redesign of the program.

Naturally there are tradeoffs between speed of execution and amount of memory committed to data storage in any of the organization methods. If speed is most important and there is sufficient memory available, then a table or list might be indicated. On the other hand, if memory requirements are critical you might wish to consider an algorithm to compute the necessary data as you go through the program. This would naturally slow down execution of the program.

These decisions must be made early in the design process and must take into account all the requirements of the program as outlined in the problem definition stages. As the author of the program, it is your task to decide what can be tolerated by the application in terms of speed and program size. Your job is to devise the best possible compromise between the various conflicting requirements of your program.

I am sure you are familiar with many of the common data structures used, but a brief review here will establish a common terminology with which to discuss the various data structures and their uses.

Generally, theoreticians divide data structures into two groups. These are *linear* structures, in which the data items are arranged serially one after another; and *nonlinear* structures, in which the items are linked or organized in some other manner.

In discussing data structures, let's follow this grouping as it suits our purpose but also reserve the right to depart from it to clarify a point or make a distinction.

The most common linear structure is the *sequential list,* or more commonly *list.* This consists of data items placed one after the other into designated memory locations as they are received by the program. Whenever an item is needed, the program goes to the start of the list and searches through the items until the correct one is obtained.

Two variations on this idea are the *linked list* and the *circular list.* A linked list is a list whereby the location in memory of the next item is included into the data. This allows storage of the list items in the most convenient locations, rather than in a contiguous block of memory needed for the sequential list. If the location of the previous item is also stored as a part of the data, the list is then referred to as a *doubly linked list.* A circular list is arranged to automatically shift back to the beginning when the program reaches the end of the list.

These shifts and designations are made possible by the memory addresses incorporated in the data item. The addresses are termed *pointers* because they point to, or designate, the next memory location to be accessed.

A *table* is a list that is ordered in some specific way, either alphabetically or numerically. This permits us to find particular items faster and more easily.

The sequential list forces us to start at the beginning and search through each entry until we find the item we are looking for.

This is like looking for the definition of a word in a dictionary where all the words have been printed in random order. An alphabetical ordering of the list on the other hand permits faster location of any specific item. The same argument can be applied to numerical ordering.

Two other structures much used in assembly-language programming are the *stack* and the *queue*. I am not implying that these are limited to assembly-language programming. They are used in all levels of programming. But assembler programming is the place where most programmers become involved with these structures for the first time.

The stack is classed as a last-in-first-out *(LIFO)* structure. The usual analogy is that of a stack of plates sitting on a counter. As in the stack of plates, the first item to be withdrawn or used is the one on the top of the stack. This is usually the last item to have been placed there.

In microcomputer programming the stack is used in two ways. Its primary use is as a temporary storage place for memory addresses to which program control is returned following execution of subroutines. (A *subroutine* is a segment of code that can be used in more than one place in a program without rewriting it each time.)

A second use of the stack is for temporary data storage. This must be done very carefully, however, as you are mixing data and program addresses. If a data item is put back as an address, the computer won't know the difference. The result of such executions are unpredictable, but almost certainly catastrophic.

The queue is a first-in-first-out *(FIFO)* structure. The analogy here is the ticket line at the theater; the first person in line is the first to obtain service.

A common use of a queue in microcomputers, is in executive or supervisory programs where several peripheral devices are placed in a queue awaiting access to the central processing unit (CPU). In such cases the first device requesting service will be the first to obtain access when the processor becomes available. Each of the others, then, gain access as the one ahead completes its task.

The lists and table structure we have discussed are linear structures. Although all data structures are implemented this way within the computer memory, it is often convenient to think of them as multidimensional in nature.

The *array* is one of the most common of these multidimensional structures. Consider a table as an array with a single dimension. Another way to think of an array is as a numerically ordered table.

Each item is indexed with a number (called a *subscript*) used to designate which particular item of information (called an *element*) you want the program to use. In most computer languages the number of dimensions possible in an array is unlimited. Practical limitations on the amount of computer memory available for these structures, and the task of keeping the various items in mind, will limit the number of dimensions to a maximum of three.

Each dimension of the array is represented by a numerical subscript. In most high-level languages these multidimensional subscripts are separated by commas and enclosed in parentheses. For example, the element occupying the third position in the second row of a two-dimensional array would be designated in BASIC as ARRAY (2,3). Here array is used as the variable name. The numerals inside the parentheses represent the second row and the third position in that row respectively. As in other ordered structures, the objective is to increase the efficiency of the data acquisition process and reduce the amount of time spent in this activity.

Another of these multidimensional structures is the *directory*. It has been referred to by some authors as a "list of lists." This system is used to gain access to or load into the computer memory files stored on magnetic disks. The directory itself is a list of various locations on the disk in which the file information is stored. When called, the contents of a specific location is loaded into memory.

Another example of a directory structure is the data base file system illustrated in Fig. 4-1. The access level might have a list of names, search keys, or access codes. The next level would contain a

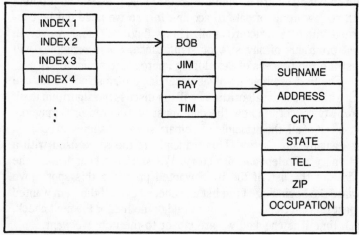

Fig. 4-1. Two-level directory.

table or list of data items for each access entry, while the third level contains the data itself. This is termed a two-level directory since we must go through two levels to get to the actual data wanted. A more flexible system might include additional, intermediate levels to whatever degree is useful.

A more general case of the directory structure can be defined as a *tree*. This type is used whenever a logical relationship exists among all data elements. Such a relation is called a *syntax*. A typical noncomputer example of such a structure is the family tree or genealogical chart. Here, the relationships between each element (person) and all the others follows a fixed structure. Therefore it is easy to determine the relationship between any two persons listed on the chart.

While tree structures can be constructed in any computer language, some high-level languages—most notably LISP—make implementation of these structures easy even to high levels of complexity. It is this feature which has made LISP the choice of those programmers and researchers interested in the fields of artificial intelligence and language study.

These structures are not mutually exclusive. They can be combined in any way desired to design forms for data enabling us to most easily process the information. These combinations are limited only by your ingenuity as a programmer and designer.

In the short program we have been using as an example, no significant data structures exist to complicate the design. There are only three simple variables which can be handled completely by the built-in list structure of the interpreter. This presents no problem with so few items of data to account for, so we need not be concerned with data structure at all. This will not be true, however, in most programs of any size or significance. Some examples will illustrate the process of developing appropriate structures.

The first example involves designing a data structure for use with a binary search algorithm. I will not discuss the algorithm itself here. My concern is how the data must be ordered or arranged.

First of all, the principle of a binary search assumes an ordered list (usually alphabetic). This principle is the same used with a dictionary or telephone directory. We start the search near the middle of the list. If the item wanted preceeds this spot move toward the beginning of the list and check again. If the item wanted is past this check point, move the end of the list for the next check. Each time it is checked we are closer to the item we want.

Second, to make the search process easier, let's assume that each entry takes up an equal amount of space in computer memory. This can be arranged in one of several ways, depending on the amount of memory available for the task. Which of our data structures will prove most appropriate in this example? Let's examine the alternatives. The best structure for this application is an ordered list or table. None of the nonlinear structures would work here at all, or would they? Let's take a close look at the data structure requirements. We need an ordered list, and a list which has a fixed number of characters for each entry. Nothing I have said so far requires these two to be in the *same* list. We have assumed that the data is in this list, but the program won't care where it is as long as the search process obtains the correct data by the program.

Suppose we had a group of data items which were not all the same length. Further, suppose we set up an alphabetic code in which three alphabetic characters represented a particular entry no matter what its total length. Now if we set up a table where each entry is five bytes long and use the character code above as the first three bytes, with the memory address of the actual data as the last two bytes, then we can search this table of five byte entries for the code of the data item we wanted. The search can be binary because we have an alphabetized list of codes to use, but we are still accessing unequal data items with the program.

Naturally this would require more memory since we are using one list to point to where the actual data is stored. But what is wrong if the idea solves the problem of unequal entry length and is acceptable to the other program requirements?

You will recognize the type of data structure discussed here as a directory structure with two levels. Do not limit your applications by formal definitions. Structures are not mutually exclusive. The only criteria to apply is the utility of a structure in meeting the requirements of the program.

The next program example is considerably more complicated, because there is more to be done to obtain a result. This is the design of a lookup table for a disassembler; a program which inputs Z-80 machine code and outputs the manufacturers mnemonic opcodes. The following things were considered during design:

1. Mnemonic opcodes can be one, two, three, or four characters or bytes long.

2. Operands can be any combination of register names and punctuation including parentheses and other characters.

3. The program will have to copy the data to another area where each element can be combined with the rest into a complete opcode.

The main constraint on the design of this data structure was that the entries were not all the same length. The different operands and opcodes had a discrepant number of characters. Some way was needed to tell when the program had arrived at the end of the data item. In addition, the number of characters in the complete opcode plus operands varied from three to four, and up to eight characters. Since the program had to know how many characters to copy to the assembly area, each data entry was set up to designate how many characters made up that particular item.

The final design set up a modified directory structure. Three numerically ordered tables were created. The first, to which the program goes initially, contains coded instructions for creating all possible Z-80 mnemonics. Each entry contains the number of characters (bytes) in the entry, the code for the Z-80 opcode, and codes for each of the characters in the operands in order from left to right. Two other lists were also set up, which were numerically ordered and contained the data for creating the opcode and each element of an operand.

The mnemonics were created using these three lists or tables. First, the program determined the numerical position of the desired code from a list of approximately seven hundred possible Z-80 opcodes. It then went and counted through the first list until the count equalled the position determined earlier. Since the entries could be different lengths, the program kept track of the memory location being accessed by adding to the memory counter the first byte in each entry (the number of bytes or length of that entry). Thus, when the position count was correct the program was at the correct location to obtain the codes for that instruction.

The other two lists also contained numerically ordered information. These were accessed by using information from the entry found in the first list. In this first list, each code or byte was in position of the correct information in either the second list for the opcode, or the third list for the operands.

The first level contained the instructions which the second level used in the two tables to create the opcodes and operands for the various instructions. The number of characters contained in each of the data items in the second and third lists were also included so the program would know how many bytes of code made up any instruction. Figure 4-2 will help to illustrate the relationship between the three lists.

Here again, the method in which the data was organized for use by the program was dictated by the needs of the processing se-

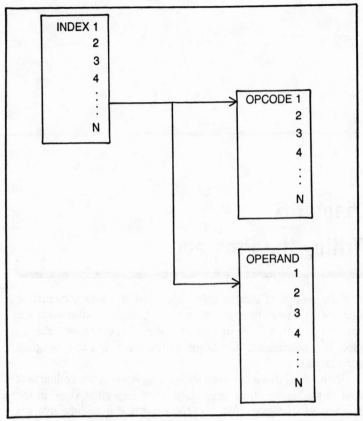

Fig. 4-2. Disassembler data structure.

quences in the program. In many programs the form the data takes
depends on the requirements of such already completed segments.
This will be especially true if you attempt to use or adapt some
program or subroutine to your current needs.

In going about the task of efficient design, don't worry about
what form will be required by the program instructions, or about
what forms the data might assume. Instead, decide what form the
data is to assume to insure an efficient display when the results are
complete. Then experiment with various forms of data organization
to see which are most easily converted to the desired format.

Work back and forth between data structure and algorithm
design until an acceptable solution is devised for both. There will
probably be compromises on both sides, but in the end you will have
a workable algorithm which leaves useful and not awkward data to
work with.

Chapter 5
Writing the Program

Once the design of the program algorithm and data structure is complete, it's time to begin coding the program. After so much effort has gone into the design process, it might seem now that what is left is a mechanical translation of the algorithm into program instructions.

In the past, there has been an overemphasis of the coding task given to the novice, thus neglecting other important steps in the designing of a program. Much of the expertise in coding involves familiarity with the language being used. It would be impossible to adequately discuss another computer language, in addition to our present topic, in a book of this size.

What I shall do is cover some of the general highlights in efficient coding and refer you to the many good reference manuals available for more detailed study.

As you continue to program in any language, you will discover or invent sequences of code helpful to perform various tasks. Keep a record of these and your coding task will become easier. As an example, here are two expressions in BASIC which are generally useful. The first expression

$$A = INT(100*A+.5)/100$$

gives true 5/4 rounding to two decimal places. Use of the INT or FIX commands alone merely truncates the expression either to an integer or to the specified number of places. They do not increase the value of the final digit to show that the lost digit or digits were more than half the value of the remainder. If each occurrence of 100 in the above expression were changed to 1000, then the expression rounds to three decimal places. By the proper choice of multiplier and divisor (which should be the same) we can round to any number of places required.

The next expression requires more attention to detail while you are entering it because of the number and placement of the parentheses. It is a print formatting statement* which places information in a columnar display. The expression is

```
PRINT TAB((((A−INT((A−1)/3)*3)−1)*28)+1);
IF INT(A/3) = A/3 THEN PRINT
IF INT(A/42) = A/42 THEN PAUSE
```

This expression is usually placed within a loop. The variable A is the loop counter variable. The "3" represents the number of columns on the screen and may be varied to suit the application. The "28" in the tab expression is the spacing constant, and can also be changed to suit the application. As it stands, this expression formats the entire screen. The tab expression can be adjusted to start at any specified column merely by adding the above expression to the beginning position you wish to designate. The second line ensures that when all columns in a row have been filled, the cursor goes to the next row, and then the next, etc., and pauses at the end of a full screen display. You should understand that the "PAUSE" is not a BASIC command. You will have to create your own pause routine to insert here.

Every programmer is constantly on the lookout for such sequences. Each time you examine a program listing there may be another new idea you will find useful. Whenever you talk with fellow programmers, be alert to learn from their experiences. You will be surprised how quickly your list will grow.

All computer languages have instructions allowing you to control the sequence of execution. These are the keys to effective program design, and you should become familiar with them and their results. These include jumps, subroutines, branching instructions, case structures, and iterative or repeating loops. The forms they take will vary from language to language, but their actions are similar.

---

*This print formatting statement is from "The Electronic Librarian," *Kilobaud Microcomputing*, p. 53. Copyright 1979 by Kilobaud Microcomputing. All rights reserved, used by permission.

A *jump* will transfer control from one location to another within the program. On its execution, the program starts processing in accordance with the instructions at the new location.

The *subroutine* permits execution of a single segment of code (usually performing some common task or function) from more than one place in the program without duplicating the set of instructions. On completion of the segment, control is transferred back to the instruction immediately following the one which called the subroutine.

Branching instructions permit altering the sequence of program execution according to the results of a test made by the program. These tests are logical in nature. That is, they are usually a comparison of a program variable with some test value. If the test is true, a branch to some new location is made. If the test fails (or is false), program execution continues with a second designated instruction. If only a true branch is designated, in most cases the program continues normal execution on a false result.

Case structures compute a branching address according to the value of a designated variable which has been computed or provided by the program.

Iterative loops permit the repetition of a code sequence a specified number of times. Such loops can also repeat the sequence until a given condition is satisfied. They are useful where the same operation must be performed on a number of values.

The principles involved in structured programming also apply here. Use of these principles is one way to avoid logical programming errors while coding the program. This is especially important if the logic is complex or there are a number of nested loops or branching structures. If you have not just coded the segment, it is often difficult to determine where each of the nested levels end. These basic structures will help you avoid such errors if they are carefully adhered to while coding the program.

JUMPS

Jumps are useful in directing program flow, especially in simpler programs. They should be used carefully. Many advocates of structured programming techniques recommend replacing jumps with subroutine calls. This does have advantages. For one thing, it forces better design of program modules. The functions must be clearly defined in order to be used as subroutines. For another, the exit address is set by the call instruction. Executing the call automatically stores the next program address or program line number in the stack for access following the return. This permits faster execution since the central processor, or the interpreter program, does not have to locate the address or line number through a search. It is already available from the stack. Another advantage is that it reduces the amount of time needed in debugging and in redesign if necessary.

Sparing use of jumps in programming also reduces interaction between various parts of the program. Then it is easier to trace the sequence of instructions through the program. This leads to an easier understanding of what the instructions are attempting to accomplish and also makes any errors in program design obvious.

Consider the segment of code in Fig. 5-1 as an example. This segment of code was written on a Radio Shack TRS-80 Model II microcomputer and uses language available in its BASIC interpreter. It's function is to print the string array items designated in the input portions of the program (not included in the figure). The external references to line 100 returns program control to the main command menu under various specified conditions.

The subroutine beginning at line 3370 aborts the printout when ESC is pressed. If aborted, the program sends a top of form command to the printer making subsequent print commands start at the top of a page. The loop from line 3324 in line 3328 provides for variable spacing of the lines on the printed page. SP is obviously the spacing variable and is designated when the page format is set up at the start of the run.

Following the sequence of program execution here is not difficult. There are a few places whereby, rearranging the coding a bit could improve our grasp of what the program is doing. There is nothing wrong with the segment as it stands. It will execute properly. But the logical sections and their boundarys may be varified to improve understanding of how the program segment operates.

The most obvious example is the spacing loop from lines 3324 to 3328. This is a simple loop performing an elementary function in the segment. If it were made a subroutine and placed outside the main flow sequence of the segment, it could then be called a subroutine in line 3320, and line 3322 could be eliminated entirely. Then there is a single statement referring to the segment which is a remark or comment for that line. This makes remembering its function much easier than checking the sequence of code each time and analyzing its operation.

```
3260 PP=PG-1
3262 FOR K=0 TO LA STEP PL
3265 PP=PP+1
3270 PRINT @ 1160, "PRINTING PAGE";PP;
3274 IF PN < 1 THEN 3300 ELSE LPRINT T$;
3280 IF NM$ <> "" THEN LPRINT TAB(75-LEN(NM$))NM$:
                              GOTO 3290
3282 LPRINT
3290 LPRINT TAB (LL-7) "PAGE ";
3295 LPRINT USING "###";PP
3300 FOR J=K TO K+PL-1
3310 IF J > LA THEN 3360
3320 IF SP > 0 THEN 3324
3322 GOTO 3330
3324 FOR M = 1 TO SP
3326 LPRINT
3328 NEXT M
3330 IF N$= "Y" THEN LPRINT J;
3340 LPRINT TAB(T1) A$(J);
3345 GOSUB 3370
3350 NEXT J
3351 SYSTEM "FORMS {T}"
3352 PRINT @1160, CHR$(23);
3355 IF PN < 1 THEN 100
3360 IF PF=1 AND PA$="S" THEN 100
3362 NEXT K
3364 SYSTEM "FORMS {T}"
3366 GOTO 100
3370 FOR M=1 TO 5
3375 A$ = INKEY$
3380 IF A$ = "" THEN 3410
3390 IF ASC(A$)=27 AND PA$="P"THEN SYSTEM "FORMS {T}"
3400 IF ASC(A$)=27 THEN 100
3410 NEXT M
3420 RETURN
```

Fig. 5-1. Program segment to print the string array items designated.

In this trivial case, it does not matter which way segment is
coded. In more complex segments, or in longer programs, it becomes more important to understand how a program operates.

In the case of the abort subroutine, jumps have been eliminated
where possible. This makes the logic of the segment more discern-
ible. We are leaving the main sequence of the program to check
some specific function, but will continue the program following the
interruption.

The main point to be made is that excessive use of jumps leads
to difficulty in understanding programs. Not only for another programmer who must work with what you have written, but also for
yourself as the one who codes the program. It can lead to both
coding errors (when a wrong line is specified) and design errors due
to incomplete or erroneous assumptions about the program logic or
the coding to implement it. Many of these difficulties can be eliminated by the simpler subroutine construction which helps to
minimize opportunity for error.

SUBROUTINES

I have been talking about substituting subroutines for jumps without discussing the forms such segments should take, or how they are designed. Subroutines can be very useful provided certain restrictions are kept in mind. Each subroutine should be written to perform a single specific task. Some of these tasks can be fairly complex and be composed of a number of simpler subtasks, which may or may not be subroutines themselves.

There is a second restriction if subroutines are nested (one subroutine being called while in the middle of executing another). The inner or last-called subroutine must be completed and a return executed before the outer subroutine is completed. This limitation is due to the way in which the returns are handled by the various programming languages.

Figure 5-2 illustrates this point using BASIC programming language. A subroutine is set up at line 10. Line 20 prevents the program from running directly into the subroutine without a Call. This point is important since doing so will cause an error forcing the program to cease operation. Line 30 starts the "outer" subroutine which continues until the return at line 90. The return here is the delimiter for the second subroutine which begins at line 100 and is called at line 70 in the "outer" subroutine. Note that the "inner" subroutine (100) completes execution and returns to line 80 before the "outer" subroutine can complete its processing and return from line 90.

This may be obvious, but if a conditional jump were set up from the inner to the outer subroutine, under certain conditions it might be possible to create such errors.

```
     10 GOSUB 30

             30 PRINT "TEST EXAMPLE"
             40 PRINT
             50 FOR I = 0 TO 3
             60     PRINT"OUTER LOOP"
             70     GOSUB 100

                 100 FOR J=1 TO 2
                 110     PRINT "INNER LOOP"
                 120 NEXT J
                 130 RETURN

             80 NEXT I
             90 RETURN
     20 END
```

Fig. 5-2. Nested subroutine.

```
10 IF SUM > 10 THEN 20 ELSE 40
20 SUM = (SUM-5)/2
30 GOTO 50
40 SUM = SUM + A
50 PRINT SUM
```

Fig. 5-3. Branching code segment.

BRANCHING INSTRUCTIONS

When coding branching instructions, the branches can often be coded to eliminate use of the alternate statement. For example, in BASIC the branching instruction has the form:

IF (COND) THEN <ALT #1> ELSE <ALT #2>

Figure 5-3 shows a portion of the addition example from Chapter 3 coded so that line 10 provides the branching instruction for the alternate processing paths after the first addition.

Since line 20 would execute without going to line 40, the branching instruction can be shortened by setting up the test so that the jump to line 40 occurs when the test is true. This saves in execution time as well as memory.

To do this, first test for the opposite or *inverse* of the above condition. Since in line 10 the sum is greater than 10, its inverse would have to be the sum less than or equal to 10. The new version is shown in Fig. 5-4. Both sequences give exactly the same result and execute in precisely the same way. This makes coding simpler and easier to follow.

Figure 5-5 displays each of four logical operators and its inverse. Each set of symbols on a line is the inverse of the other. The rule for creating the inverse of a given conditional expression is to replace any of the above eight symbols with its inverse. The following expressions provide a few illustrative examples of this.

Conditional Expression	Inverse
X > 3	X < 3
Y = 0 OR X < 1	Y < > 0 AND X = > 1
C > (X + 3)	C < = (X + 3)

These can be combined, as desired, with any other structures mentioned. And any condition or type of logical structure needed

Fig. 5-4. Branching example, inverse logic.

```
10 IF SUM <= 10 THEN 40
20 SUM = (SUM-5)/2
30 GOTO 50
40 SUM = SUM + A
50 PRINT SUM
```

Symbol	Inverse
=	<>
>	<=
=>	<
AND	OR

Fig. 5-5. Logical operators and inverses.

can be created. The only limits are ingenuity in combining them and the logical requirements of the program in design.

The use of standard structured coding can aid greatly in displaying the clarity and logic of a set of nested branching instructions and possibly of sets of nested branches combined with other types of coding structures. For example, which of the two examples of coding in Figs. 5-6 and 5-7 is easier to understand? As in earlier examples, both segments of code perform the same function and both produce the same result in the variables on exit from the segment. To understand what is being done during processing, it is obvious that the first example is the better choice.

If our selection is the segment that optimizes the processing—either runs faster or uses least memory—then the

```
100 IN$="":W$=INKEY$:W=14:WD=0:WS=WD:WL%=WD:IF
    FL=WD THEN FL=1
105 PRINT STRING$(ABS(FL),136);STRING$(ABS(FL),24);
110 PRINT CHR$(W);:FOR W%=1 TO 25:W$=INKEY$: IF
    W$ <> "" THEN 115 ELSE NEXT:PRINT CHR$(15);:
    FOR W%=1 TO 25:W$=INKEY$: IF W$ <> "" THEN 115
    ELSE NEXT:GOTO 110
115 PRINT CHR$(W);:IF ABS(FL)=WL% THEN 125 ELSE IF
    FL > 0 AND W$ => " " AND W$ <= "Z" THEN 170 ELSE
    IF FL < 0 AND W$ > "/" AND W$ < ":" THEN 170
117 IF W$ = "," THEN PRINT W$;:WL% = WL%+1:GOTO 175
120 IF W$ = "." AND WD = 0 THEN WD = 1: GOTO 170
123 IF (W$ = "-" OR W$ = "+") AND WS = 0 AND WL% = 0
    THEN WS = 1: GOTO 170
125 IF W$ <> CHR$(8) THEN 150 ELSE IF WL% = 0 THEN
    110 ELSE PRINT CHR$(24);:IF L > 0 THEN 135 ELSE
    IF PEEK(16418) = 44 THEN 140
130 IF PEEK(16418) = 46 THEN WD = 0:GOTO 135 ELSE IF
    PEEK(16418) = 43 OR PEEK(16418) = 45 THEN WS = 0
135 IN$ = LEFT$(IN$,LEN(IN$)-1)
140 WL% = WL%-1:POKE(16418),136:GOTO 110
150 IF W$ = CHR$(24) THEN PRINT
    STRING$(WL%,CHR$(24));:GOTO 100
155 IF W$ <> CHR$(13) THEN 110 ELSE PRINT
    STRING$(ABS(FL)-WL%,32);
160 PRINT CHR$(15);:W% = 25:NEXT:RETURN
170 PRINT W$;:IN$ = IN$+W$:WL% = WL%+1
175 IF ABS(FL) = 1 THEN 160 ELSE 110
```

Fig. 5-6. Optimized INKEY subroutine. (Courtesy of The Tandy Corporation.)

45

```
090   IN$ = ""
092   W$ = INKEY$
094   W = 14
095   WD = 0
096   WS = WD
098   WL% = WD
100   IF FL = WD THEN FL = 1
105   PRINT STRINGS$(ABS(FL),136);STRING$(ABS(FL),24);
106   PRINT CHR$(W);
107   FOR W% = 1 TO 25
108       W$ = INKEY$
109       IF W$ <> "" THEN 117
110   NEXT W%
111   PRINT CHR$(15);
112   FOR W% = 1 TO 25
113       W$ = INKEY$
114       IF W$ <> "" THEN 117
115   NEXT W%
116   GOTO 106
117   PRINT CHR$(W);
118   IF ABS(FL) = WL% THEN 125
119       IF FL > 0 AND W$ =>" " AND W$ <="Z" THEN 170
120           IF FL < 0 AND W$ > "/" AND W$ < ":"
                  THEN 170
121   IF W$ = "," THEN PRINT W$
                        WL% = WL%+1
                        GOTO 175
122   IF W$ = "." AND WD = 0 THEN WD = 1
                                  GOTO 170
123   IF (W$ = "-" OR W$ = "+") AND WS = 0 AND WL%
      = 0 THEN WS = 1
                GOTO 170
125   IF W$ <> CHR$(8) THEN 150
126       IF WL% = 0 THEN 106
127       PRINT CHR$(24)
128       IF FL > 0 THEN 135
129           IF PEEK(16418)=44 THEN 140
130   IF PEEK(16418)=46 THEN WD = 0
                                  GOTO 135
131       IF PEEK(16418)=43 OR PEEK(16418)=45 THEN
                                                  WS=0
135   IN$ = LEFT$(IN$,LEN(IN$)-1)
140   WL% = WL%-1
141   POKE 16418,136
142   GOTO 106
150   IF W$=CHR$(24) THEN PRINT STRING$(WL%,CHR$(24));
                        GOTO 090
155   IF W$ <> CHR$(13) THEN 106
156   PRINT STRING$(ABS(FL)-WL%,32);
160   PRINT CHR$(15);
161   W% = 25
162   NEXT
163   RETURN
170   PRINT W$
171   IN$ = IN$+W$
172   WL% = WL%+1
175   IF ABS(FL) = 1 THEN 160
176   GOTO 106
```

Fig. 5-7. Indented INKEY subroutine. (Courtesy of Tandy Corporation.)

choice is not as clear. In fact, with some examples it might be difficult to make a choice at all. Under such circumstances, all you can do is to exercise your best judgment at the time. Personal judgment must play a major part in deciding what is better for your purposes. I said in the beginning that programming is personal and that everyone must use an approach they feel comfortable with.

The only general rule to suggest is to design and code the segment using the structured form shown in these examples. When the segment is completely debugged and running correctly, then start to combine the statements into multistatement lines where possible. It is also good to develop test data while debugging the original version. After each change run the test data to be sure you haven't introduced any bugs while converting the coding. This is easy to do, especially in conditional statements.

THE CASE STRUCTURE

The case structure is used where a program needs alternative command inputs that will branch to respective segments or modules of code. A typical example is a command menu for an applications program.

The flowchart of a case structure is diagrammed as a series of branching instructions. An identical result can be obtained in a program by using as many branching instructions as there are alternate routines to be executed. The case structure is a simpler way to implement the task. It saves memory and execution time over the branching method. The usual format in BASIC is the following syntax.

ON <variable> GOTO/GOSUB <addr>, <addr>, . . .

For example:

ON X GOTO 20,50,80,1220

or

ON X GOSUB 150,300,400,500

In either example the value of X, the variable, is computed before executing the instruction. If X equals one, then the program branches to the first address in the line. If X equals two, it goes to the second, and so on. If the value of X is zero or is greater than the number of addresses in the instruction then the program goes to the next line following the instruction.

LOOPS

The loop is one of the most powerful and useful structures in any programming language. It permits enormous compression of coding since the same sequence of code can be repeated over and over without the necessity to rewrite the coded sequence.

```
10 FOR I = 1 TO 4
20 PRINT "OUTER LOOP"
30 FOR J = 1 TO 2
40 PRINT "INNER LOOP"
50 NEXT J
60 NEXT I
```

Fig. 5-8. Nested for-next loops.

As mentioned earlier, there are two types of loop structures. The *do-until* structure forces execution of the loop coding at least one time and continues until the given condition is satisfied. The *do-while* structure permits the program to skip the loop coding entirely if the exit condition is satisfied on entry.

The *for-next* loop BASIC is an automated do-until structure. It will always execute at least once. These loops may be nested so long as a NEXT instruction is inserted for each FOR instruction in the coding. The other thing to be careful of is that each loop can sometimes be contained within any present outer loop structures.

For example, in Fig. 5-8 the J loop is entirely contained within the I loop. If the program were changed, as in Fig. 5-9, so that the termination of the I loop came before the completion of the J loop, an error would be generated and the program fails to run.

For better clarity in program design structured and indented coding can be used to insure each loop is terminated properly. The example here is much easier to keep track of if indented structure is used for our coding. See Fig. 5-10. In this example everything to the right of the beginning of each loop is included within that loop, and there is less chance of confusion in terminating them properly.

Even with these precautions it is still possible, in some versions of BASIC, to encounter execution error. An article in the January, 1981, issue of *BYTE* magazine, entitled "A Bug in Basic,"

```
10 FOR I = 1 TO 4
20 PRINT "OUTER LOOP"
30 FOR J = 1 TO 2
40 PRINT "INNER LOOP"
50 NEXT I
60 NEXT J
```

Fig. 5-9. Incorrect for-next nesting.

```
10 FOR I = 1 TO 4
20      PRINT "OUTER LOOP"
30      FOR J = 1 TO 2
40          PRINT "INNER LOOP"
50      NEXT J
60 NEXT I
```

Fig. 5-10. Indented for-next loops.

describes a software bug which produces errors in some versions of BASIC. If the program jumps out of a loop before completion and is still inside an outer loop, the program may confuse the NEXT of the outer loop for the NEXT of the inner loop. This leaves the outer loop FOR statement without a termination.

To correct such an error, it is necessary to change the loop counter variable to a designation not used elsewhere in the program. This eliminates the confusion and the supposed error.

Some programmers think the way to avoid this problem would be not to terminate such loops prematurely. This restricts the use of these structures and so is not necessary. The only prohibition is to jump abnormally *into* such loops. Premature termination of loops is necessary for correct operation of certain tasks such as searching, or in ending a computation given a specified condition. Such termination should never produce errors.

According to the *BYTE* article, six of fifteen popular microcomputers tested on November 12 and 13, 1980, exhibited this bug in the same test program which ran without error on the rest. The article details exactly what happens in the computer to produce such an error and tells which systems tested did or did not exhibit the problem.

Don't worry about it unless you are having problems with these loops and no one can resolve them for you. Be aware that it is possible to use commercial software that is not error free.

If desired, the same loop structure can be created without the use of the for-next statements. If you remember, the do-until loop consists of a process block followed by a branch test. An example of this structure is the sequence of code in Fig. 5-11.

This is the conditional loop equivalent of the for-next loop. The counter variable I is initialized to zero in line 10, the processing is implemented and the counter is incremented in lines 20 and 30. Then compare the value of the counter variable with some pre-

```
```

```
10 I=0
20 PRINT "TEST CODE"
30 I=I+1
40 IF I < 4 THEN 20
50 END
```

Fig. 5-11. Do-until loop structure.

determined value (here it is 4) and repeat if the condition is met (or is true). Note that the number of times the processing instruction is executed within the loop depends on the relative placement of the processing instruction and the incrementing instruction for the counter variable. If the processing is completed first and the counter incremented as in the above example, then the loop will print the message four times. If the counter is incremented before the processing is begun then only three will appear.

The do-while loop first executes the test and then does the processing as in Fig. 5-12. Because the test is at the beginning of the sequence, inverse logic is used for the test. The test is set up to jump to the end of the segment if its value becomes equal to or greater than four.

In some versions of BASIC an automated do-while loop, the *while-wend* instruction is included, Fig. 5-13 illustrates one application. Here the number of passes through the loop is specified at the beginning. Start the loop and decrement the counter after each iteration. When the counter reaches zero, the loop terminates. In this instruction the test is always for zero. The coding must arrange for the counter to eventually arrive at zero. If this is not done the program will never exit from the loop.

Another example of the way in which a while-wend loop can be useful is illustrated in Fig. 5-14. This segment sorts a list (B$) into ascending order using a sorting algorithm known as a *bubble sort*.

```
10 I=0
20 IF I => 4 THEN 60
30 PRINT "TEST CODE"
40 I=I+1
50 GOTO 20
60 END
```

Fig. 5-12. Do-while loop structure.

```
10 I=4
20 WHILE I
30 PRINT "TEST CODE"
40 I=I-1
50 WEND
60 END
```

Fig. 5-13. While-wend loop example.

This sorting technique is not very efficient, but it is simple and is useful when the number of elements is not large.

Line 10 forces a pass through the loop the first time. Future looping is determined by the results of the sort comparison in line 50. Line 30 sets the counter to zero. If no exchanges are made, as the for-next loop from lines 40 to 60 compares all elements of the list, assume that the entire list is sorted, the counter remains zero, and the while-wend loop terminates. If an exchange occurs on any pass through the list then the loop is repeated at least one more time.

In this example the for-next loop is nested inside the while-wend loop. These and any other structured blocks can be nested to any number of levels required by the program. The only restriction is that each loop or structure must be completely contained within a single level.

Another type of loop structure is an *endless loop*, with a user-controlled escape instruction. This allows continued execution of the loop instructions until exit and is convenient when it is impossible to tell in advance how many times it takes to execute a given segment of code.

```
10 C=1
20 WHILE C
30 C=0
40 FOR I = 1 TO J-1
50 IF B$(I) > B$(I+1) THEN
          SWAP B$(I),B$(I+1):C=1
60 NEXT I
70 WEND
80 END
```

Fig. 5-14. While-wend bubble sort.

Suppose you want to input data and store it in a list. The sequence of code in Fig. 5-15 allows us to input a variable number of items up to the maximum number specified in the program for that list. In this segment transfer the input item (in Z$) to the list slot A$(I), then move the counter to the next slot. The escape instruction is in line 50. The loop ends if either the escape character (here @) is input in the program, or if the number of slots equals the maximum number available to the program.

An example of this loop integrated into a program appears in the data input subroutine of the Correlation and Linear Regression program in Chapter 10.

ASSEMBLER CODING

In the previous chapters there has been no distinctions made between assembly-language programming and programming in high-level languages. Those topics are done in the same way no matter what the level of language used. It makes no difference which language is being used when defining the problem adequately, or in designing the program algorithms. These are general tasks which are not dependent on any language structure.

Naturally, you will become intimate with the particular language you choose. The first portion of this chapter, which dealt with high-level languages, provides some insights into the general structures commonly used. If you decide to use assembly language, you do not have these easily defined sequences to rely on. There are some equivalent instructions, but by no means are they all present in assembly language.

I mentioned in Chapter 2 that high-level instructions are usually equivalent to many assembly-level instructions. If wished, certain assembler routines, sequences of code to perform specific functions, can be created to use in a similar manner as the high-level instruction they represent. In essence you write your own compiler routines for the functions needed. Whether or not this is an efficient procedure will depend on the function you wish to implement and the way it is used in the program.

It may be better to look carefully at the program logic to see if some of the innate features of the assembler language can be used to perform these tasks. If so you can complete these same tasks in less time and with less program memory. What functions in high-level languages have direct counterparts in assembler? Let's examine the Z-80 instruction set for some clues.

```
10 I=0
20 INPUT Z$
30 A$(I) = Z$
40 I=I+1
50 IF Z$ = "@" OR I=> MAX THEN 70
60 GOTO 20
70 END
```

Fig. 5-15. Variable input loop.

Jumps

The *jump* in assembler performs the same function as a GOTO command in BASIC. The jump is more versatile since in assembler it can be made conditional on the results of certain tests. This is all within a single instruction. Because of this the assembler jump can serve the same functions as both the GOTO and branching instructions.

The GOTO makes jumps in reference to program line numbers. In assembler, the jump is to a specific memory address. The jump can also be computed relative to the current instruction location with the use of special relative jump instructions. Since a single byte is used to store the information used in computing the offset, the maximum offset is -127 or $+128$ bytes from the current instruction.

Subroutines

The *call* is the assembler equivalent of the GOSUB command in BASIC. It also can be made conditional on the status of the *flag* bits stored in the central processing unit (CPU). This makes the call instruction considerably more versatile. For instance, suppose you had a subroutine which produced an error message. In assembler, you could make the calling of the routine dependent on the condition of the flag which indicates the error. In BASIC you would need to use an if-then structure along with the subroutine to achieve this purpose.

A second way in which the subroutine structure in assembler is made more powerful is the existence of the conditional return. That is, the return from a subroutine can be made conditional on the status of any of the various testable flag bits. This allows termination of a subroutine at any number of places depending on circumstances. It is a more useful routine when proper planning has gone into its design.

Branching

In the high-level languages, branches are made conditional on the existence of certain logical conditions between designated program variables tested for by the program. These have no direct counterparts in the assembler instruction set.

Assembler branches are made conditional on the status of specified bits in the flag register. The *flag register* is a special register or storage location within the CPU of the microprocessor. The bits in this register are individually addressed by the CPU. They maintain a record of the status of certain conditions which could change depending on what program instructions are being executed. Figure 5-16 lists the names of the flags and their function. Not all of these are accessible to the programmer. The half-carry and the add/subtract flags are used internally by the CPU for special processing instructions.

The Z-80 instruction set provides transfer of program control which can be specified by the status of the four testable flag bits— the carry, zero, sign, and parity/overflow bits.

The *carry* flag indicates that a carry has been generated in addition or a borrow in subtraction. It is also used as a ninth bit in shift and rotate instructions. To prevent errors in results, the carry is reset before performing any calculations. This is done by executing a logical AND or a logical OR instruction on the accumulator or "A" register. A logical XOR will do it as well, but will also zero the accumulator. The other two only clear the carry. The two instruction sequences set carry (SCF) and complement carry (CCF) can also be used, but the logical instructions are shorter and more efficient.

The *zero* flag indicates when the result of a comparison or subtraction is a value of zero in the accumulator. This of course, is an equality test.

The *sign* flag indicates the sign of the value in the accumulator, either plus (+) or minus (−). A zero indicates a positive number; a one, a negative number.

The *parity/overflow* flag has a dual function. Parity is a count of the number of ones in a byte. If the number of ones is even, then the byte is said to have *even* parity. And if the number is odd, then the byte has ODD parity. This has its main use in verifying data received from peripheral devices, or over communication links.

54

Name	Function
CARRY	Holds carry status of result (0 if no carry, 1 if carry generated). Also used in rotates and shifts.
ZERO	Indicates whether result was zero (1) or nonzero (0).
SIGN	Holds numerical sign of result (0 if positive, 1 if negative).
PARITY/ OVERFLOW	Holds parity of result or overflow condition. If used as parity, P=1 if the number of 1 bits in the result is even, or 0 if they are odd. If used as overflow flag, V=0 if no overflow, 1 if overflow occurred.
ADD/ SUBTRACT	Add or subtract for decimal instructions. Not testable.
HALF CARRY	Holds half-carry status of result (from right to left nibble). Not testable.

Fig. 5-16. CPU flags and functions.

The overflow function indicates when the value of a result is too large to be placed into the accumulator. It also indicates, during execution of block transfer and block search instructions, when the instruction has reached the end of the block of data.

Branching instructions are constructed by using a subroutine call or by use of a conditional jump to the desired location. The logic for these branches is created by use of the flag bits associated with the accumulator. To summarize the main use of the zero and carry see Fig. 5-17. Assuming in the future that A is the accumulator and that X is the second operand for a CP (or ComPare) instruction, any of the logical operators can be created by a careful study and use of this figure in association with the conditional instructions.

As an example, suppose you want your program to jump if the value of the accumulator becomes greater than 10. If you used the instruction sequence:

```
CP    10
JR    NC,ADDR
```

it would also jump if the accumulator equalled 10 and an error would be generated. In this case you can either reverse A and X or add 1 to A.

```
A = accumulator
X = other operand
Zero flag is:
    1 if A = X
    0 if A ≠ X
Carry flag is:
    1 if A < X
    0 if A ≥ X
```

Fig. 5-17. Summary of flags in compare instructions.

Case Structures

The nearest thing to the case structure in assembler is the *automated block compare instruction*. A number of other conditions still must be set up in order to make it useful. So far as a direct equivalent is concerned, none of the assembler instructions come close.

Loops

Loop structures in assembly-language are set up using conditional tests and jumps. Whether the loop is a do-while or do-until structure is not important, as this is determined by the arrangement of the coding within the loop and not by the instructions used. The only exception to this is the DJNZ instruction. This instruction is an automated loop which continues execution until the contents of the "B" register becomes zero.

Chapter 6
Testing and Debugging

Once the program is designed and coded, the operation must be verified. You might say that at this point if the program was designed and coded properly there should be no need for verification. Theoretically this is true, but there are several sources of possible error, both in design and coding, which make such verification prudent before you use or release for use any program.

There is an adage known as Murphy's law. It states: Anything that can go wrong will go wrong at the worst possible time.

This chapter will help you eliminate as many errors as possible before they can cause some catastrophic loss of data or time during program use.

TESTING

The best way to check all possibilities is to prepare a checklist of procedures and tests to be done after coding. If you use *top-down* design, then prepare a list for each stage of the design.

The first step is to compare the program design with the actual coding you have written to implement the program. Does every section in the design have its counterpart in the code? It is easy to forget or skip over a section especially when working on a large or complex program taking many weeks to design. Try to make sure that the code does what you intended it to. If you are programming in a high-level language, check the code carefully for spelling and punctuation errors. This type of check of course is only preliminary Its purpose is to insure that the program will run on the interpreter.

Once the program will run (don't worry about validity up to this point), you can determine the correctness of the output whatever its form.

If the output doesn't seem reasonable, or is obviously incorrect (assuming that the design algorithms are correct) the first items to check are the loops. Make sure that each loop includes only those instructions you intended, that the number of iterations is correct, that the variables are correct, and that they change properly as the loop repeats the sequence. It might be good to work through a couple of iterations by hand just to make sure your design is logically correct.

Next, check the branches and decision points. Do they branch to the correct instruction? Are the branches set up on the correct test? If you coded a branch when the variable is equal to or less than a certain value, sooner or later you are going to branch to the wrong instruction when the value comes up equal to your test value.

Watch especially for which *then* and *else* statements go with which *if* statements. Here is where your structuring or modular indenting can be of help, especially if there are a series of nested structures or if the logic for the jump is complex.

Look again at the examples in Figs. 5-6 and 5-7 of the *INKEY* subroutine. In the design of this subroutine, you can get confused by the nested if-then-else statements in this segment of code. Without a clearly structured or indented outline to follow, it could take three or four times as long to get it working correctly as it would otherwise.

Check all special cases. Make sure that they branch to the correct address or line number. Also make sure that you have made provision in the program for all situations which might occur. Failing to consider a particular case invariably causes problems and errors in program execution. When this type of error occurs, you may be able to correct it by adding some code to handle it. This can be done economically in correcting minor flaws. In many cases, though, it will be easier, and in the long run, simpler to redesign the program logic to include such cases. Then rewrite the portion of the program which is involved.

DEBUGGING

Let's take a look at a typical example. Figure 6-1 is a code listing of a short program in BASIC. If you have a computer with a

BASIC interpreter you might enter the program and work through the debugging process. One note; the program is written in Microsoft BASIC for the Radio Shack Model II microcomputer. Other versions of BASIC may require modification of the program to run.

This program was designed to aid in creating alphabetized lists of data such as a list of variables for a program or an index or glossary for a book. A unique feature of the program is that correspondence is maintained between the two associated variable lists: one for the key symbol or word, and one for its definition. It orders them without needing to connect them and later separating them again. This saves considerable time and programming effort.

The program is rather elementary. It can read in a data file or input data from the keyboard. The data is sorted, and the user is given the option of a video display, or hard copy, followed by options to repeat the display and to save the present data in a disk file. If desired, it would not be difficult to redesign the program to incorporate additional features and options.

A careful initial hand check of the original listing, (Fig. 6-1), reveals that a hyphen is missing in line 12. It should have been inserted between the I and K. As it reads, the instruction defines the variables beginning with I as integer instead of I, J, and K as was intended. Next, the semicolon required to separate the message prompt from the input variable in line 21 is missing. In line 61, the ASCII string designator ($) for the input variable is omitted and in line 76 the jump is incorrectly designated as going to the input subroutine at line 120. It should go to line 110.

Now that these changes have been made, let's try the corrected program given in Fig. 6-2 to see if all the bugs are corrected.

The program ran all right until the entry of the definition was completed. Instead of giving us a prompt for the next variable, the program stopped with a no-for error in line 2370. What could have happened? Let's look at the no-for error first since the line number was designated. Aha! The two next statements are reversed so that the inner nested loop (K) is not completely enclosed within the outer (I) loop. Changing this was the easy part. Now let's find out why the program ended up here. You start out entering data and keep repeating the data input statements until entering the asterisk (*) escape characters. Line 50 should steer us back to the beginning of the input loop. To do this, go to line 55. The program actually went into the subroutine where it stopped from line 53. It must be jumping the wrong way from the if-then-else statement. To correct this, invert the logic of the statement.

```
10 CLEAR 10000
11 DEFSTR X,L
12 DEFINT IK
13 DIM X(200),L(200)
15 I=1
16 CLS
17 INPUT"IS THIS AN UPDATE";A$
19 IF A$ = "Y" THEN GOSUB 120: I=I+1
20 CLS
21 INPUT"WHAT IS VARIABLE NAME"X(I)
30 INPUT"ENTER ITS DEFINITION";L(I)
50 IF X(I) = "*" AND L(I) = "*" THEN 55
51 I=I+1
52 J=I
53 GOSUB 2290
54 GOTO 60
55 I=I+1
56 GOTO 20
60 CLS
61 INPUT"SEND DATA TO PRINTER OR VIDEO DISPLAY (P/V)";C
64 FOR I = 1 TO J
65 IF C$ = "P" THEN 67
66 LPRINT X(I); TAB(10) L(I)
67 PRINT X(I)
68 PRINT L(I)
69 NEXT I
70 CLS
71 INPUT"DO YOU WISH TO REPEAT (Y/N)";B$
```

Fig. 6-1. Initial version of program.

If you remember from the last chapter, logic is inverted by
replacing each logical operator in the statement with its inverse. In
this case, the corrected line reads:

$$\text{IF } X(I) <> \text{"*" OR } L(I) <> \text{"*" THEN 55}$$

```
73 IF B$ = "Y" THEN 60
74 INPUT"DO YOU WISH TO SAVE DATA (Y/N)";C$
76 IF C$ = "N" THEN 120
80 OPEN "O",1,"CHVAR/TXT"
90 PRINT #1, J
91 FOR I = 1 TO J
95 PRINT #1, X(I);",";L(I)
98 NEXT I
100 CLOSE
101 PRINT TAB(32)"FILE CLOSED"
110 END
120 OPEN,"I",1,"CHVAR/TXT"
125 INPUT #1,J
130 FOR I = 1 TO J
135 INPUT #1, X(I),L(I)
140 NEXT I
148 CLOSE
150 RETURN
2290 IF J <= 1 THEN 2380
2291 JL = J-1
2292 FOR I = 1 TO JL
2295     KL = I+1
2300     FOR K = KL TO J
2330          IF X(I) <= X(K) THEN 2360
2340          SWAP X(I),X(K)
2350          SWAP L(I),L(K)
2360     NEXT I
2370 NEXT K
2380 RETURN
```

Now let's check this section by inserting a "stop" command at the beginning of lines 51 and 55. This allows you to check which way the statement executes the jump without worrying whether the rest of the program is correct.

```
10 CLEAR 10000
11 DEFSTR X,L
12 DEFINT I-K
13 DIM X(200),L(200)
15 I=1
16 CLS
17 INPUT"IS THIS AN UPDATE";A$
19 IF A$ = "Y" THEN GOSUB 120: I=I+1
20 CLS
21 INPUT"WHAT IS VARIABLE NAME";X(I)
30 INPUT"ENTER ITS DEFINITION";L(I)
50 IF X(I) = "*" AND L(I) = "*" THEN 55
51 I=I+1
52 J=I
53 GOSUB 2290
54 GOTO 60
55 I=I+1
56 GOTO 20
60 CLS
61 INPUT"SEND DATA TO PRINTER OR VIDEO DISPLAY (P/V)";C$
64 FOR I = 1 TO J
65 IF C$ = "P" THEN 67
66 LPRINT X(I); TAB(10) L(I)
67 PRINT X(I)
68 PRINT L(I)
69 NEXT I
70 CLS
71 INPUT"DO YOU WISH TO REPEAT (Y/N)";B$
73 IF B$ = "Y" THEN 60
```

Fig. 6-2. Hand-checked version of the program.

Now that the stops are in, run the program again. Good! After entering the first data pair there is a break at line 55. This is where you want to be. To double check, enter a "continue" command. This allows execution of the program to continue normally. Now see the prompt for your second data pair. Enter the asterisks to escape the

```
74 INPUT"DO YOU WISH TO SAVE DATA (Y/N)";C$

76 IF C$ = "N" THEN 110

80 OPEN "O",1,"CHVAR/TXT"
90 PRINT #1, J

91 FOR I = 1 TO J

95 PRINT #1, X(I);",";L(I)

98 NEXT I

100 CLOSE

101 PRINT TAB(32)"FILE CLOSED"

110 END

120 OPEN,"I",1,"CHVAR/TXT"

125 INPUT #1,J

130 FOR I = 1 TO J

135 INPUT #1, X(I),L(I)

140 NEXT I

148 CLOSE

150 RETURN

2290 IF J <= 1 THEN 2380

2291 JL = J-1
2292 FOR I = 1 TO JL

2295     KL = I+1

2300     FOR K = KL TO J

2330         IF X(I) <= X(K) THEN 2360

2340         SWAP X(I),X(K)

2350         SWAP L(I),L(K)

2360     NEXT I

2370 NEXT K

2380 RETURN
```

loop. Is there a break at line 51? If both these are correct, then delete the stops from the program.

Now reenter the data since it was lost in the editing process. Enter two or three data pairs to check the operation of the sort routine also.

Let's look at what has happened. You entered the data pairs and the escape characters. The program stored them correctly, but two problems present themselves. First, and most important, when we tried to have them displayed on the video display they were printed on the line printer. Secondly, the escape characters also appeared in the printout. This is certainly not what you wanted.

Looking at Fig. 6-2 again the segment of code which controls the display functions is the loop in lines 64 through 69. Concentrating on this segment reveals that line 65 is the one which controls routing of the output to a particular display device. The condition variable in the branching statement is not correct for the way in which the loop operates. Making the jump on "V" (video display) gives you what you want here. That way, you have a video display on "V", and both video and printout on "P".

Now to our escape character. So what! It doesn't make any difference to the program output whether the escape characters appear. Anyone unfamiliar with the program wouldn't know what they represented. However, look at it as a character which normally would not appear in the output. What happens in the entry sequence under these conditions? First, the two associated inputs are entered. Second, the list counter is increased by one, and the prompts are repeated. The program sequence is as follows: lines 20, 21, 30, 50, 55, 56, and then back to 20. The lines which change the list counter are line 55 in the repeat entry portion of the branching instruction, and line 51 in the exit portion.

Both listings are the same, so how can this be? The exit statement in line 51 must be changed to $I=I-1$. By doing this the list slot containing the escape characters will be ignored by the program. Neither the sort or display segments will recognize them since J, the total number of entries in the list, is set equal to I in line 52.

The next item is really a design modification, but consider it a "bug" of sorts. When you call the video display routine, the characters appear on the screen. The computer is so fast we have no time to see what they are before they are erased and the repeat prompt appears. This is minor and can be remedied by changing the CLS in line 70 at the end of the display loop to a print statement. This will separate the prompt from the end of the list and permit both to remain on the screen.

Everything is checked now except the use of the file input and output routines. Knowing that the data will enter correctly from the keyboard; that the sort routine is working; that the branches are all right; and that the program terminates properly, let's enter some data and save it to a disk file.

First check the file entry routine. Run the program to start over and enter "Y" at the update prompt. It appears there is another spelling or punctuation error in line 120. Inspecting this line reveals an extra comma after the open, and before the rest of the statement. Removing this comma clears the problem. Now the program will run in all sections and not stop because of syntax or logic errors. The corrected program is listed in Fig. 6-3.

At this point in the process of program verification, testing and debugging are complete. The program will run under normal circumstances with the expected inputs. It is unrealistic to expect, however, that all users will remember exactly what to enter at any particular place. Now our job as programmers is to anticipate all possible incorrect operator responses and provide ways for the program to handle such errors. Figure 6-3 has five places where errors occur in places where the operator has to input information to the program, either as data or as branching choices for the program. In the prompt statements, it must be decided what erroneous inputs are most likely. Obviously, it would be impossible to provide responses for all errors. But since the prompt statements contain some clues (the Y/N prompt), you can most likely, expect something similar. The most portable error would be either a single character, which is not a "Y" or "N," due to pressing a wrong key by mistake; entering the "Y" or "N" as lowercase; or spelling out the response as "YES" or "NO."

What will the computer do in such cases? If the single desired character (in uppercase) is entered, the jump will be made. If anything else is entered, the *else* branch will be executed. Therefore, if an incorrect response is made, the program executes the *else* branch of the statement.

There are two problems here. First, assure that only a single character is present at the start of the branching statement. Second, distinguish between correct and incorrect responses in the else branch of the comparison. The first problem is simple. Truncate whatever has been input to the left-most single character and make this the variable. A solution to the second involves redesign of the condition logic in the branching instruction.

You want to see a situation in which an incorrect response has no apparent effect on program operation, but yet the program will not proceed until a proper response has been entered. Since a single character is assured by the truncation, set up the branches so that

```
10 CLEAR 10000
11 DEFSTR X,L
12 DEFINT I-K
13 DIM X(200),L(200)
15 I=1
16 CLS
17 INPUT"IS THIS AN UPDATE";A$
18 A$ = LEFT$(A$,1)
19 IF A$ = "Y" THEN GOSUB 120: I=I+1
20 CLS
21 INPUT"WHAT IS VARIABLE NAME";X(I)
30 INPUT"ENTER ITS DEFINITION";L(I)
50 IF X(I) <> "*" OR L(I) <> "*" THEN 55
51 I=I-1
52 J=I
53 GOSUB 2290
54 GOTO 60
55 I=I+1
56 GOTO 20
60 CLS
61 INPUT"SEND DATA TO PRINTER OR VIDEO DISPLAY (P/V)";C$
62 C$ = LEFT$(C$,1)
64 FOR I = 1 TO J
65 IF C$ = "V" THEN 67
66 LPRINT X(I); TAB(10) L(I)
67 PRINT X(I)
68 PRINT L(I)
69 NEXT I
70 CLS
71 INPUT"DO YOU WISH TO REPEAT (Y/N)";B$
```

Fig. 6-3. Intermediate version of the sort program.

the "Y" branch is activated only by upper- or lowercase "Y", and the "N" branch on upper- or lower-case "N". If anything else is input,

```
72 B$ = LEFT$(B$,1)
73 IF B$ = "Y" THEN 60
74 INPUT"DO YOU WISH TO SAVE DATA (Y/N)";C$
75 C$ = LEFT$(C$,1)
76 IF C$ = "N" THEN 110
80 OPEN "O",1,"CHVAR/TXT"
90 PRINT #1, J
91 FOR I = 1 TO J
95 PRINT #1, X(I);",";L(I)
98 NEXT I
100 CLOSE
101 PRINT TAB(32)"FILE CLOSED"
110 END
120 OPEN"I",1,"CHVAR/TXT"
125 INPUT #1,J
130 FOR I = 1 TO J
135 INPUT #1, X(I),L(I)
140 NEXT I
148 CLOSE
150 RETURN
2290 IF J <= 1 THEN 2380
2291 JL = J-1
2292 FOR I = 1 TO JL
2295     KL = I+1
2300     FOR K = KL TO J
2330          IF X(I) <= X(K) THEN 2360
2340          SWAP X(I),X(K)
2350          SWAP L(I),L(K)
2360     NEXT K
2370 NEXT I
```

return to tne prompt for reentry. This requires a two-level nested branching statement which has the form:

IF (A$="Y" OR A$="Y") THEN GOSUB 120:I=I+1
IF (A$="N" OR A$= "n") THEN 20 ELSE 17

This statement replaces the branching statement in line 19 of Fig. 6-3. Similar formats can be used for the other prompt statements and corresponding branches in lines 61 and 65, 71 and 73, and 74 and 76. Write your own statements for these lines and then compare them with the statements in Fig. 6-4. Don't worry if they are not exactly the same. The important thing is that they perform the task you set for them. Note also that in these nested statements the second if-then-else statement is the else of the first if-then-else statement.

To use the extra memory, you can provide a prompt telling the user what has happened, and remind him of the correct response in the situation. This prompt could be written as a short subroutine and inserted just before returning to the input prompt again.

Before leaving the program, let's review what has made this an operational program.

1. You reviewed the listing as entered into the computer for spelling and punctuation errors, but still, errors creep in. You can estimate about one error for every six lines of code. Most can be found by a careful hand check before running. Some, however, will slip through until attempting the program. The computer is the final judge.

2. You checked for jumps to incorrect locations; incorrect nesting of loops; incorrect branching logic; and failure to increment or decrement counter variables, or doing so at the wrong times. These errors will account for most of the time spent in debugging. Naturally, the more complex your program the more time required to find these problems. This is where modular or structured design will help in tracking down the source of the problem.

3. Finally, you determined what effect incorrect entries to the various prompt statements had on program operation. And ran all the various branches and options provided in the program to assure they worked correctly. Do not assume that a particular section of a program is error free until it has been tested within the working program, and has performed desirably. These design modifications take care of conditions or inputs ignored in the design process. It is best then to go back to the design material, and redesign it to take the new items into account. This way there is less chance of correcting one problem while at the same time introducing two

other problems, because of interactions unconsidered when coding the new material.

The final working version of the program is shown in Fig. 6-4. This version has most, if not all, of the possible errors removed or taken into account.

Now that the program is working properly there is one final task: to optimize the program. It is not necessary in a program of this size, but the practice will do us good.

To begin, combine program statements into multistatement lines if your system permits it. In TRS-80 BASIC, each line number takes up five bytes of memory; so the fewer lines used the less memory used. Be careful when doing this. Whenever you have an instruction to jump a branch, make sure that instruction begins a line. A number of statements can usually be combined by separating them with colons. You can enter up to 256 characters on a single line.

If additional space is still needed, you can eliminate any remarks from the running version of the program and, in TRS-80 BASIC, eliminate blank spaces from between the words making up instructions and statements. Elimination of blanks cannot be done on all systems. Check the version of BASIC you are using to find out if this is allowed.

Make sure, when you have finished, that you check the program operation again. You may have created some additional bugs in the optimization process. This can be especially troubling in nested if-then-else structures and in loops. Figure 6-5 shows an optimized version of the program. Figures 6-6 through 6-11 are the design flowcharts as the program gradually developed.

ASSEMBLY LANGUAGE

In assembly language, there is so much detail to deal with that a different approach is taken. The design of a machine-language program is handled in the same way as any other. The most common approach is a combination of modular and structured programming techniques, along with top-down design to provide an overall picture of the progress of the program.

Once the program is coded, however, even the simplest function is a complex sequence of code. As a consequence, many assembly-language programmers will start the debugging process with the simplest primitive routines they have in the program. Each routine and each section is subjected to testing until it is completely

69

```
10 CLEAR 10000
11 DEFSTR X,L
12 DEFINT I-K
13 DIM X(200),L(200)
15 I=1
16 CLS
17 INPUT"IS THIS AN UPDATE";A$
19 (IF A$ = "Y" or A$="y") THEN GOSUB 120: I=I+1 ELSE
   IF (A$="N" OR A$="n") THEN 20 ELSE 17
20 CLS
21 INPUT"WHAT IS VARIABLE NAME";X(I)
30 INPUT"ENTER ITS DEFINITION";L(I)
50 IF X(I) <> "*" OR L(I) <> "*" THEN 55
51 I=I-1
52 J=I
53 GOSUB 2290
54 GOTO 60
55 I=I+1
56 GOTO 20
60 CLS
61 INPUT"SEND DATA TO PRINTER OR VIDEO DISPLAY
   (P/V)";C$:C$=LEFT$(C$,1)
64 FOR I = 1 TO J
65 IF (C$ = "V" or C$ = "v")THEN 67 ELSE IF (C$<>"P" OR
   C$<>"p") THEN 61
66 LPRINT X(I); TAB(10) L(I)
67 PRINT X(I)
68 PRINT L(I)
69 NEXT I
70 PRINT
71 INPUT"DO YOU WISH TO REPEAT (Y/N)";B$:B$=LEFT$(B$,1)
```

Fig. 6-4. Corrected sort program.

```basic
73 IF (B$ = "Y" OR B$ = "y") THEN 60 ELSE IF (B$<>"N" OR
   B$<> n") THEN 71
74 INPUT"DO YOU WISH TO SAVE DATA (Y/N)";C$: C$=LEFT$(C$,1)
76 IF (C$ = "N" OR C$ = "n") THEN 110 ELSE IF (C$<> "Y" OR
   C$ <> y") THEN 74
80 OPEN "O",1,"CHVAR/TXT"
90 PRINT #1, J
91 FOR I = 1 TO J
95 PRINT #1, X(I);",";L(I)
98 NEXT I
100 CLOSE
101 PRINT TAB(32)"FILE CLOSED"
110 END
120 OPEN "I",1,"CHVAR/TXT"
125 INPUT #1,J
130 FOR I = 1 TO J
135 INPUT #1, X(I),L(I)
140 NEXT I
148 CLOSE
150 RETURN
2290 IF J <= 1 THEN 2380
2291 JL = J-1
2292 FOR I = 1 TO JL
2295     KL = I+1
2300     FOR K = KL TO J
2330          IF X(I) <= X(K) THEN 2360
2340          SWAP X(I),X(K)
2350          SWAP L(I),L(K)
2360     NEXT K
2370 NEXT I
2380 RETURN
```

```
10 CLEAR10000:DEFSTRX,L:DEFINTI-K:DIMX(200),L(200)

15 I=1

16 CLS:INPUT"IS THIS AN UPDATE";A$:A$=LEFT$(A$,1):IF
   A$="Y"THENGOSUB2400:GOSUB120:I=I+1

20 CLS:LINEINPUT"WHAT IS VARIABLE NAME";X(I)

30 LINEINPUT"ENTER ITS DEFINITION";L(I)

50 IFX(I)="*"ANDL(I)="*"THENI=I-1:J=I:GOSUB2290:GOTO60

55 I=I+1:GOTO20

60 CLS:INPUT"SEND DATA TO PRINTER OR VIDEO DISPLAY
   (P/V)";C$:C$=LEFT$(C$,1)

64 FORI=1TOJ:IFC$="V"THEN68

65 LPRINTX(I);TAB(10)L(I)

68 PRINTX(I):PRINTL(I):NEXTI

69 CLS:INPUT"DO YOU WISH TO REPEAT (Y/N)";B$:B$=
   LEFT$(B$,1):IFB$="Y"THEN60

70 INPUT"DO YOU WISH TO SAVE DATA (Y/N)";C$:C$=
   LEFT$(C$,1):IFC$="N"THEN100

75 GOSUB2400

80 OPEN"O",1,F$
```

Fig. 6-5. Optimized version of sort program.

reliable under all program conditions. Then, it is combined into the next level of coding. As the programmer builds toward a complete program, he doesn't want any of the previously tested segments to interfere in the present level of testing.

In assembler, there are more things to check for when debugging a program. You check all the things mentioned in connection with high-level languages. They can happen in assembly language just as easily as in BASIC or any other language. In addition, there are a number of peculiar things which can disrupt program operation in assembly language. Some of these are; failure to initialize variables, counters, pointers, and other program items; reversing the order of the operands; accidentally reinitializing a register or memory location; changing flags before they are used; confusing values and addresses, numbers, and characters, or binary and decimal numbers; failing to change or reinitialize flags when you intended to; reversing the order of compares and subtracts; using shift instruc-

```
90 PRINT#1,J:FORI=1TOJ:PRINT#1,X(I);",";L(I):NEXTI
100 CLOSE:PRINTTAB(32)"FILE CLOSED"
110 END
120 OPEN"I",1,F$
130 INPUT#1,J
140 FORI=1TOJ
142 LINE INPUT #1,X(I)
144 LINE INPUT #1,L(I)
146 NEXT I
150 CLOSE:RETURN
2290 GOTO2310
2310 IFJ<=1THENRETURN
2320 JL=J-1:FORI=1TOJL:KL=I+1:FORK=KLTOJ
2330 IFX(I)<=X(K)THEN2360
2340 SWAPX(I),X(K)
2350 SWAPL(I),L(K)
2360 NEXTK
2370 NEXTI:RETURN
2400 INPUT"    ENTER FILE NAME";F$:RETURN
```

tions improperly; confusing the stack and stack pointer; confusing registers and register pairs; ignoring the effects of subroutines and macros on registers and especially on flags; and changing a register or memory location before you use it in the program. These are some of the errors which can occur.

Illustrating the debugging of a complete assembler program would take more space than is available here. The following short program illustrates a few of these points and gives a feel for the debugging process implemented in machine-language programs.

The purpose of this routine is to convert one byte (two hexadecimal digits) into their ASCII equivalents. Figure 6-12 is the assembly-language source listing in Z-80 mnemonics.

A number of items are specified in the assembler listing which are not necessary in high-level coding. In particular, note the specifications for what the various registers must contain on entry and exit from the routine. The programmer needs this information so that the information processed in the routine is not destroyed

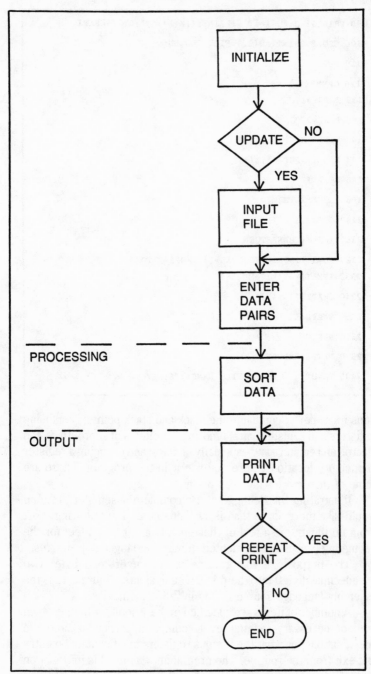

Fig. 6-6. Overall design of sort program.

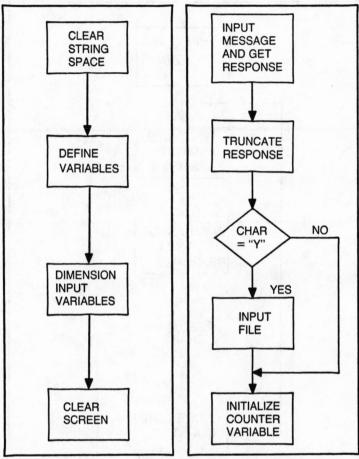

Fig. 6-7. Initialization of sort program.   Fig. 6-8. Update flowchart.

before it can be used in other portions of the program. Subroutines called by the routine are also listed so that a complete picture of its operation appears in the listing. It is also a good idea to include a name for the routine along with a description of its purpose. This gives you an easy handle for future reference.

Comments can be included in the listing for every significant instruction, and should explain what the instruction is doing in terms of the overall purpose of the routine. In the example, the instruction "and ofh" won't say very much about what is happening at that point in the program. It must be explained that the instruction masks off the previously converted digits so that you are working with the four least significant digits. If these comments are not

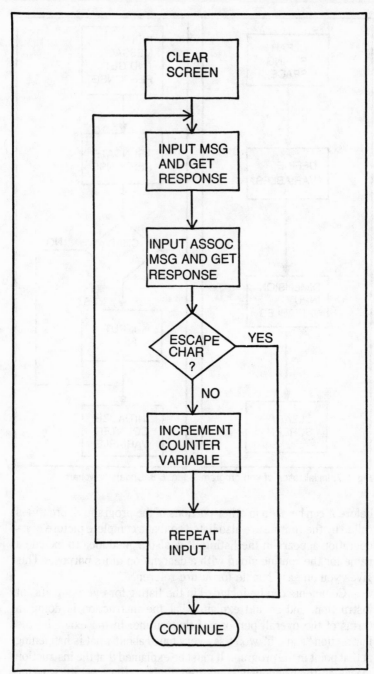

Fig. 6-9. Data entry routine.

76

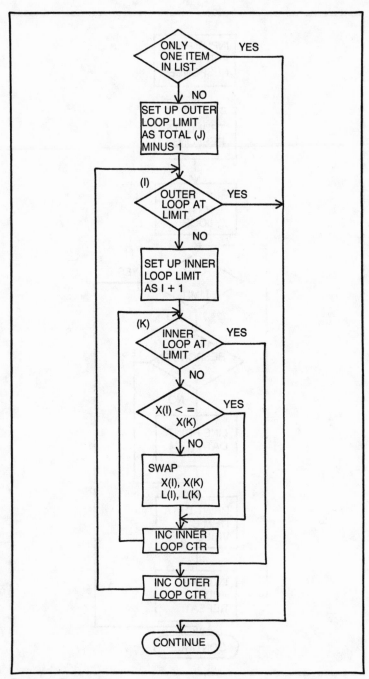

Fig. 6-10. Sort routine.

77

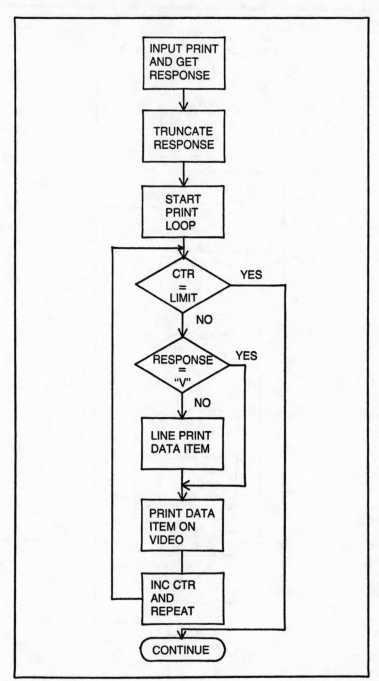

Fig. 6-11. Print routine.

```
                        HEXCV

          ROUTINE TO CONVERT FROM HEX TO ASCII

          ENTRY:  (A) = 8 BIT VALUE TO CONVERT

          EXIT:   (H) = ASCII CHARACTER FOR HIGH NIBBLE

                  (L) = ASCII CHARACTER FOR LOW NIBBLE

                  (A) = DESTROYED

                  (C) = DESTROYED

          SUBROUTINE CALLS: CONVERT
-----------------------------------------------------------------
3000      00100           ORG     3000H    ;CHANGE ON
                                           ;REASSEMBLY

3000      00110 HEXCV     LD      C,A      ;SAVE 2 HEX
                                           ;DIGITS

3001      00120           SRL     A        ;ALIGN HIGH

3003      00130           SRL     A        ;DIGIT

3005      00140           SRL     A

3007      00150           SRL     A

3009      00160           CALL    CONVERT  ;CONVERT TO
                                           ;ASCII

300C      00170           LD      H,A      ;SAVE DIGIT

300D      00180           LD      A,C      ;RESTORE ORIG
                                           ;BYTE

300E      00190           AND     OFH      ;GET LOW DIGIT

3010      00200           CALL    CONVERT  ;CONVERT 2ND
                                           ;DIGIT

3013      00210           LD      L,A      ;SAVE DIGIT

3014      00220           END

3015      00230 CONVERT   ADD     A,30H    ;CONVERSION

                                           ;FACTOR

3017      00240           CP      3AH      ;TEST FOR 0-9

3019      00250           JP      M,TST    ;GO IF 0-9

301C      00260           ADD     A,7      ;CORRECT FOR A-F

301E      00270 TST       RET              ;RETURN

301E      00280           END
```

Fig. 6-12. Assembler source listing for hexadecimal conversion routine. This routine converts one byte of code into two ASCII-coded hexadecimal characters, which together represent the original byte in ASCII representation.

included, no one will know what the individual instructions were intended to accomplish, or even how the overall routine was designed to work.

Before assembling the source code, let's double check a few things. We've saved the original byte in the first instruction, then shifted to get the four most significant bytes in the next four identical instructions, and then called the conversion routine for the first time. Now store the conversion and get the original byte back to convert the other half. You get rid of the converted code and then convert the remaining bytes. The routine then stores the second conversion and exits.

The conversion subroutine adds the conversion factor, tests the conversion for alphabetic characters, and then, either completes the conversion or, if already complete, returns to the calling routine. It appears to be all there so you are ready to hand check the code.

A hand check uses the checklist procedure to verify that the instructions are doing what intended. In checking our source list in Fig. 6-12 these were the following errors:

1. After converting and saving the first character the order of operands was reversed and the original data destroyed by loading the converted character over it.

2. The compare test in the subroutine is incorrect. In this case, add the 7 to 39 or nine in ASCII. The jump is made if the value is equal to or less than 39. The correct coding should compare with 3AH.

Once these changes have been made the routine is ready to assemble.

Figure 6-13 is an assembled listing of the program. The source listing and comments appear on the right. On the left side of the page appear the memory location and hexadecimal code for each instruction. Now let's enter the code into computer memory and test it. Remember, no program or routine can be guaranteed to run until you test it on your own microcomputer. This is the ultimate test and, in the long run, the only one that counts.

First test the conversion subroutine. This is the only subroutine within the program, and is called twice. Be certain that if problems occur in the program they are not originating here. The subroutine requires the data to be in the four least significant bits of register A (the accumulator). For this test, simply enter the data there and see what is produced. The results will also appear in the accumulator.

Let's enter the subroutine using the machine-language monitor program. Once in memory, test the subroutine using values of 0, 5, 9, A, and F. Zero and F give a check on the limits expected of the routine; five gives a test on a representative case; and nine and A check the proper routing of the jump instruction. Since all give the correct result, the subroutine is operating correctly. Now incorporate it into the rest of the routine.

When trying a value in the complete routine, the second ASCII character is correct, and the first one is not. There must be a problem in the first part of the routine. The subroutine tested all right by itself and gives the correct results the second time through. The problem, then, must be either in what is input to the routine, or in the transfer of the results to the "H" register.

To test this, put a breakpoint (a temporary halt in program execution inserted by the monitor) at the beginning of the subroutine, and another just after return. Inserting 34 in the "A" register and running the routine gives the answer. The shift instructions are incorrect. At the beginning, the subroutine should have 03 (hex) in the accumulator. Instead it has 40 (hex). Looking carefully at the shift instructions you'll find that a left shift was coded instead of a right shift. Changing this corrects the problem, and the remainder of the routine works correctly.

These kinds of difficulties are typical of problems encountered in assembling and testing machine-language programs. You had incorrect instructions, inversion of operands, incorrect jumps, and incorrect use of flags. Careful checking and testing in small steps minimizes the effects of these errors.

SUMMARY

The purpose of testing and debugging is to insure correct program operation. Errors can occur in both design and coding. Both should be checked thoroughly, and checklists are the best way to insure that nothing is left out or forgotten. Make a checklist for each level of design if using top-down design techniques. These lists should contain the following items as a minimum.

1. Check coding against the design. Is it all there? Does it do what was intended?

2. Check for punctuation and spelling errors in coding.

3. Check any loops which occur in the code. Do they contain only the instructions you intended? Is the number of iterations correct? Are the variables correct and do they change as necessary?

```
                         HEXCV

        ROUTINE TO CONVERT FROM HEX TO ASCII

        ENTRY:  (A) = 8 BIT VALUE TO CONVERT

        EXIT:   (H) = ASCII CHARACTER FOR HIGH NIBBLE

                (L) = ASCII CHARACTER FOR LOW NIBBLE

                (A) = DESTROYED

                (C) = DESTROYED

        SUBROUTINE CALLS: CONVERT
------------------------------------------------------------------
3000          00100          ORG     3000H   ;CHANGE ON
                                             ;REASSEMBLY

3000 4F       00110 HEXCV    LD      C,A     ;SAVE 2 HEX
                                             ;DIGITS

3001 CB3F     00120          SRL     A       ;ALIGN HIGH

3003 CB3F     00130          SRL     A       ;DIGIT

3005 CB3F     00140          SRL     A

3007 CB3F     00150          SRL     A

3009 CD1530   00160          CALL    CONVERT ;CONVERT TO
                                             ;ASCII

300C 67       00170          LD      H,A     ;SAVE DIGIT

300D 79       00180          LD      A,C     ;RESTORE ORIG
                                             ;BYTE

300E E60F     00190          AND     0FH     ;GET LOW DIGIT

3010 CD1530   00200          CALL    CONVERT ;CONVERT 2ND
                                             ;DIGIT

3013 6F       00210          LD      L,A     ;SAVE DIGIT

3014          00220          END

3015 C630     00230 CONVERT  ADD     A,30H   ;CONVERSION
                                             ;FACTOR

3017 FE3A     00240          CP      3AH     ;TEST FOR 0-9

3019 FA1E30   00250          JP      M,TST   ;GO IF 0-9

301C C607     00260          ADD     A,7     ;CORRECT FOR A-F

301E C9       00270 TST      RET             ;RETURN

301E          00280          END
```

Fig. 6-13. Assembler output including machine code and addresses.

82

4. Check all branches and decision points. Do they go to the correct instruction? Is the logic correct? Are there any special cases which are not accounted for?

5. Check for proper nesting in loops and conditional branches.

6. Check any other design errors or omissions which may show up during testing and debugging.

Testing will generally proceed from top to bottom in high-level languages, and from the bottom (the simplest subsegments) to the complete program in assembly-language programs.

Debugging assembly-language programs requires much more attention to detail than debugging high-level programs. The following things can cause problems in assembly-language:

1. Failing to initialize variables, pointers, and other program values before use. Or accidentally reinitializing them before they can be used in the program.

2. Confusing similar items such as values and addresses, numbers and characters, data and pointers, registers and register pairs and so on.

3. Reversing the order of operands in comparisons, subtraction, or other non-commuting operations.

4. Not taking into account the effects of macros and/or subroutines on the flag register.

5. Using instructions improperly, or using the wrong instruction for what you wish to accomplish.

Chapter 7
Documentation and Redesign

Documentation is one of the least considered facets in programming. Many program designers ignore it until after the program is written and running. As a result, the documentation packages supplied with such programs tend to be superficial and perfunctory.

To many programmers, writing documentation is an onerous and boring task, but in reality, nothing could be further from the truth. No program is worth a nickel unless someone other than the original programmer can understand and use it. Futhermore, without adequate documentation, even the author of the program could probably not use it after a lapse of a few weeks.

Preparing complete program documentation is one of the most vital tasks in the programming process. This task can be easy if notes are kept during the program development process. In addition, the program itself can be self documenting. Let's examine some of the forms which documentation can take.

COMMENTS
One of the most obvious self documentation forms is the *remark* or *comment*. These are explanatory statements ignored by the compiler or assembler, but which appear in the source listing explaining the purpose of a particular instruction or sequence of instructions. They do take up memory space when run on an interpreter, even though these lines are not executed. Figure 7-1 illustrates use of remarks in a BASIC program. Figure 7-2 does the same for an assembler listing.

Good comments or remarks explain the purpose of an instruction or sequence rather than repeat what the instruction is doing at that particular time. Make comments as clear as possible. Explain how the data is being handled, what the variables are and how they are affected by the sequence. Comments such as "increment counter" are worthless unless they include statements explaining what the counter is referring to in the particular instruction or sequence. Comments such as "count items in array until all have been checked and sorted" are usually more meaningful when looked at after a period of time.

Comments should also be in plain English. Attempts to save space by abbreviating or using acronyms only confuses the user. If the meaning of a comment is not obvious after three or four weeks, then it is not a good comment.

It is not necessary to comment every line when the purpose of the instruction is obvious in the context. This clutters the program with useless detail obscuring the important information making it difficult to recognize. Proper use of comments helps you to pick out significant program structures and understand their interrelations. In addition, comments highlight any special or unusual conditions; use of instructions in ways not normally envisioned; confusing variables or data structures, and generally, to clarify points confusing to those unfamiliar with the basic assumptions underlying the design of the program.

FLOWCHARTS

The flowchart can be an important documentation aid so long as it does not become too detailed. Flowcharts can have the same problems as comments: too much detail obscures the basic structure and confuses the reader. One way to avoid this is to decide in advance what the flowchart is to show. If there is much information, perhaps several flowcharts can be constructed for different purposes.

As mentioned in Chapter 3, the basic advantage of the flowchart is to provide a picture of the overall system and its interrelations. And that it is easily understood by the nonprogrammer, makes its use imperative. Emphasize these primary advantages when considering their use.

STRUCTURE DIAGRAM

The structured form of a program listing also provides a clear picture of the logical organization of a program or a module of the

```
1'          DATA ENTRY SECTION
2'          Initialize program
10 CLEAR 10000
11 DEFSTR X,L
12 DEFINT I-K
13 DIM X(200),L(200)
15 I=1
16'         Check for update
17 CLS
18 INPUT"IS THIS AN UPDATE";A$
19 (IF A$ = "Y" or A$="y") THEN GOSUB 120: I=I+1 ELSE
   IF (A$="N" OR A$="n") THEN 20 ELSE 17
20          Enter new data
21 CLS
22 INPUT"WHAT IS VARIABLE NAME";X(I)
30 INPUT"ENTER ITS DEFINITION";L(I)
50 IF X(I) <> "*" OR L(I) <> "*" THEN 55
51 I=I-1
52 J=I
53'              PROCESSING
54 GOSUB 2290 'Sorts data into alphabetical order
55 GOTO 60
56 I=I+1
57 GOTO 20
58'              PROGRAM OUTPUT
59'          Output display options
60 CLS
61 INPUT"SEND DATA TO PRINTER OR VIDEO DISPLAY
   (P/V)";C$:C$=LEFT$(C$,1)
62'          Print data
64 FOR I = 1 TO J
```

Fig. 7-1. Commented BASIC program.

```
55 IF (C$ = "V" or C$ = "v")THEN 67 ELSE IF (C$<>"P" OR
   C$<>"p") THEN 61
66 LPRINT X(I); TAB(10) L(I)
67 PRINT X(I)
68 PRINT L(I)
69 NEXT I
70 PRINT
71'                  Repeat option
72 INPUT"DO YOU WISH TO REPEAT (Y/N)";B$:B$=LEFT$(B$,1)
73 IF (B$ = "Y" OR B$ = "y") THEN 60 ELSE IF (B$<>"N" OR
   B$<> n") THEN 71
74'                  Save option
75 INPUT"DO YOU WISH TO SAVE DATA (Y/N)";C$: C$=LEFT$(C$,1)
76 IF (C$ = "N" OR C$ = "n") THEN 110 ELSE IF (C$<> "Y" OR
   C$ <> y") THEN 74
78'             Data save subroutine
80 OPEN "O",1,"CHVAR/TXT"
90 PRINT #1, J
91 FOR I = 1 TO J
95 PRINT #1, X(I);",";L(I)
98 NEXT I
100 CLOSE
101'            Exit from program
102 PRINT TAB(32)"FILE CLOSED"
110 END
115'            Data read subroutine
120 OPEN "I",1,"CHVAR/TXT"
125 INPUT #1,J
130 FOR I = 1 TO J
135 INPUT #1, X(I),L(I)
140 NEXT I
148 CLOSE
```

```
150 RETURN

2280'              Sort subroutine

2290 IF J <= 1 THEN 2380

2291 JL = J-1

2292 FOR I = 1 TO JL

2295     KL = I+1

2300     FOR K = KL TO J

2330         IF X(I) <= X(K) THEN 2360

2340         SWAP X(I),X(K)

2350         SWAP L(I),L(K)

2360     NEXT K

2370 NEXT I

2380 RETURN
```

Fig. 7-1. Commented BASIC program (continued from page 87).

program. This is especially true if the following things are kept in mind when designing the program.

1. Describe the function or purpose of each section. This can be done with comments or in a special header for the segment.

2. Make it clear, either through the structures or by comments, which statements are included within each loop or conditional structure. Indenting can aid greatly in this.

3. Use consistent language in your comments. Use the same names for the same structures in the different parts of the program, and make the total structure as well as its descriptions as simple as possible.

THE MEMORY MAP

A memory map is simply a list of the areas of memory used by the program. This includes space used for the program instructions, the data, any tables or other structures used by the program, areas reserved for workspace, the stack, and other program needs. As is evident from the discussion so far, the memory map is most often used as documentation with assembly-language programs.

This does not imply it is inappropriate to use a memory map to document high-level programs. There are times when it is essential to know where the data is stored and how much space is taken up

```
                        HEXCV

        ROUTINE TO CONVERT FROM HEX TO ASCII

        ENTRY:  (A) = 8 BIT VALUE TO CONVERT

        EXIT:   (H) = ASCII CHARACTER FOR HIGH NIBBLE

                (L) = ASCII CHARACTER FOR LOW NIBBLE

                (A) = DESTROYED

                (C) = DESTROYED

        SUBROUTINE CALLS: CONVERT
--------------------------------------------------------------
3000          00100          ORG     3000H  ;CHANGE ON

                                            ;REASSEMBLY

3000 4F       00110 HEXCV    LD      C,A    ;SAVE 2 HEX

                                            ;DIGITS

3001 CB3F     00120          SRL     A      ;ALIGN HIGH

3003 CB3F     00130          SRL     A      ;DIGIT

3005 CB3F     00140          SRL     A

3007 CB3F     00150          SRL     A

3009 CD1530   00160          CALL    CONVERT ;CONVERT TO

                                            ;ASCII

300C 67       00170          LD      H,A    ;SAVE DIGIT

300D 79       00180          LD      A,C    ;RESTORE ORIG

                                            ;BYTE
300E E60F     00190          AND     0FH    ;GET LOW DIGIT

3010 CD1530   00200          CALL    CONVERT ;CONVERT 2ND

                                            ;DIGIT

3013 6F       00210          LD      L,A    ;SAVE DIGIT

3014          00220          END

3015 C630     00230 CONVERT  ADD     A,30H  ;CONVERSION

                                            ;FACTOR

3017 FE3A     00240          CP      3AH    ;TEST FOR 0-9

3019 FA1E30   00250          JP      M,TST  ;GO IF 0-9

301C C607     00260          ADD     A,7    ;CORRECT FOR A-F

301E C9       00270 TST      RET            ;RETURN

301E          00280          END
```

Fig. 7-2. Commented assembler output.

with the program. It is only that this type of documentation is more common in assembly-language programming.

VARIABLE LISTS

A variable list is usually an alphabetical list of all variables used by the program. Often included are some or all of the following items.

1. A definition of the variable and its use in the program.
2. The memory locations or program lines at which it appears.
3. A cross reference index of line numbers and names ordered by line number.

PROGRAM DESCRIPTION

One of the most important of these documentation aids is a clearly written description of exactly what the program was designed to do, the algorithms employed to perform these tasks, how the program operation was verified, and what provisions have been made to avoid or correct operator errors. Clarity is emphasized here. This is not strictly a programmer's aid. You can expand this for the programmer in the program logic manual.

A concise description is important for both the programmer and the user to understand what the program has been designed to do without overwhelming them with detail. A description of the test plan and its results also aids in understanding the limits of the design. It also gives a standard against which to test if they have problems with any part of the program.

The items mentioned so far are considered by many to be the *minimum* acceptable set of documents for a program which is not to be released to others. If the program is to be released commercially, or even distributed among your friends or associates, then at least three more documents need to be produced.

PROGRAM LOGIC MANUAL

The first of these is the program logic manual I mentioned earlier. This manual explains in detail the design goals of the program, what algorithms were chosen to implement them, and why those particular ones and not others were used. It explains in detail, what data structures are used and how they are manipulated in the program. Coding is explained in a step-by-step fashion so that the programmer reading this manual knows exactly what each instruction does in advancing the processing of the data to its conclusion. Any special tables, graphs, or other aids in understanding the logic or the coding in the program are also included.

THE USER'S GUIDE

The user's guide is the most important document of all, but unfortunately, one of the most overlooked. In writing the user's guide remember that the operator reading it will not have any extensive background in programming, nor will he or she be aware of or care about the elegant subtleties of the program. The main emphasis is to explain as clearly and as simply as possible all the commands and functions available to the user. This includes what procedures to follow if incorrect entries are made at any point, what the program expects to accomplish from the user's point of view, and any features or functions requiring special attention. Also remember that some operators are more experienced than others and explain how an experienced operator can take advantage of any procedural shortcuts available.

Since the user will most likely be inexperienced in programming and its language, it is imperative that all explanations be clear and simple. Use as many illustrations as possible. Simple flowcharts of the overall program organization can be helpful if they show the relation between the various commands. Some user's guides contain pictures or diagrams of the video display. These show the operator what to expect as a program prompt, and what response is expected for the step-by-step explanation of the commands. Use examples freely. A good example can solidify understanding of a whole section of step-by-step explanation.

Once you have the instructions on paper, test the guide. Follow exactly the instructions you have given and see if they are what you intended. Better yet, have someone else test the manual. When you are familiar with the program and its design, take shortcuts not apparent to the first-time user. This way you can see how clear your instructions really were. You may be surprised, perhaps upset, but the user's guide will be the better for the experience. More could be said here but keeping in mind these highlights a minimally satisfactory document can be produced.

Remember, the user's guide is the most useful of all the program documents. You can never spend too much time insuring that it is clear, concise, and above all simple to use.

MAINTENANCE MANUAL

The Maintenance Manual is designed for the programmer who needs to adapt the program to new uses or conditions. Provisions for future expansion of the program are fully explained here. The procedures for modifying the program are included as step-by-step instructions, along with explanations of any other items such as the effect on data structures, data manipulation, interaction between program segments, and the like.

DOCUMENTATION EXAMPLE

Not let's put the information to use with the program in Fig 6-4 of Chapter 6. In developing a program, all the items discussed in this chapter, except for the program logic manual, the user's guide, and the program maintainance manual, have been completed. These were omitted in Chapter 6 in order to concentrate on testing and debugging without additional topics intruding. As you probably see by now, such artificial separation of the various program phases is purely for convenience in discussing them. Actually, many of them are carried on simultaneously during the development process.

Let's begin by commenting the program listing of Fig. 6-4. The initial remarks at the beginning indicate the name and a brief summary of the program's purpose. The name assigned can be arbitrary but should relate to the function the program performs. Then indicate the various modules or blocks of code by separating them with blank lines and providing header remarks for them. This stage of the process is shown in Fig. 7-3. Then comment all loops and decision blocks listing destinations in all cases. The final commented version appears in Fig. 7-4.

You already have your flowcharts from Chapter 6 (see Figs. 6-6 through 6-11) and so do not need to repeat them here.

Our next documentation task is the structure diagram. This will give us an alternate form of program organization and is shown in Fig. 7-5.

A memory map is not necessary here. The compiler or interpreter handles such details for us, and the size of the program presents no trouble in fitting in the available space. The variable list for the program appears in Fig. 7-6. It is fairly simple with only a few variables to account for.

The following pages illustrate a typical program description, logic manual, user's guide, and maintenance manual.

VARSORT Program Description

This program creates an alphabetically sorted list of items, while maintaining correspondence between items in the sorted list and associated items in a second list. This is done without the usual amount of manipulation ordinarily necessary. The items are input initially with functions permitting the inclusion of commas and other punctuation marks within the entries. The entries are sorted, displayed, and saved in a data file on a disk. Different file names can be specified so the program can be used for more than one purpose at the same time.

The program was tested by entering a series of pairs of data items, having the program sort them in alphabetic order, saving them to disk, reading the file back in again, and displaying them on the screen and printing them on a dot matrix printer. In this way, all features and segments of the program were tested for correct operation and the data can be checked for alphabetic ordering. The program accepts only those prompts specified as input in branching between the various segments. Incorrect inputs will have no apparent effect on program operation.

VARSORT Program Logic

The program was originally designed to aid in creating variable lists for program documentation. By changing the prompt statements to those appropriate for a particular purpose, the program can be adapted to sort and display any set of associated data items. For example, the Bibliography, Glossary, and Index of this book were all created with this program.

The central algorithm of the program is the sorting routine. The sort begins at line 2290 with a check of the number of data items. If only one is present, the sort is bypassed since there is no need to sort a single item. In addition, the algorithm assumes at least two items in the list to be sorted. Then set up the comparison of the data items in the initial list. These are sorted. Each item in the associated list maintains correspondence with the proper item in the original list.

Set up two counters for the comparisons. The first sequences from one (1), to one less than the maximum number of items. The second compares each of the first sequence counter items with every other one in the second sequence. If the first data item is greater than the second, then the items are exchanged and their associated items are exchanged.

When the exchanges occur go to the next item in the first sort sequence. If the items are not exchanged, compare the current item in the first counter sequence with the remainder of the items in the second sequence. The program also includes standard disk input and output routines for sequential files. The output sequence is set up to simulate line input statements to include punctuation in the data items.

```
1'              DATA ENTRY SECTION
2'                Initialize program
10 CLEAR 10000
11 DEFSTR X,L
12 DEFINT I-K
13 DIM X(200),L(200)
15 I=1
16'           Check for update
17 CLS
18 INPUT"IS THIS AN UPDATE";A$
19 (IF A$ = "Y" or A$="y") THEN GOSUB 120: I=I+1 ELSE
   IF (A$="N" OR A$="n") THEN 20 ELSE 17
20             Enter new data
21 CLS
22 INPUT"WHAT IS VARIABLE NAME";X(I)
30 INPUT"ENTER ITS DEFINITION";L(I)
50 IF X(I) <> "*" OR L(I) <> "*" THEN 55
51 I=I-1
52 J=I
53'                  PROCESSING
54 GOSUB 2290
55 GOTO 60
56 I=I+1
57 GOTO 20
58'                PROGRAM OUTPUT
59'          Output display options
60 CLS
61 INPUT"SEND DATA TO PRINTER OR VIDEO DISPLAY
   (P/V)";C$:C$=LEFT$(C$,1)
62'          Print data
64 FOR I = 1 TO J
```

Fig. 7-3. VARSORT/BAS program listing.

```
 65 IF (C$ = "V" or C$ = "v")THEN 67 ELSE IF (C$<>"P" OR
    C$<>"p") THEN 61
 66 LPRINT X(I); TAB(10) L(I)
 67 PRINT X(I)
 68 PRINT L(I)
 69 NEXT I
 70 PRINT
 71'                 Repeat option
 72 INPUT"DO YOU WISH TO REPEAT (Y/N)";B$:B$=LEFT$(B$,1)
 73 IF (B$ = "Y" OR B$ = "y") THEN 60 ELSE IF (B$<>"N" OR
    B$<> n") THEN 71
 74'                 Save option
 75 INPUT"DO YOU WISH TO SAVE DATA (Y/N)";C$: C$=LEFT$(C$,1)
 76 IF (C$ = "N" OR C$ = "n") THEN 110 ELSE IF (C$<> "Y" OR
    C$ <> y") THEN 74
 78'                 Data save subroutine
 80 OPEN "O",1,"CHVAR/TXT"
 90 PRINT #1, J
 91 FOR I = 1 TO J
 95 PRINT #1, X(I);",";L(I)
 98 NEXT I
100 CLOSE
101'                 Exit from program
102 PRINT TAB(32)"FILE CLOSED"
110 END
115'                 Data read subroutine
120 OPEN "I",1,"CHVAR/TXT"
125 INPUT #1,J
130 FOR I = 1 TO J
135 INPUT #1, X(I),L(I)
140 NEXT I
148 CLOSE
```

```
150 RETURN

2280'              Sort subroutine

2290 IF J <= 1 THEN 2380

2291 JL = J-1

2292 FOR I = 1 TO JL

2295     KL = I+1

2300     FOR K = KL TO J

2330         IF X(I) <= X(K) THEN 2360

2340         SWAP X(I),X(K)

2350         SWAP L(I),L(K)

2360     NEXT K

2370 NEXT I

2380 RETURN
```

Fig. 7-3. VARSORT/BAS program listing (continued from page 95).

Program flow is controlled by conditional statements in the appropriate places, since only two choices are available at any single point. The program can be designed so that all inputs are entered at the beginning of the program. This requires a series of multiple-condition conditional instructions. I feel that the programming effort required to produce such complicated code is not justified by the slight convenience such a scheme provides.

The data is set up in two equally dimensioned lists. The first list {X} holds the key items to be sorted. The second {L} contains the data associated with the corresponding key item. Each key and its associated data maintains the same relative position in the list no matter what the current position of the key item is.

Detailed Logic

The initialization segment contains lines 10 through 15. Here, set up the initial conditions required by the program to run. If the program is running under TRSDOS 1.2, reserve space for storage and manipulation of alphanumeric data (line 10). Next, define the variable types, string or alphanumeric for X and L, and numeric integer for I, J, and K (lines 11 and 12). Line 13 sets up the number of list slots needed for the data, and line 15 sets the data counter variable to its initial value of one.

Now is the first decision point of the program. Clear the screen and display a prompt asking if the file desired is to be created as a new file or to be added to an existing file. If the existing file is updated, the input subroutine is called and the designated file is read into memory. The data counter is set at the number of data items input plus one, and now go to the data input prompts to enter additional data. If a new file is created, go directly to the data input section with the counter remaining at the initial value of one to begin input.

In either case, when all the new items have been entered, the entire list is sorted in order to integrate the new items into the proper places within the lists. The input loop is terminated by entering asterisks {*} for data. On termination, the termination characters are eliminated from the list in line 51, and the sort data counter {J} initialized before calling the subroutine in line 53.

On completion of the sort, clear the screen again and display the second decision prompt. This is the display option. Give yourself the choice of putting the sorted lists on the video display, or outputting the data to both line printer and video display.

This is implemented in the for-next loop beginning at line 64. The limits of the loop are the limits of the entered data. The distinction between the two is whether the information is output to the line printer or not. The video display occurs in any case. The form of the output is entered and conditioned in lines 61 and 62. The decision is implemented in line 65 where the line printer output instruction, line 66, is skipped if the conditional statement indicates only video output. If not, both forms of output are executed and the loop continues until all items have been output.

On completion of the output loop the next prompt appears. This gives the option to repeat the display. If you do not want to repeat then our final prompt appears. This one gives us the option to save the current data in a sequential file. If you want to save the data designate the name you are assigning to the file. The program then writes it to the disk. If the data is temporary and unimportant, skip the file creation routine. Following this, the file is closed and program control returns to either the BASIC interpreter or to the operating system.

VARSORT User's Guide

This program was designed originally to aid in creating variable lists for program documentation. By changing the prompt statements for a specific purpose you can adapt the program to sort and display any set of associated display items.

```
1'              DATA ENTRY SECTION
2'              Initialize program
10 CLEAR 10000
11 DEFSTR X,L
12 DEFINT I-K
13 DIM X(200),L(200)
15 I=1
16'              Check for update
17 CLS
18 INPUT"IS THIS AN UPDATE";A$
19 (IF A$ = "Y" or A$="y") THEN GOSUB 120: I=I+1 ELSE
   IF (A$="N" OR A$="n") THEN 20 ELSE 17
20              Enter new data
21 CLS
22 INPUT"WHAT IS VARIABLE NAME";X(I)
30 INPUT"ENTER ITS DEFINITION";L(I)
50 IF X(I) <> "*" OR L(I) <> "*" THEN 55
51 I=I-1
52 J=I
53'                   PROCESSING
54 GOSUB 2290 'Sorts data into alphabetical order
55 GOTO 60 'Continue to program output
56 I=I+1
57 GOTO 20 'Repeat data entry
58'                   PROGRAM OUTPUT
59'            Output display options
60 CLS
61 INPUT"SEND DATA TO PRINTER OR VIDEO DISPLAY
   (P/V)";C$:C$=LEFT$(C$,1)
62'              Print data
64 FOR I = 1 TO J
```

Fig. 7-4. VARSORT/BAS program listing.

98

```
65 IF (C$ = "V" or C$ = "v")THEN 67 ELSE IF (C$<>"P" OR
   C$<>"p") THEN 61
66 LPRINT X(I); TAB(10) L(I)
67 PRINT X(I)、
68 PRINT L(I)
69 NEXT I
70 PRINT
71'                  Repeat option
72 INPUT"DO YOU WISH TO REPEAT (Y/N)";B$:B$=LEFT$(B$,1)
73 IF (B$ = "Y" OR B$ = "y") THEN 60 ELSE IF (B$<>"N" OR
   B$<> n") THEN 71
74'                  Save option
75 INPUT"DO YOU WISH TO SAVE DATA (Y/N)";C$: C$=LEFT$(C$,1)
76 IF (C$ = "N" OR C$ = "n") THEN 110 ELSE IF (C$<> "Y" OR
   C$ <> y") THEN 74
78'             Data save subroutine
80 OPEN "O",1,"CHVAR/TXT"
90 PRINT #1, J
91 FOR I = 1 TO J
95 PRINT #1, X(I);",";L(I)
98 NEXT I
100 CLOSE
101'           Exit from program
102 PRINT TAB(32)"FILE CLOSED"
110 END
115'             Data read subroutine
120 OPEN "I",1,"CHVAR/TXT"
125 INPUT #1,J
130 FOR I = 1 TO J
135 INPUT #1, X(I),L(I)
140 NEXT I
148 CLOSE
```

```
        150 RETURN

        2280'          Sort subroutine

        2290 IF J <= 1 THEN 2380

        2291 JL = J-1

        2292 FOR I = 1 TO JL

        2295    KL = I+1

        2300    FOR K = KL TO J

        2330        IF X(I) <= X(K) THEN 2360

        2340        SWAP X(I),X(K)

        2350        SWAP L(I),L(K)

        2360    NEXT K

        2370 NEXT I

        2380 RETURN
```

Fig. 7-4. VARSORT/BAS program listing (continued from page 99).

The program was written on a Radio Shack TRS-80 Model II using a TRSDOS 1.2 operating system. The line printer output is from the parallel port. We enter the program with the following sequence of instructions:

1. Turn on the printer and computer and insert the program diskette into drive zero (the one built into the computer). Close the drive door.

2. Enter the date when the prompt appears on the screen. Then enter the time if desired. If you wish to skip a time entry, press <ENTER >.

3. Load and run the program by entering the following command string when the TRSDOS READY prompt appears.

Basic Varsort/BAS −F:1

When the above has been typed in, press ENTER. This will bring you into the program.

The first question asked by the program is, Is This An Update? Your response is "Y" or "N". You enter a "Y" for yes if the file you want has been created and saved on disk previously. If there is no file and you are entering fresh data, enter "N" for no. If the response was "Y" enter the name of the file you wish to put into memory. No matter which branch taken prompts appear for you to enter new data. When all desired data has been entered, continue with the program by entering asterisks {∗} for each of the prompts. The two prompts appearing in sequence for each entry are; What is Variable

Name? Enter it's Definition. Following exit from the data entry section there is a delay while the program sorts the key list into alphabetic order.

The next prompt occurs after the sort has been completed. The screen is cleared and this prompt appears. Send Data to Printer or Video Display (P/V). This permits you to direct the list output to the line printer, and video display, or only the video display. During the display, scrolling can be halted by pressing HOLD. To restart scrolling of the display, press HOLD again or press any other key on the keyboard.

When the end of the list is reached and all items have been displayed the following prompt appears. Do You Wish to Repeat (Y/N) Entering "Y" repeats the display sequence. Then, select a printer/video display option again. The program does not provide for storing responses on repeats. If "N" is entered the program continues.

```
DATA ENTRY
    INITIALIZE
        Clear String Space
        Define Variable Types
        Dimension Arrays
    CHECK FOR UPDATE
        Read Old Data
            open file
            read number of items in file
            read all data items
            close file
    ENTER NEW DATA
PROCESSING
    SORT DATA
OUTPUT
    DISPLAY OPTIONS
        Printer and Video
        Video Only
    REPEAT DISPLAY
    SAVE DATA
        Open File
        Print Number of Items in Memory
        Print All Data in Memory to Disk
        Close File
    EXIT PROGRAM
```

Fig. 7-5. Structure diagram for VARSORT/BAS program.

A$	Input variable used with update prompt
B$	Input variable used in repeat option
C$	Input variable used in output display and Data save routines
I	Counter variable used throughout program
J	Counter variable used in output display and Disk save routines
JL	Temporary variable used in sort routine
K	Counter variable in sort routine
KL	Temporary variable used in sort routine
L	Associated data array
X	Primary data array

Fig. 7-6. Variable list for VARSORT/BAS program.

The final question you must respond to is; Do You Wish To Save Data (Y/N) "N" entered here skips the file creation segment immediately following the prompt, closes the file, and exits the program. If "Y" is entered, the program writes the data to a disk file to be named at this point, closes the file, and again exits the program.

VARSORT Maintenance Manual

No specific provisions have been made for additions or modifications to the program. The most obvious improvement is the inclusion of a module, or section to permit changing the data for a particular item already in memory.

A convenient way to implement such a change is to convert each of the present function segments into either subroutines, or modules with a command menu inserted after the update segment. Write the change data segment as an additional module and add its starting address as an additional command in the menu. With this method, coding is rearranged but little rewritten, except for the new segment, the update coding (included as a command), and the display and inputs for the menu itself.

Another desirable modification is to permit data items longer than 256 characters input into the program. To implement this, set up a third list of items including the overflow data from the "L" list. It requires a major modification of each of the program segments. By doing this, you are modifying the data structure of the program. As mentioned in Chapter 4, changing the data structure often requires major modification or rewriting of the program.

What needs to be done in this case? Initially, the input of the second entry prompt is altered to place the data into the third list whenever the second list slot is full, 256 characters. This is not true in all cases, still, it is necessary to insure that if no data is input, the third list remains empty.

Second, the display functions in the for-next loop will have to be modified to print the third list item if present. This will require conditional print statements for the third list in both video and line printer instructions.

Third, modify the input and output routines so that the third item is saved and read back into memory. The input program has no way of distinguishing an item belonging to the second or third list, so it must supply some type of routine for this function. Another alternative to this problem is to insure that all list slots have at least one character. If the third list has no input for a particular item, substitute a blank giving no apparent change to the display.

REDESIGN

It often happens that when finished coding, testing, debugging, etc., you are not completely satisfied with the program's operation. Perhaps it is the appearance of the output on the screen or the printer; perhaps some other feature should be included in the program capabilities and you feel hampered using the program. Perhaps the program takes up too much memory, or is too slow in execution. In these cases a fresh look at the overall design of the program needs to be taken. If the changes are minor, or the improvement in speed or reduction in memory size too little, then these reductions may be achieved through careful rewriting of the present code.

If the changes are major; the improvement in performance greater than twenty or twenty-five percent, then it's best to redesign the entire program, perhaps using better algorithms. Certainly the new requirements will have to be integrated into the overall design.

If our requirements do not necessitate major reorganization, then a number of things can be done to improve performance. To save as much memory as possible when programming in a high-level language, try to implement as many of the following suggestions as possible.

1. Condense redundant segments of code into subroutines to avoid writing the same segment of code several times.

2. Make modules as general as possible. Consider using a module in several places if possible. This gives the same advantage as a subroutine.

3. Delete all remarks from the program listing when running the program on an interpreter.

4. Delete extra spaces from the program listing where possible. Each space takes up extra memory and contributes nothing to the program.

5. Combine program instructions into multi-statement lines wherever possible. Each line number takes five bytes of storage.

6. Use integer variables wherever possible. Integers take only two bytes per variable, single or double precision variables use eight and sixteen bytes respectively.

7. Use as few parentheses as possible. You will need twelve bytes of storage for every level of parentheses.

8. Dimension arrays sparingly. Unused array storage is wasted and cannot be used for other purposes.

9. Define variable types during initialization where possible. This saves the program memory used to designate them each time they appear in the program listing.

If the program is written in assembly language, then investigate to see if these items can help.

1. Again, use subroutines where possible to reduce the total amount of code necessary in the program.

2. Use register operations whenever possible to reduce the overhead involved in transferring values back and forth between memory locations.

3. Use the stack when possible for temporary memory storage. Pushes and Pops are single-byte instructions, and you can reduce the memory overhead so long as you are careful in their use.

4. Eliminate jumps. Use relative jumps instead whenever possible. Use the short form of an instruction whenever you can.

5. Use leftover results from previous operations where the program permits. This eliminates some initialization instructions.

6. Use direct memory instructions where possible to reduce both space and execution time.

7. If values can be computed, rather than found from a table,

this can save memory. The relative effectiveness will depend on how much memory can be saved.

8. Use the alternate registers as temporary storage rather than memory.

If the problem is slow execution, fairly common in BASIC, these suggestions might help.

1. Use integer variables as loop counters. This is the most effective and important item on the list of suggestions. Depending on the design of the program, this can speed up execution as much as thirty times.

2. Use variables instead of constants for program values. It takes less look-up time for variables than for constants.

3. Define the most used variables first. When variables are defined they are stored by the interpreter in a sequential list. Those variables closer to the beginning of the list can be found in less time.

4. If the program is still too slow, consider converting the largest and most frequently used segments into assembly-language subprograms called by the main high-level program.

If the entire program is written in assembly language and still too slow, check the following suggestions in your attempts to improve speed.

1. Concentrate on all loops. Since any individual assembly-language instruction executes in microseconds, millions of executions must be saved to create any appreciable difference in execution time. This can best be done by reducing the time to execute the most frequently used loops.

2. Eliminate jumps to the extent possible. These take up extra time in transferring control.

3. Use the stack for temporary data storage instead of storing it in memory. Data access is faster when using single byte instructions.

4. Use look-up tables for values instead of computing them with some algorithm. Accessing a table is much faster.

5. Avoid indexed and relative addressing. These take up extra time.

Let's take a look at the program to see which category it fits. What is found objectionable in the program as it stands? In reality, there are two major flaws.

First, there is no way to change any of the data once it has been entered. If an entry was erroneously entered, or some change in the description or definition of any entry was necessary, there is no way in the present program to correct these errors. This is a major change requiring design of an entire new section of code. This was one of the things I referred to in Chapter 6 by calling the program elementary.

Let's not be concerned here with its design. You have enough background by now to design and integrate such a segment. This will provide you with some practice in applying the techniques discussed in this book.

The second problem is the format or layout of the data on the line printer. You can enter up to 256 characters in any one definition. Ordinary 8½-by-11-inch paper displays approximately seventy to eighty characters per line. Either you run off the side of the page on long entries, or format the printer to eighty characters, confusing the reader by mixing the definitions with the data they represent. A good example of this confusion is Fig. 7-7. How can things be arranged so they can keep the titles and publishing information separate from the authors?

One way is to separate the authors and the data by a vertical space. Another might be to indent the data by a fixed amount in order to set apart the beginning of the author lines from the beginning of the data. Whichever is decided, there is still the problem of the long lines. The best solution is to design a segment of code that breaks the lines into shorter segments. It can fit on a single line and print the segments all with the original indenting.

What is needed to implement such a change? First, some sort of loop structure to count characters in the line is needed. A good character to test such as loop is a space. This way, the program will put a word either on one line or the other, and not split it into parts.

The rest of the segment is a set of conditional structures disallowing a line no longer than sixty characters to print. Sixty plus the ten space indent at the beginning of the line from the calling program will give evenly spaced margins.

Now let's start the design. You don't want to disturb the integrity of the data variables (they may have to be put back into the disk file), so begin by designating a temporary string variable (T$) to hold the line wanted to print, and a variable to designate the total number of characters in the working line (JT).

The length of the line can be checked initially and printed directly if it is less than sixty characters. Short lines will enable you to skip the counting routine entirely.

Now that the variables are set up, let's see what the loop coding will look like. To set up the for-next loop with a counter variable—

say JJ—count from the end of the line. The step will be minus one. Here is our loop:

```
FOR JJ = JT TO 1 STEP −1 IF MID$(T$,JJ,1) = "Blank Space"
then 'Exit'
NEXT JJ
```

Naturally the 'Exit' specified is to the remainder of the segment. The MID$ function is used for looking at one character at a time in the line. The words "blank space" of course are not used in the actual coding but are replaced with one space enclosed in quotation marks.

The conditional structures are next. They seem complicated, but only because of the number of things to be done in each leg of the branch. Their purpose is to insure that no line longer than sixty characters is ever printed.

The first conditional level tests if the character count from the loop is greater than sixty. This is necessary since the routine exits the loop every time a space is encountered. If the count is not sixty or less, the statement reinitializes the maximum count length to the present value and goes through the loop again. On long lines go through the count loop several times before the count is less than or equal to sixty.

If the count at the conditional statement is not greater than sixty, a number of actions are taken. First, the line is separated into the part less than sixty characters (T1$), and the remainder of the line (T2$). Next, the short part (T1$) is printed. Finally, the remainder in the second conditional statement is tested.

In the second test, if the length is greater than sixty characters, set the temporary variable (T$) equal to the remainder (T2$), and the maximum count equal to its length. Then go back to the loop and separate the remainder into sections as explained above. If the length of the remainder is not greater than sixty characters, print the remainder. Be certain that the entire line is eventually printed. This is done by making our only exit from the routine which includes the printing of the remainder. If the remainder is less than or equal to sixty characters it will be printed, and that no more characters remain in the line. This is the exit.

When exiting there is one more thing to do before returning to the main program sequence. Include a vertical space instruction to separate the beginning of the next entry from the end of the present one. Our conditional coding looks like this:

```
CHAPLIN,N

FLOWCHARTS

DAHL,O.J.,HOAVE,A.R., & DIJKSTRA,E.W

STRUCTURED PROGRAMMING

DALTON,W.F

DESIGN MICROCOMPUTER SOFTWARE LIKE OTHER SYSTEMS - SYSTEMA
TICALLY - ELECTRONICS 1/19/78 PP 97-101

DEMILO,R.A

HINTS ON TEST DATA SELECTION - COMPUTER 4/78 PP 34-41

DIJKSTRA,E.W

A DISCIPLINE OF PROGRAMMING

DOLLHOFF,T

MICROPROCESSOR SOFTWARE - DIGITAL DESIGN 2/77 PP 44-51

HALSTEAD, M.H

ELEMENTS OF SOFTWARE SCIENCE

HUGHES,J.K., & MICHTOM,J.I

A STRUCTURED APPROACH TO PROGRAMMING

KNUTH,D.E

THE ART OF COMPUTER PROGRAMMING (3 VOLS)

MORGAN,D.E & TAYLOR,D.J

A SURVEY OF METHODS FOR ACHIEVING RELIABLE SOFTWARE - CO
MPUTER 2/77 PP 44-52

MYERS, W

THE NEED FOR SOFTWARE ENGINEERING - COMPUTER 2/78 PP 12-25

PARNAS, D.L
```

Fig. 7-7. Incorrect VARSORT formatting.

```
IF JJ > 60 THEN JT=JJ GOTO 'LOOP' (else)T1$=
LEFT$(T$,JJ)
  T2$= RIGHT$(T$,LEN(T$)-JJ)
  LPRINT TAB(10) T1$
  IF LEN(T2$) > 60 THEN T$=T2$ JT=LEN(T2$) GOTO
'LOOP' (else)LPRINTTAB(10)T2$ ENDIF
ENDIF
LPRINT
'EXIT'
```

ON THE CRITERIA TO BE USED IN DECOMPOSING SYSTEMS INTO MODULES - COMMUNICATIONS OF THE ACM 12/72 - PP 1053-1058

PARNAS, D.L

TECHNIQUE FOR THE SPECIFICATION OF SOFTWARE MODULES WITH EXAMPLES - COMMUNICATIONS OF THE ACM 5/73 PP 330-336

PETERSON, W.W

INTRODUCTION TO PROGRAMMING LANGUAGES

ULRICKSON,R.W

SOLVE SOFTWARE PROBLEMS STEP BY STEP - ELECTRONIC DESIGN 1/18/77 PP 54-58

ULRICKSON,R.W

SOFTWARE MODULES ARE THE BUILDING BLOCKS - ELECTRONIC DESIGN 2//1/77 PP 62-66

VAN TASSEL

PROGRAM STYLE,DESIGN,EFFICIENCY,DEBUGGING, AND TESTING

WALSH,D.A

STRUCTURED TESTING IN DATAMATION 7/77 PP 111-118

WELLER,W.J

ASSEMBLY LEVEL PROGRAMMING FOR SMALL COMPUTERS

WIRTH,N

ALGORITHMS + DATA STRUCTURE = PROGRAMS

WIRTH,N

SYSTEMATIC PROGRAMMING: AN INTRODUCTION

YOURDON, E.U.

TECHNIQUES OF PROGRAM STRUCTURE AND DESIGN

If correct, the design should work. Let's enter it and see. Keep in mind that this is a new segment of code, and you are in the testing and debugging stage of design. First set up the segment as a subroutine in order to keep the program flow clear in your minds. Figure 7-8 is a flowchart of the design. Figure 7-9 is the code as it will appear starting at line 3000.

When you run the program and activate the print function a few lines appear. Although the printer stops, the computer is still running. Looking at the output all the printed lines were less than a full line and the program stopped (or seemed to) when entering the first multi-line entry. Hit break to regain control of the computer,

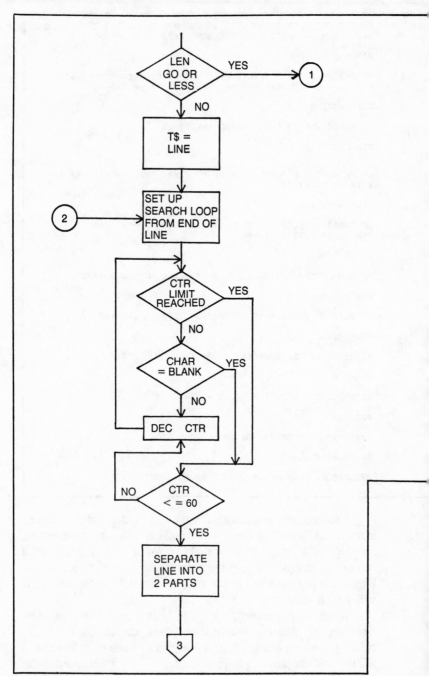

Fig. 7-8. Line separation flowchart.

110

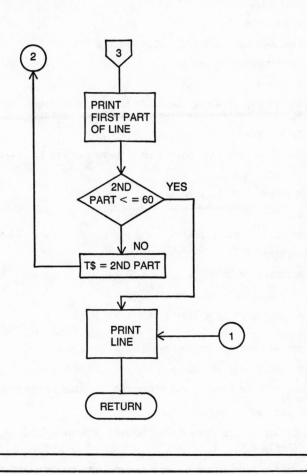

```
3000 IF LEN(L(I)) <= 60 THEN LPRINT TAB(10)L(I):RETURN
3010 T$=L(I)
3020 FOR JJ=LEN(T$) TO 1 STEP -1
3030  IF MID$(T$,JJ,1) <> " " THEN NEXT JJ
3040         IF JJ <= 60 THEN T1$=LEFT$(T$,JJ):
T2$=RIGHT$(T$,LEN(T$)-JJ):LPRINTTAB(10)T1$:IF LEN(T2$)
<=60 THEN LPRINTTAB(10)T2$:RETURN ELSE T$=T2$:GOTO 3020
3050 RETURN
```

Fig. 7-9. Line separation module for VARSORT program.

```
CHAPLIN,N

FLOWCHARTS

DAHL,O.J.,HOAVE,A.R., & DIJKSTRA,E.W

STRUCTURED PROGRAMMING

DALTON,W.F

DESIGN MICROCOMPUTER SOFTWARE LIKE OTHER SYSTEMS -
SYSTEMATICALLY - ELECTRONICS 1/19/78 PP 97-101

DEMILO,R.A

HINTS ON TEST DATA SELECTION - COMPUTER 4/78 PP 34-41

DIJKSTRA,E.W

A DISCIPLINE OF PROGRAMMING

DOLLHOFF,T

MICROPROCESSOR SOFTWARE - DIGITAL DESIGN 2/77 PP 44-51

HALSTEAD, M.H

ELEMENTS OF SOFTWARE SCIENCE

HUGHES,J.K., & MICHTOM,J.I

A STRUCTURED APPROACH TO PROGRAMMING

KNUTH,D.E
THE ART OF COMPUTER PROGRAMMING (3 VOLS)

MORGAN,D.E & TAYLOR,D.J

A SURVEY OF METHODS FOR ACHIEVING RELIABLE SOFTWARE -
COMPUTER 2/77 PP 44-52
MYERS, W

THE NEED FOR SOFTWARE ENGINEERING - COMPUTER 2/78 PP 12-25
PARNAS, D.L
```

Fig. 7-10. Correctly formatted VARSORT output.

and turn on the trace function of the interpreter. When continuing, see that the computer is in an endless loop between the first conditional statement and the counting loop.

Insert a *stop* just before the conditional statement and reinitialize the program. When it stops check the value of JJ and JT. Since the counter (JJ) is being reduced by one on each pass through the loop, it must be less than JT whenever the loop exits. This time the relation between them is correct.

Restart the program and check again when you get to stop. What's this! Both are equal. A moment's reflection reveals a subtle

ON THE CRITERIA TO BE USED IN DECOMPOSING SYSTEMS INTO
MODULES - COMMUNICATIONS OF THE ACM 12/72 - PP 1053-1058

PARNAS, D.L

A TECHNIQUE FOR THE SPECIFICATION OF SOFTWARE MODULES WITH
EXAMPLES - COMMUNICATIONS OF THE ACM 5/73 PP 330-336

PETERSON, W.W

INTRODUCTION TO PROGRAMMING LANGUAGES

ULRICKSON,R.W

SOLVE SOFTWARE PROBLEMS STEP BY STEP - ELECTRONIC DESIGN
1/18/77 PP 54-58

ULRICKSON,R.W

SOFTWARE MODULES ARE THE BUILDING BLOCKS - ELECTRONIC
DESIGN 2//1/77 PP 62-66

VAN TASSEL

PROGRAM STYLE,DESIGN,EFFICIENCY,DEBUGGING, AND TESTING

WALSH,D.A

STRUCTURED TESTING IN DATAMATION 7/77 PP 111-118

WELLER,W.J

ASSEMBLY LEVEL PROGRAMMING FOR SMALL COMPUTERS

WIRTH,N

ALGORITHMS + DATA STRUCTURE = PROGRAMS

WIRTH,N

SYSTEMATIC PROGRAMMING: AN INTRODUCTION

YOURDON, E.U.

TECHNIQUES OF PROGRAM STRUCTURE AND DESIGN

but important point in the operation of for-next loops which caused the error. The loop counter is incremented or decremented after the test has been made. On the previous pass the loop stops the count on a blank space. If the counter is not changed, test that blank space again without changing the counter at all. This was the problem here. To correct this, decrease the count by one before going back into the loop, so you start on the next space or character before the one you ended with.

To do this one more instruction is inserted between the end of the counting loop and the beginning of the first conditional state-

```
10 CLEAR10000:DEFSTRX,L:DEFINTI-K:DIMX(200),L(200)

15 I=1

16 CLS:INPUT"IS THIS AN UPDATE";A$:A$=LEFT$(A$,1):IF A$="Y"
   THENGOSUB2400:GOSUB120:I=I+1

20 CLS:LINEINPUT"WHAT IS VARIABLE NAME";X(I)

30 LINEINPUT"ENTER ITS DEFINITION";L(I)

50 IFX(I)="*"ANDL(I)="*"THENI=I-1:J=I:GOSUB2290:GOTO60

55 I=I+1:GOTO20

60 CLS:INPUT"SEND DATA TO PRINTER OR VIDEO DISPLAY
(P/V)";C$:C$=LEFT$(C$,1)

64 FORI=1TOJ:IFC$="V"THEN68

65 LPRINTX(I):LPRINT

66 GOSUB 3000

68 PRINTX(I):PRINTL(I):NEXTI

69 CLS:INPUT"DO YOU WISH TO REPEAT (Y/N)";B$:B$=
LEFT$(B$,1):IFB$="Y"THEN60

70 INPUT"DO YOU WISH TO SAVE DATA (Y/N)";C$:C$=
LEFT$(C$,1):IFC$="N"THEN100

75 GOSUB2400

80 OPEN"O",1,F$

90 PRINT#1,J:FORI=1TOJ:PRINT#1,X(I);",";L(I):NEXTI

100 CLOSE:PRINTTAB(32)"FILE CLOSED"

110 END
```

Fig. 7-11. Improved VARSORT program listing. This version of the program assures that entries longer than 60 characters will be printed on multiple lines in intelligible form by separating the text only between words.

ment. If the instruction $JJ = JJ - 1$ is inserted here, the program will run normally. Figure 7-10 illustrates the output of the revised line print section just completed. Figure 7-11 is the revised program listing.

If you are familiar with all the instructions in the language and aware of each effect and action, such redesign and debugging is not necessary. However, it's hard to remember the action of every program instruction used and its effect on output.

If such a change as the one above is desirable, it can be made

```
120 OPEN"I",1,F$
130 INPUT#1,J
140 FORI=1TOJ
142 LINE INPUT #1,X(I)
144 LINE INPUT #1,L(I)
146 NEXT I
150 CLOSE:RETURN
2290 GOTO2310
2310 IFJ<=1THENRETURN
2320 JL=J-1:FORI=1TOJL:KL=I+1:FORK=KLTOJ
2330 IFX(I)<=X(K)THEN2360
2340 SWAPX(I),X(K)
2350 SWAPL(I),L(K)
2360 NEXTK
2370 NEXTI:RETURN
2400 INPUT"    ENTER FILE NAME";F$:RETURN
3000 IF LEN(L(I)) <= 60 THEN LPRINT TAB(10)L(I):RETURN
3010 T$=L(I)
3020 FOR JJ=LEN(T$) TO 1 STEP -1
3030  IF MID$(T$,JJ,1) <> " " THEN NEXT JJ
3040          IF JJ <= 60 THEN T1$=LEFT$(T$,JJ):
T2$=RIGHT$(T$,LEN(T$)-JJ):LPRINTTAB(10)T1$:IF LEN(T2$)
<=60 THEN LPRINTTAB(10)T2$:RETURN ELSE T$=T2$:GOTO 3020
3050 RETURN
```

without throwing everything out and starting from scratch. Only consider how it will interact with the remainder of the program.

SUMMARY

Writing documentation for a program is one of the least considered yet most important aspects of programming. If careful notes are kept during program development, documentation can be much easier to write.

Programs can be self-documenting. Such self-documentation can take the form of comments or remarks in the program listing, flowcharts or structured forms of the program logic designed during the development process, memory maps, and variable lists.

Minimum documentation contains a clearly written description of what the program is designed to do, and any special precautions or procedures to be used in working with the program. It is also a good idea to include in this description the test plan used in testing and debugging the program along with a correct set of test results.

Additional documentation is supplied with software for use by others. This includes the program logic manual, the user's guide, and the program maintenance manual.

The program logic manual explains in detail the workings of the program, what it was designed to do, what algorithms were used, and the data structures designed into the program.

The User's Guide is the most important document written for the program. Remember that it is written for the general user and not for other programmers. It is simple and clearly written with numerous examples explaining each command and its use. If shortcuts are included for the experienced operator, these should also be explained. Provide appropriate pictures and diagrams to illustrate what you are saying. The guide should be tested to insure clear explanations and illustrations before release.

The maintenance manual explains to another programmer what provisions have been designed into the program for future expansion or modification. Step-by-step instructions for program modification must also be included. Program redesign can be for any of three purposes.

1. To reduce memory usage.
2. To increase speed of execution.
3. To include other desirable features or modifications.

To reduce memory usage by the program a few helpful things such as converting over used segments of code into subroutines, deleting remarks, comments, or extra spaces; combining instructions into multistatement lines where possible; and using as few levels of parentheses as possible.

To increase speed, use integer variables as counters in loops. In assembly language, try reducing execution time within loops as much as possible. Most time can be saved here because of the many repetitions of the code. If more than a twenty or twenty-five percent increase is sought, it is easier to redesign the program with a faster algorithm, than try to squeeze this much improvement out of your present program.

Chapter 8
Computer Languages

Chapter 2 briefly mentioned a few computer languages available for microcomputers; this chapter discusses each more fully. In this way you will be aware of what languages are available and the advantages and disadvantages associated with each of them.

ASSEMBLY LANGUAGE

Why would a programmer elect to use assembly-language? Using assembly language creates some problems for the programmer but is used in cases where the special needs of the program are more important than the inconvenience to the programmer. Assembly language is usually chosen as the programming language in a project for one of several reasons.

You want to write a game program. Perhaps something like the space war games often seen in the arcades across the country. These simulate real movement of objects in response to operator input. They must provide an immediate response to the player's actions. In this situation, called real time simulation, you cannot wait for the instruction translation required by a high-level language. It is simply too slow. There is no other alternative.

Another example is in controlling some external device. Suppose you want the computer to turn on your lawn sprinkler whenever the temperature rose above eighty degrees and the soil humidity was low. Designing such a program is not difficult, but writing the code in any high-level language might be awkward.

High-level languages are not well adapted to coding such tasks. Assembly language provides a simpler and more compact way to generate required control sequences to whatever interface provided.

These are typical examples of assembly-language applications. Whenever a program in which speed of execution is essential, such as the game, then the disadvantages of assembly-language can be tolerated.

Control applications, as in our second example, are another area where assembly language has definite advantages. The control programs are easier, and take less memory in assembler.

You can see here which types of programs benefit from assembler. In general, assembly language is useful for high execution speed, minimum use of memory, real time, interactive or control applications, and in programs having a limited amount of data processing.

The major advantages in assembler are its speed, small amount of memory used, i.e., efficiency, and the detailed control it provides over the way data is handled during processing.

The main disadvantages are that it is not portable (cannot be used on any microprocessor except the one it was written for) and requires more programming effort in design, coding, and debugging.

HIGH-LEVEL LANGUAGES

Generally, high-level languages are easier for the programmer to use because they are closer to English. The major disadvantage, however, is their speed. They're usually slower and more cumbersome than machine and assembly language. It is purely the preference of the user which language works best.

APL

APL, for A Programming Language, was developed by Dr. Kenneth Iverson while he was teaching at Harvard in 1962. Like BASIC and FORTRAN it is a procedure-oriented language, that is it is used to express procedures for solving problems. It is one of the most widely used of this class of languages. BASIC and APL are the two most widely used of the interactive languages.

APL is a powerful interactive language resulting from the basic data element of the language, the array. Another powerful element of the language is its remarkable set of operators available for manipulating the arrays. All operators operate on scalers (single dimension quantities) and exist in forms operated directly on the arrays.

One unusual feature of APL is that there is no hierarchy of operations. Instead, expressions are evaluated from right to left as they are encountered. For example, the expression

$$3 + 4 * 7 + 3$$

evaluates to 43 instead of the usual 52 because in the right to left evaluation, the right-most three is added to the seven before the multiplication takes place. Then the left-most three is added to the product.

There are operators which transpose matrices, rotate the rows or columns of an array, and perform number base conversion. These are designated with a symbol which is one small part of an APL statement. Matrix multiplication is designated by three symbols in addition to the names of the matrices.

As you can see, the APL is designed mainly for algebraic and mathematical manipulation. Within this context the language is quite attractive since a beginner can get started doing meaningful work very quickly and still have features of great power and range available.

BASIC

BASIC was developed in the mid-60s at Dartmouth college. It's authors, John Kemeny and Thomas Kurtz, designed it as a teaching language to introduce students to the structures of computer languages. It was intended to be very simple to learn and inexpensive to implement and use. It was this purpose which generated the acronym BASIC from Beginners All-purpose Symbolic Instruction Code.

Over the years, and especially since the era of inexpensive personal microcomputers, the number of variants of BASIC have increased tremendously. Its advantage as a first language is the ease with which it can be learned. Almost everyone learns one or another version supplied with almost every microcomputer. The power of the microcomputer versions of BASIC has increased over the years as more features have been added. The Appendix contains a comparison of the versions of BASIC found on six of the popular microcomputers sold nationwide. This will provide some idea of the variations you can encounter.

The main objections to BASIC can be summed up in two categories. First, since most BASICs found on microcomputers are interpreters to provide interaction with the user, execution is slow. As features are added to the interpreter execution becomes even slower and more memory must be used thereby reducing memory space for user applications.

Second, and perhaps more important, many users are convinced that is extremely difficult to write good structured code in BASIC. As the cost of memory decreases through technological advancement, the development of good applications programs becomes more important and necessary. To write understandable programs requires clear and concise organization of logic. The best way to do this is through structured programming.

Even with these objections it seems BASIC will be with us for some time to come. The ease in which it is learned by the novice and its general-purpose nature make it a logical choice for an initial programming language. So much hobbyist software is available in BASIC that, for many people, the above objections will not receive much consideration.

COBOL

COBOL is the standard language for business applications. It was developed in the late 1950s by a group of computer manufacturers and the U.S. Government. Major design goals in developing the language were to make the programs easy to read and to make it independent of the particular computer it happens to be running on at the time.

The name COBOL is an acronym for COmmon Business-Oriented Language. It uses terms and syntax which more closely approximate natural English. This is in contrast to the terser and more mathematical approach of FORTRAN, the other major language at the time.

A COBOL program is composed of four divisions each with a distinct function. The *identification* division names the program. The *environment* division links the *data* division and the *procedure* division with the actual equipment to be used. This designates the input and output devices. The data division describes all the files used by the program along with the arrangement of the information they contain. The procedure division specifies the processing to be done.

An important difference in COBOL from previous languages is the rigid separation of data and processing sections. In this way, only certain portions of the program need to be altered if program specifications must be changed.

120

FORTH

FORTH was developed during the 1960s by Charles S. Moore. In reading "The Evolution of FORTH, An Unusual Language,* Charles S. Moore's description of its development in the August, 1980, issue of *BYTE* magazine, it is obvious that he did not start out to design a new programming language. He states on page 88, "at no point did I sit down to design a programming language. I solved the problems as they arose." He describes his dissatisfaction with certain aspects of then existing programming languages and the gradual development of concepts to overcome those difficulties. As these concepts evolved they gradually assumed their present forms.

Moore's major goal was to increase the speed at which programs could be written. He claims that by using FORTH, one's programming output can be increased by a factor of ten. The language can be either a boon or a bane depending on your understanding and skill as a programmer. Moore states on page 76 of the same article, "FORTH is an amplifier. A good programmer can do a fantastic job with FORTH; a bad programmer can do a disastrous job." This puts quite a burden on you as a programmer, but if you can meet the challenge the results can be exciting.

FORTH as a language has five major elements or concepts. None of them is unique to FORTH, but together they form a system with unexpected power and flexibility. The first is the dictionary.

The dictionary takes up most of the program memory space. As the word implies, the dictionary is a list of definitions. These form the vocabulary of the program and are referenced during execution. New words may be added at any time. These dictionary words are similar to subroutine or function calls in other languages. A word in FORTH can also be a part of the definition of another word. In this way many sophisticated functions can be built up by combining simpler functions (words) into more complex ones.

The stack is present in almost all languages. The difference here is that the user controls the stack directly while in most other languages it is used only under program control. The stack is the temporary storage area for the data immediately operated on by the program. This feature makes numeric operations somewhat slower than in other languages due to the extra steps involved.

The interpreter in FORTH has a two-level structure which enables it to run faster than other languages. The first level (called the text interpreter) parses text strings input from the terminal, or from disk, looking up each word in the dictionary. When a word is found, the second level (the address interpreter) is called. The address interpreter executes strings of addresses. These point to the words previously compiled. If a word has other words in its definition, there is no need to go back to the text interpreter since its address can be executed directly.

FORTH's assembler also permits new word functions to be created directly in machine-language. These are included in the dictionary in the same way as other words.

The final element is virtual memory. FORTH organizes the disk space into fixed length blocks of 1024 bytes. These may contain data or program material. These blocks are read into buffers maintained in memory as they are referenced in the program. Because of this, if a block is referenced it will be placed in memory automatically. This means large programs, loaded in their entirety, can fit into available computer memory.

Obviously there are a number of important advantages to such a system. The language itself forces highly structured programming. It is compact and transportable to other systems. It has a self contained operating system, allowing much more memory for other tasks. If desired, it can also run as a task under other operating systems. It is recursive; that is, a function can call itself at any level. And finally; program, interpreter, and operating system is written in FORTH and available for use or modification if necessary. You don't need to be a systems analyst to change the system to meet your needs.

Naturally there are also disadvantages to FORTH. For one thing, there was no floating-point arithmetic available before 1980, though that may have changed by now. The language does not have numeric typing, i.e., integer, single precision, double precision, and no automatic error checking for this, though user routines can be written to add this function. The language does not use a directory structure for file access. This means that you have to know the block where your program or data is stored in advance.

Perhaps the most important fact is that source programs in FORTH are difficult to read, due to the compactness of the code and the fact that variable names are not used. The programming style is also different. No named variables are used, and modular programs emphasize top down design and short definitions. Post fix notation is used in arithmetic expressions. Also called reverse polish notation, the operators are placed following the data items in the command string.

The language was developed for control applications, data

bases, and general business use. It is less useful in mathematical applications, though subroutines in other languages can be written to perform these functions.

FORTRAN

FORTRAN, an acronym for FORmula TRANslation language, developed in the 1950s by IBM, as an alternative to assembly-language, the only way to program in those early days of computer development. Several versions were developed throughout the 1950s and early 1960s. In 1966 the FORTRAN IV version was accepted as the standard implementation of the language by the American National Standards Institute (ANSI). This did not mean, however, that all versions of FORTRAN IV were the same or compatible. The basic FORTRAN IV was there, but other versions were merely extensions. These offered extra features or, in some cases, unique, non-standard ways of handling the basic features. Because of this, anyone using a program written in FORTRAN must examine it carefully to see what features of the language are used, and exactly how they are implemented in that particular version of the language. This is true for versions used with large computers and with the versions of FORTRAN available for microcomputers. For this reason, much of the portability advantage of high-level languages is lost. The programs can be used but may have to be modified in order to run on a particular computer.

As the name suggests, FORTRAN was developed primarily for the manipulation of mathematical expressions in scientific research. FORTRAN is still the main language used for programs in the technological fields. It is unlikely that this language will change much in the near future due to the large library of programs developed over the past two decades.

LISP

LISP was developed by John McCarthy at MIT during the late 1950s and early 1960s. The name is derived from list processing, since the list is the primary data structure of the language. It was originally developed for research in artificial intelligence and has proved excellent for that purpose as well as other fields where large amounts of data must be organized into complex inter-related hierarchies. In recent years several LISP programs developed can perform symbolic math operations such as simplification of equations, algebraic, differential, and integral transformations, etc.

An excellent and concise definition of the language can be found in the following quote by John Allen from his article "An Overview of Lisp" printed in the August, 1979, issue of *BYTE* magazine. "The best description of the LISP programming language is that it is a high-level machine language. That is, it shares many of the facets of contemporary machine-language—the necessity for attention to detail and the freedom to manipulate the machine's data and programs without restriction—yet LISP is high-level in that the language contains the expressive power and convenience of traditional high-level languages. The contradiction is resolvable: a LISP machine is just a higher-level machine whose data items are organized differently from the binary bit patterns of most machines, and the LISP programming language is the assembly language for this machine."

The language has two forms of expression, S (or symbolic) expressions, and M (for meta) expressions. The S expressions are the primitive data items of the language. These can be compared with a microcomputer assembly language. S expressions are sometimes referred to as the internal syntax of the language.

The M expressions, the so-called external syntax, are used for programming and data notation. They are comparable to the higher-level languages. Both must be understood in order to program effectively in LISP. S expressions are the most common. The numerous parentheses used are easily recognized.

Features of LISP include the fact that the list is the basic data structure; Lambda notation, which permits description and manipulation of functions, and even programs as data items; the use of recursion permitting routines to call themselves; and the use of a dynamic scope rule as a default value. This rule specifies that the value used with a function is the value assigned at the time the function is called. Static scope, the alternative, assigns the value assigned at the time the function was defined. Finally, many LISP systems for microcomputers combine the functions of the interpreter and compiler into a single program.

PASCAL

PASCAL is a language developed in the late 1960s and early 1970s by Nicholas Wirth. It is an offshoot of ALGOL 60, a programming language developed in the early 1960s as an alternative to FORTRAN. Algol 60 was not used much in the United States due to the vested interest that IBM had in FORTRAN. It enjoyed greater success in Europe. Since Wirth is Swiss, the connection is logical.

PASCAL was originally developed to serve as a language for

teaching programming as a systematic body of knowledge. At the same time proved that reliable and efficient programs could be created on then available computers.

It is one of the few programming languages designed to help the programmer to isolate coding errors quickly. A good deal of checking is done during compilation. Once syntax errors are eliminated it is not unusual for a program to execute error free. The programmer is forced to define how each symbol he introduces is to be used, plus the existence of a variety of data types as well as different programming structures. These permit programs to be written in structured forms so they are easy to read and understand. They also permit the program structures to reflect more closely the meaning of the logical forms implemented in the programs.

PASCAL programming structures include case, repeat-until, if-then-else, while-do, and for-do. The goto is also permitted, however it can be avoided by a suitable choice of program organization.

Early PASCAL systems for microcomputers had problems making any serious use of them difficult. These have since been eliminated and present day PASCAL systems seem to work well.

PASCAL's main advantage is insistence on good, structured programming techniques in order to develop the source code. Its permanence as a general purpose programming language seems assured both by its format and the numerous program structures and data types available.

Chapter 9
A Programmable Calculator Program

This program was written for use on Texas Instruments' TI-59 programmable calculator. Several program modules are combined here; the operator selects the proper sequence for the result desired. This is done by pressing the appropriate sequence of programmable function keys located across the top of the keyboard. The purpose of the program is to convert hexadecimal numbers into their decimal equivalents, and conversely, to convert decimal numbers into hexadecimal notation.

Since the TI-59 cannot display alphabetic characters without an optional printer attachment, the hexadecimal digits "A" through "F" are input and displayed as their decimal equivalents 10 through 15. They are output to the calculator display similar to the decimal to hexadecimal conversion.

Because of its small size and limited intended purpose, the TI-59 does not have the memory capacity of a general-purpose microcomputer. To overcome this limitation, its instruction set is compressed to a series of two-digit numbers corresponding to the various combinations of keys available for programming. The total available dynamic memory (RAM) is divided between program memory and data memory. Partitioning into the two segments is alterable for specific applications. You must set it in advance if necessary before you enter or run a program.

The language of the TI-59 is best characterized as a simple-looking language oriented toward mathematical computation. It has several features such as the ability to increment and decrement registers, set and test flags, detailed control over data structures, and an automated looping DSZ instruction comparable to assembly-language instructions. All of the mathematical functions operate like a high-level language with a single instruction calling a function routine.

It has all the usual features of a programming language; the ability to alter program sequence in a number of ways, to call up to six levels of subroutines, to make logical comparisons and branch to alternate program segments in response, and to create iterative or repeating loops. It permits labeling of program segments and has the capability to jump to segment names, or name codes as well as designated memory locations. The full set of instruction codes is listed in Fig. 9-1. Further details on the way in which specific instructions are implemented can be found in *Personal Programming,* the TI-59 owner's manual.

PROBLEM DEFINITION

Program design began as decisions about operations and functions to be performed. These were conversion of hexadecimal numbers to decimal notation and the opposite, conversion of numbers from decimal to hexadecimal. One additional function was needed; the clearing of the display and data storage locations in preparation for new calculations. Fig. 9-2 shows this initial phase in structured format. In this case there are two programs combined in one; alternate routes for the two functions are shown by a solid line, and the dotted line issues from it to the alternate box.

The data structure needed is not complex and is defined within the program. Data is accessed under program control by placing the data in the display register. This is similar to assembly-language programming in general-purpose computers. Data registers are assigned specific functions within the program during design. The program merely places the data from a particular register in the display register when instructed by the instructions. It is up to the designer to insure that the correct data is available. To help, a list of data registers and their uses within a program is created. There is less apt chance to call a wrong register when coding the program. Figure 9-3 shows the use of each data register used by our program.

PROGRAM DESIGN

With these points decided, you begin the actual design of the program. The first module, Data Initialization, is used by both

KEY	CODE	KEY	CODE	KEY	CODE	KEY	CODE	KEY	CODE
A'	16	B'	17	C'	18	D'	19	E'	10
A	11	B	12	C	13	D	14	E	15
		INV	27	LOG	28	CP	29	CLR	20
2ND MERGED		INV	22	LNX	23	CE	24	CLR	25
PGM	36*	P>R	37	SIN	38	COS	39	TAN	30
LRN	NONE	$\triangleleft$	32	SQR	33	$\sqrt{}$	34	$\frac{1}{X}$	35
INS	NONE	CMs	47	EXC	48*	PRD	49*	IND	40 (OR MERGED)
SST	NONE	STO	42*	RCL	43*	SUM	44*	y^X	45
DEL	NONE	ENG	57	FIX	58*	INT	59	|X|	50
BST	NONE	EE	52	(	53	)	54	÷	55

KEY	CODE	KEY	CODE	KEY	CODE	KEY	CODE	KEY	CODE
PAUSE	66	X=T	67*	NOP	68	OP	69*	DEG	60
GTO	61*	7	07	8	08	9	09	×	65
LBL	76*	X≥T	77*	SUM	78	MEAN	79	RAD	70
SBR	71*	4	04	5	05	6	06	-	75
ST FLG	86*	LF FLG	87*	DMS	88	PI	89	GRAD	80
RST	81	1	01	2	02	3	03	+	85
WRITE	96	DSZ	97*	ADV	98	PRT	99	LIST	90
R/S	91	0	00	.	93	+/-	94	=	95

Fig. 9-1. TI-59 programmable calculator keyboard and instruction key codes. Key codes followed by an asterisk require instructions or addresses to be complete. Also the IND instruction is sometimes numerically merged with the code of the key it is used with.

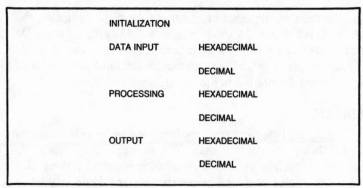

Fig. 9-2. Structure diagram of hexadecimal/decimal conversion.

functions of the program. Memory must be cleared no matter what type of conversion. Most of the modules have simple sequences. This enables you to design and code at the same time. In more complex modules this might not be advisable.

Register	Function
00	Indirect addressing of digit storage in decimal to hexadecimal conversion
01	Loop counter for number of times through inner loop (power of 16 computation) in module D.
02	Temporary storage for intermediate results in string packing routine (A').
03	Power of 16 storage in hexadecimal to decimal conversion.
04	Permanent storage for packed digits in hexadecimal conversion.
05	Digit counter for hexadecimal input.
06	Indirect addressing for decimal to hexadecimal output routine.
07	Power of 16 storage in decimal to hexadecimal conversion.
09	Number of digits stored in decimal to hexadecimal output routine.
11	Temporary storage for initial hexadecimal input
13	Storage locations for hexadecimal digits.
14	These are accessed indirectly from registers 00 and 06 in the two appropriate
15	routines.
16	
17	
18	Output for hexadecimal to decimal conversion.
30	Storage for computer power of 16 in decimal to hexadecimal conversion.
50	Storage for decimal input value.

Fig. 9-3. Data register functions in the program.

The registers necessary to clear are the display register, the test (or T) register, and the data registers used by the program. Do this by entering and defining these instructions as a separate module called by pressing the E' programmable function key at the top of the keyboard. Figure 9-4 is the initialization flowchart.

DATA ENTRY

Data entry is set up as two modules, one for hexadecimal data and the other for decimal data. The decimal entry routine is straightforward. The desired decimal value is entered. When C is pressed the value is stored in register 20, and 12 is entered in register 00 for use by the processing module.

In order to conserve memory space, the hexadecimal input routine employs a technique known as "string packing." This allows several digits to be placed in a single register for storage. How is this accomplished? When the value of a hexadecimal digit is input, it is divided by 100 and stored in a temporary location. At the same time, a second register is incremented to indicate the total number

Fig. 9-4. Program initialization.

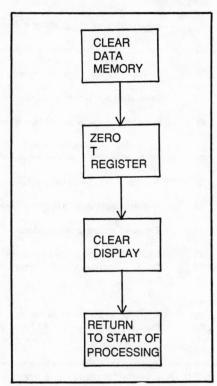

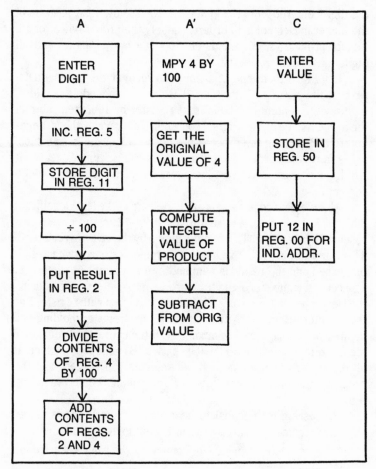

A	A'	C
ENTER DIGIT	MPY 4 BY 100	ENTER VALUE
INC. REG. 5	GET THE ORIGINAL VALUE OF 4	STORE IN REG. 50
STORE DIGIT IN REG. 11	COMPUTE INTEGER VALUE OF PRODUCT	PUT 12 IN REG. 00 FOR IND. ADDR.
÷ 100	SUBTRACT FROM ORIG VALUE	
PUT RESULT IN REG. 2		
DIVIDE CONTENTS OF REG. 4 BY 100		
ADD CONTENTS OF REGS. 2 AND 4		

Fig. 9-5. Data entry routines.

of digits entered thus far. The value in the permanent storage location for the numbers is also divided by 100 and then the two are added together becoming the new value in the permanent location.

In the program, the initial entry is stored in register 11. Register 5 is used to store the hexadecimal digit count, register 2 stores the initial value after division, and register 4 holds the permanent value used by the processing routine. Figure 9-5 shows flowcharts for the entry routines.

PROCESSING

In converting hexadecimal to decimal notation first do a number of things in this program. Get back in original form each of

131

the digits entered from the keyboard. Next know what position in the numeral each holds in order to supply the proper power of 16. Finally, provide a storage register to hold the partial answer until all digits have been computed.

Let's take them one at a time. To recover the original data, reverse the process of storing it. This is done in module A'. Here, multiply the contents of the storage register by 100, then subtract the integer value of the original contents. This reveals the last digit entered. Repeating the process provides each of the hexadecimal digits in reverse order. This is important to remember because it will be necessary to convert the digits in this same order to get a correct result.

Module B is the processing module. It gets the least significant digit with module A', and multiplies it by 16 to the power represented by that digit. This is determined by the value in register 3. This is initially zero. The register is incremented once for each digit processed and the result is summed into register 18 for storage. The correct number of digits to be processed is determined by using the Decrement and Skip on Zero (DSZ) instruction with register 5 as the counter. Remember that this was the register holding the number of digits entered in module A. If the contents of register 5 are not zero, the instruction will go back to B and repeat the loop. If all digits have been processed the register will be zero and the program will continue. The flowchart for module B is shown in Fig. 9-6.

Processing for decimal to hexadecimal conversion is somewhat more complicated. Use the following logical structure:

1. Set up a loop structure for computing the value of each digit in the following manner.

Compute powers of 16 starting with zero. Register 7 is used to store the value of the current power. Also increment register 1 on each pass to store the number of times we go through the loop.

Compare the entered decimal value with the computed value.

If the computed value is less than the entry, compute the next higher power (increment register 7) and repeat the loop.

If the computed value is equal to or greater than the entry, then recompute the next lower power of 16 (decrement register 7), set the loop exit flag, and repeat the loop one more time.

2. Continue by computing the number of digits in the hexadecimal number. Also set up the registers for digit storage and digit count for output.

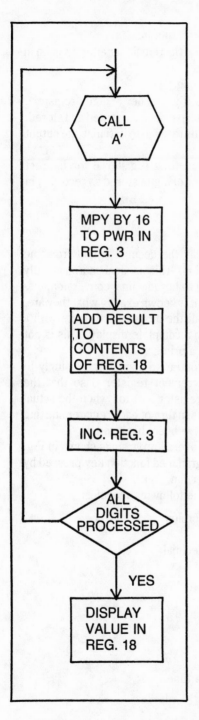

Fig. 9-6. Hexadecimal-to-decimal conversion.

133

3. Compute the integer value of the digit.

4. Compute the decimal value of the remainder after division in step 3 and store in register 20.

5. Reset the initial loop exit flag.

6. Test the value in register 1 (the number of digits register). This value goes to 0 when all digits have been computed and stored. At that point the DSZ instruction falls through to initialize the output section.

7. Output is initialized by resetting register 6 for indirect access and by displaying the number of digits stored as recorded in register 9.

OUTPUT

No action is needed to display the decimal output from the hexadecimal to decimal conversion. This is done automatically under program control. In decimal to hexadecimal conversion, display the digits one at a time so that it is known exactly what they are. If there was a way to represent all the hexadecimal digits with a single character, you could design a complete display. This is not easily done on the TI-59 without a printer.

Therefore, set up a simple routine to display them singly to insure there is no confusion. Increment register 6 so that the contents of that register are the register location when the actual data is stored. Display the contents in turn of each register starting with register 13 until all digits have been displayed.

A simplified flowchart of the overall program is shown in Fig. 9-7. Each module has its own programmed function key pressed by the user to activate that particular function.

The function keys activate the following modules:

A	Hexadecimal input for conversion to decimal
A'	Removal of incorrect hexadecimal digit
B	Processes hex to decimal conversion
C	Decimal input for conversion to hexadecimal
D	Processes decimal to hex conversion
E	Displays hex digits one at a time after calculation

134

E'   Clears data memory to initialize
          for computation

CODING

Now all the modules are defined and their logic worked out. It is now time to code the program. This is not a difficult task. Here, merely translate the logic into the appropriate key strokes on the calculator. Figure 9-8 gives the complete program. Several kinds of information are included to aid understanding and avoid mistakes in coding. The first column lists the location in program memory of each instruction. Next, find the two digit code representing that instruction. In the third column find the particular combination of key strokes which produce that code in memory. Finally, there is a comment explaining the purpose of each instruction, except in cases where the purpose is obvious.

When you enter your program into the calculator, it is a good idea to enter about ten or fifteen instructions, then go back and recheck what you have just entered to see if it corresponds to the printed listing. If the memory locations and/or instructions do not correspond to the listing, recheck the entries carefully. Such lack of correspondence can indicate extra or omitted instructions, or in certain cases, incorrect key strokes for the correct instructions. By frequent checking you can minimize the work needed to find such coding errors. It is much easier to discover them in this way than by trying to run the program.

TESTING AND DEBUGGING

Testing is done one module at a time. First, test the initialization module (E'). This is done by pressing 2nd E. When this routine is run, the display, the test (T) register, and all data memory is reset to zero. This can be checked by recalling selected memory locations at random. No matter what you display, the result should be zero.

Next test the entry routines. Enter a decimal number and press C. The numeral 12 appears in the display. Recall register 20 and the original number reappears. Then recall register 0 and 12 appears again. This completes testing of the decimal input routine.

Now test the hexadecimal input routine. As an example, pick a four-digit hexadecimal number such as 4AF5. This number is entered one digit at a time. In this example enter the 4 and then press A. If the routine is working properly .04 appears in the display. Then powers start at zero and increment once with each pass. Store this

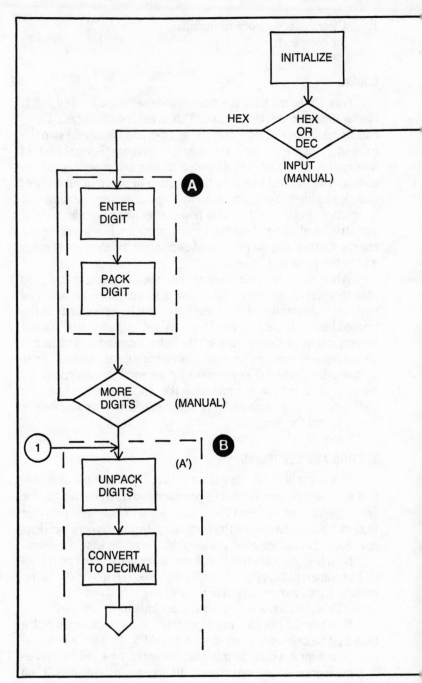

Fig. 9-7. Overall program flowchart.

(E')

DECIMAL

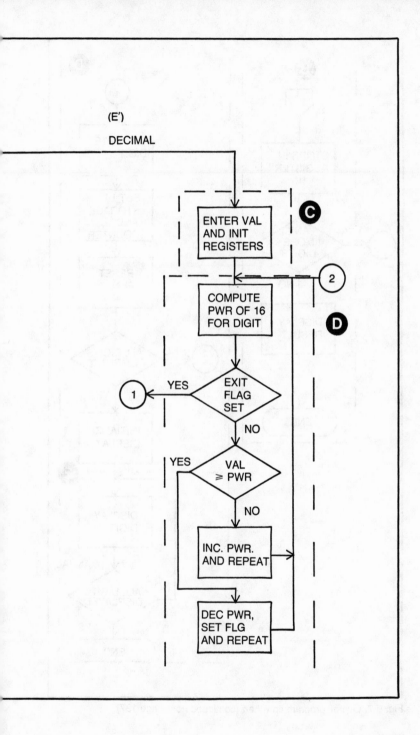

137

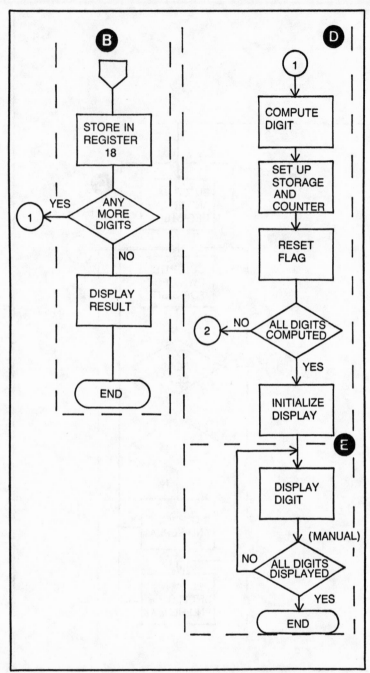

Fig. 9-7. Overall program flowchart (continued from page 137).

recall register 2 and the display remains unchanged. It should not change at this point if register 4 is recalled. Register 5 should contain 1. The original number (4) can be seen in register 11. To save time and space, Fig. 9-9 shows the contents of each of these registers as the successive digits are keyed in. If all register displays correspond with the appropriate box in Fig. 9-9, then the entry routine is correct.

Another way to check is to use the unpacking routine A' to restore the digits one at a time. This is really a double check since it assumes that the unpacking routine is operating correctly, but this cannot be verified. If the entry routine is operating properly, and the four digits are correctly entered in register 4, then unpacking them in reverse order verifies the operation of the unpacking routine. If the entry routine is to be verified later, then enter the digits into a single register in packed form as in the last column of the row labeled register 4 in Fig. 9-9.

The processing modules are next. Processing for the hexadecimal to decimal conversion is done in module B. First make sure that the unpacking routine is correct. As seen in Fig. 9-10, there are five processes carried out in the routine.

1. Each individual digit back is in reverse order with the unpacking routine A'.
2. Multiply that digit by 16 to the appropriate power for that digit.
3. Add this result to the contents of register 18, the storage register.
4. Make the exponent of 16 larger by one.
5. Check to see if all digits have been processed.

With this procedure, any errors encountered should not be difficult to trace. The idea here is to narrow the search to the items most likely to be the source of the trouble, and to ignore the remainder. These steps are not too complicated. It is also possible to work through a two or three digit number by hand. Then compare the results at each stage of the process if difficulty is encountered.

The decimal-to-hexadecimal conversion is the most complicated and, therefore, the most likely source of any trouble developed. This routine is activated by pressing D.

Let's go through the module function by function. Then you will know what to expect from the program at any point. First, set up a counter in register 1 to count the number of passes through this inner loop. Next, compute 16 to the power stored in register 7. The

Loc	Code	Key	Comments
000	76	2ND LBL	A packs the digits of the hexadecimal number. This sequence increments register 5 once for each digit entered and stores the current digit in register 11.
001	11	A	
002	69	2nd OP	
003	25	25	
004	42	STO	
005	11	11	
006	53	(	This sequence performs the actual packing. The entry digit is divided by 100 and stored in register 2 temporarily. The contents of register 4 are divided by 100 and the contents of register 2 are added to register 4.
007	43	RCL	
008	11	11	
009	55	÷	
010	01	1	
011	00	0	
012	00	0	
013	54	)	
014	42	STO	
015	02	2	
016	01	1	
017	00	0	
018	00	0	
019	22	INV	
020	49	2ND PRD	
021	04	4	
022	43	RCL	
023	02	2	
024	44	SUM	
025	04	4	
026	92	INV SBR	
027	76	2ND LBL	Routine A' unpacks the digits in reverse order of

Fig. 9-8. TI-59 commented program listing.

140

Loc	Code	Key	Comments
028	16	A'	entry for processing by routine B. This also gives us a way to correct errors when entering hexadecimal data.
029	01	1	
030	00	0	
031	00	0	
032	49	2ND PRD	
033	04	4	
034	53	(	
035	43	RCL	
036	04	4	
037	59	2ND INT	
038	22	INV	
039	44	SUM	
040	04	4	
041	54	)	
042	92	INV SBR	
043	76	2ND LBL	B computes the decimal value of each digit entered in A in reverse order and stores the result in register 18 for display. Subroutine A' is called to unpack each digit in reverse order. This is then multiplied by the correct power of 16.
044	12	B	
045	53	(	
046	71	SBR	
047	16	A'	
048	65	×	
049	01	1	
050	06	6	
051	45	y^x	
052	43	RCL	
053	03	3	
054	54	)	
055	44	SUM	This portion of B sums the result of each computation into register 18 and then increments register 3 to provide the next exponent of 16.
056	18	18	
057	69	2ND OP	

Loc	Code	Key	Comments
058	23	23	
059	97	2ND DSZ	This portion controls the loop which processes the digits. It returns to B and decrements register 5 until it equals 0. This occurs when all digits have been processed. Then we proceed to display the total.
060	05	5	
061	12	B	
062	43	RCL	Displays decimal value of hexadecimal number.
063	18	18	
064	92	INV SBR	
065	76	2ND LBL	C enters the decimal number into memory for processing and stores 12 in register 0 for indirect addressing.
066	13	C	
067	42	STO	
068	50	50	
069	01	1	
070	02	2	
071	42	STO	
072	00	0	
073	92	INV SBR	
074	76	2ND LBL	D computes the hexadecimal equivalent of the decimal value entered with C. This portion also provides for counting the hexadecimal digits generated.
075	14	D	
076	69	2ND OP	
077	21	21	
078	53	(	Compute power of 16
079	01	1	
080	06	6	
081	45	Y^X	
082	43	RCL	

Fig. 9-8. TI-59 commented program listing (continued from page 141).

142

Loc	Code	Key	Comments
083	07	7	
084	54	)	
085	42	STO	Store result for use in comparison.
086	30	30	
087	87	2ND LF FLG	Test if FLG 1 is set. To provide exit from loop at proper time. If flg not set continue processing.
088	01	1	
089	42	STO	
090	43	RCL	Get power of 16 and put in test register to compare then recall decimal value entered.
091	30	30	
092	32	X ⇄ T	
093	43	RCL	
094	50	50	
095	77	X ≥ T	Test if decimal value is equal to or greater than present power of 16. If not goto LBL LNX. This increments the exponent of 16 by one and repeats from D to compute the new power of 16.
096	23	LNX	
097	71	SBR	
098	48	EXC	
099	76	2ND LBL	
100	23	LNX	
101	69	2ND OP	
102	27	27	
103	61	GTO	
104	14	D	
105	76	2ND LBL	When the decimal value becomes less than the current value of the power of 16, the exponent is decremented. Since this determines the highest power of 16 which will divide into the decimal value; we now set flg 1 to exit the loop after computing this value.
106	48	EXC	
107	69	2ND OP	
108	37	37	

Loc	Code	Key	Comments
109	86	2ND ST FLG	
110	01	1	
111	61	GTO	
112	14	D	
113	76	2ND LBL	This instruction provides an address for branching after testing flg 1 at loc 87-89.
114	42	STO	
115	02	2	Register 1 is provided as a loop counter for determining the number of digits in the hexadecimal number. The number of passes to establish this is N+2 therefore we here subtract 2 from the total.
116	22	INV	
117	44	SUM	
118	01	1	
119	69	2ND OP	12 was stored in register 0 in C. We now increment register 0 to define the storage register for the first digit since we store indirectly in the contents of register 0. We also clear the T register for use later in this routine. Register 9 serves as a digit counter to display the number of digits computed upon completion.
120	20	20	
121	69	2ND OP	
122	29	29	
123	29	2ND CP	
124	53	(	This sequence computes the value of the current digit by dividing the decimal value by the power of 16 computed in the beginning of the sequence.
125	43	RCL	
126	50	50	
127	55	÷	
128	43	RCL	
129	30	30	
130	54	)	
131	58	2ND FIX	This sequence discards the remainder so that the integer value can be stored as a digit. It would seem simpler to use only INT for this but in some cases due to rounding errors this method produces incorrect results. This value is stored indirectly in the contents of register 0.
132	02	2	
133	52	EE	
134	22	INV	

Fig. 9-8. TI-59 commented program listing (continued from page 143).

Loc	Code	Key	Comments
135	52	EE	
136	22	INV	
137	58	2ND FIX	
138	59	INT	
139	72	STO 2ND IND	
140	00	0	
141	65	×	This sequence computes the decimal value of the remainder for use in computing the next digit.
142	43	RCL	
143	30	30	
144	54	)	
145	32	X ⇄ T	The present digit is multiplied by the present power of 16. This result is put into the T register. The original number is then put in the display and the value in the T register is subtracted. The remainder is then put in register 50 to become the starting value for the next digit.
146	53	(	
147	43	RCL	
148	50	50	
149	75	-	
150	32	X ⇄ T	
151	54	)	
152	42	STO	
153	50	50	
154	22	INV	Reset flg 1 to prepare for the new sequence.
155	86	2ND ST FLG	
156	01	1	
157	97	2ND DSZ	This instruction controls the digit loop and exits when the correct number of digits have been computed.
158	01	1	
159	14	D	

Loc	Code	Key	Comments
160	01	1	This sequence initializes register 6 which indirectly displays the digits in sequence in the following routine. The number appearing in the display as computation stops is the number of digits which has been computed.
161	02	2	
162	42	STO	
163	06	6	
164	43	RCL	
165	09	9	
166	91	R/S	
167	76	2ND LBL	Routine E increments register 6 and displays the numerical value of each hexadecimal digit computed (in sequence).
168	15	E	
169	69	2ND OP	
170	26	26	
171	73	RCL 2ND IND	
172	06	6	
173	92	INV SBR	
174	76	2ND LBL	Routine E' clears all data memory locations and the T register in preparation for a new computation.
175	10	E'	
176	47	2ND CMS	
177	29	2ND CP	
178	25	CLR	
179	81	RST	
180	92	INV SBR	

Fig. 9-8. TI-59 commented program listing (continued from page 145).

value in register 30 and test to see if the exit flag has been set. If not, compare the computed value in register 30 with the original entry in register 20. This is done by using the test register. If the computed value is less than the original entry increase the power of 16 by one and repeat the loop. The exit flag is set when the computed value is

NUMBER (HEX)	4	A (10)	F(15)	5
DISPLAY	.04	.10	.15	.05
REGISTER 2	.04	.10	.15	.05
REGISTER 4	.04	.1004	.151004	.05151004
REGISTER 5	1	2	3	4
REGISTER 11	4	10	15	5

Fig. 9-9. Register contents during string packing.

equal to or greater than the entry then the current power of 16 is reduced by one and the loop is repeated.

When this point in the program is reached, register 30 contains the highest power of 16 not larger than the original value. The exit flag is set, so continue with the remainder of the outer loop. This

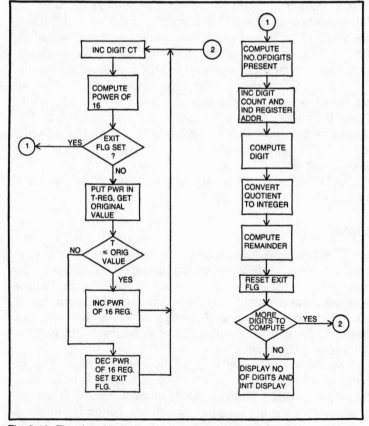

Fig. 9-10. Flowchart for decimal to hexadecimal conversion.

portion starts at label STO. The first thing to do in this section is establish the position of the digit in the number. Register 1 stores the number of passes needed to determine the highest power of 16. The position number of the digit is two less than that. You make two extra passes, the last two, to establish power no higher than 16. Then it returns to the correct value after the exit flag has been set. The adjustment consists in subtracting two from the sum, the value, in register 1.

The next step is to increment register 0. This enables you to store the result in register 13; the value is stored in the register designated by the contents of register 0. Also increment register 9 at this time to indicate a digit placed in storage.

With these preliminaries out of the way, compute the value of the digit and the remaining part of the original value. The first step is to divide the original entry in register 20 by the computed power of 16 in register 30. The sequence from memory locations 131 to 140 converts the quotient to an integer. It might seem simpler to use the INT key. When I wrote the program I kept getting random errors unless this entire sequence was used. The integer quotient is stored as the digit in the appropriate register as described above.

The remaining portion of the original value must be recovered and stored to compute the remaining digits. This is done by multiplying the power of 16 by the stored digit, and subtracting the product from original value in register 20. The remainder is stored in register 20 and becomes the new original value used in the next loop computation.

Once this has been done, reset the exit flag and check to see if all digits have been computed.

OUTPUT

The results of module B, the hexadecimal-to-decimal-conversion routine, are displayed under program control as soon as the processing has been completed. The output portion of the decimal to hexadecimal conversion is somewhat different. When processing is completed the program initializes register 6 for indirect output by storing 12 there. It also displays the contents of register 9 to show the total number of digits stored.

To display those digits, go to the display module. This is activated by pressing E. This module is simple. It increments register 6 and then displays the information pointed to by the contents of register 6. This is the desired digit. The module displays each digit as E is pressed for each successive digit. You know how many times to press the E key by the number displayed at the end of the processing sequence.

If all of the modules provide correct results, this portion of the development process is finished. If not, you can determine more easily what the errors are and where they occur.

DOCUMENTATION

Material in the previous five pages, along with the flowcharts, structure diagrams, and commented program listing are considered a part of the program logic manual. These provide a visual and verbal picture of the program. This is very important for both efficient operation and complete debugging.

The User's Guide is the most important document prepared for this program. The program is neither so long nor so complex that extensive explanation is needed. The user, however, needs to know exactly what to do in order to use the program.

Use of the program is separated into three sections. Initialization, used prior to either of the remaining sections, is called by pressing E' (2nd E). Keys A, A', and B are used with the hexadecimal-to-decimal conversion. C, D, and E are used with the decimal-to-hexadecimal conversion. Once the program has been loaded or keyed in, press the 2nd E to clear the display and initialize all data registers before beginning the program.

User's Guide: Hexadecimal-to-Decimal Conversion

This portion of the program is executed as follows. Each hexadecimal digit is entered in the order they occur from left to right. A digit is entered in the display with the calculator numeral keys. Press A after each entry. As explained previously, this puts all digits into a single register for use by the processing routine. If an error is made in entering any digit, press 2nd A (A') until the incorrect digit appears in the display. At this point, enter the correct number as described above. Then continue entering the remaining digits until all have been entered.

When all digits have been stored in memory, press B. This starts the processing routine. The result, the decimal value, is automatically displayed on completion of processing.

User's Guide: Decimal-to-Hexadecimal Conversion

The entire decimal entry is keyed in like any number on the calculator. Once it is entered, press C to transfer it to the proper memory locations and prepare for processing.

Press D to start the processing routine. When processing is completed, the display will show the number of hexadecimal digits calculated for the entry. These are then displayed by pressing E for each stored digit. The digits are displayed in order from left to right as they appear on paper.

It is important that the 2nd E initialization routine is run just before entering any new value in the program. This must be done every time with this program, and not just at the beginning of a session. Every time you want to convert a new number you must reinitialize the data memories. The following list summarizes the various commands used in the program and their meanings.

A	Used for hexadecimal digit entry when converting to decimal format.
A'	Used for error correction of hexadecimal entries.
B	Starts up the hexadecimal to decimal processing module.
C	Stores decimal value after entry for decimal to hexadecimal conversion.
D	Begins processing to convert to hexadecimal.
E	Displays single hexadecimal digit each time pressed.
E'	Clears display, test register and data registers in preparation for use by program.

REDESIGN

Certain improvements are suggested with a study of this program. First, reduce memory usage by designating the same registers to perform similar functions in both the conversion routines, rather than having separate registers in each routine. Another possibility for optimization is to use string packing to store the hexadecimal answer digits in module D, rather than using six separate registers to hold the results. It is also possible that a more efficient algorithm could be found for the conversions.

The program works as is. If you want to optimize the program, the above suggestions can serve as a starting point. Other ideas will suggest themselves from your point of view. This can only enrich your skill as a programmer.

Chapter 10
A Program in BASIC

In the next example let's compute and display statistical information for variable numbers of pairs of data. The information to be computed will include the mean and standard Deviation of each variable; the correlation coefficient and degrees of freedom between them; and the slope and Y intercept of the regression line. The user can specify the form of the display and repeat the calculations with new data or exit the program. In addition, you can enter an X value and compute the corresponding Y value.

This is an example of the somewhat vague specifications a programmer is given with a request to write a program. Now, following the outline previously developed in this book, it is necessary to amplify this specification into a useful program guide.

INPUT

Let's consider inputs. All data must be input in some form, but first, let's see what else is necessary in order to use the program effectively. From the keyboard is one way to enter the data pairs, but this would become tedious and error prone if many pairs were involved. The program would also be more useful if data could be produced by one program and the calculations performed on another without having to manually reenter every item. This might be possible if data could be input from a disk file, but it would be necessary to specify whether the data is input from a file or the keyboard.

What about the output of the program? Do you want hard copy from a printer or only video display? If you do decide on a hard copy option, what portions of the output will be included? What about supplying descriptive names for the variables? What display options are provided? All of these considerations are a part of defining the program inputs.

Now let's go back to the data itself. What is the maximum number of items entered for processing? Does the program require a set number of items, or is the number of entries variable? If the number of entries are variable, how will the program tell when all data has been entered? Is there any way for the program to check for incorrect data? What can be done in such a situation? What sort of data structure can be set up to store the input data whatever its source? In this program I made the following decisions regarding the program inputs:

1. A prompt for the user to specify input from either a disk file or the keyboard is necessary. This ensures flexibility to the program design and makes it possible to combine all, or a portion of, the program with other programs without a great amount of redesign.

2. A prompt is needed to let the user choose in advance the device on which the output will be displayed. Here again, the object is flexible design. This way you are not limited to a single device. The choices are to display on the video monitor or print on the line printer.

3. Prompts will be included to permit the user to give descriptive names to the variables, which are then displayed along with the data. The object here is readability and understanding of the final results by the user. To prevent clutter in the various displays, the maximum length of these names are limited by the program to 14 characters. If more are entered for either one or both, the program will truncate the name to the leftmost 14 characters.

4. A total of five menu options are given the user in the program.

A rectangular plot of data
Statistical computations
Prediction of Y values
Repeat the program with new values
Exit the program to BASIC

These are as specified in the original request. Compute the statistical values and provide two ways they can be displayed. Include the requested prediction routine, then provide for repeats, or exit, to make the program easier to use.

Now to the data itself. Fifty items is a reasonable limit to the number of entrys the program will accept. Since the data is entered in pairs, this means a total of twenty-five pairs of data or twenty-five data points. This number seems a good compromise between lack of detail in the plot and overcrowding on the thirteen-line-by-sixty-character plot area on the video display.

The simplest way to set up data storage is to dimension a list of fifty items. Set up the input routines to put the X variable in the first slot and the Y variable in the second slot, then increment the list counter by two. This way you will not need the extra memory for a separate list for the Y variable. These variables will need to be set to maximum precision since they are the input data and computed functions.

Data input is set up in a loop with an escape character designated in the prompt statement. This is an easy way to set up input for variable numbers of input data. Naturally, the escape character cannot be an alphanumeric character likely to be used in input.

Incorrect inputs are handled by the form of coding. Using INPUT statements for data input permits you to designate whether the input is to be numeric or alphanumeric. Once designated, the program accepts no other type. There is no way, however, for the program to determine if the numeric input entered is correct. This is the operator's responsibility. Corrections can be made before the data is entered but not after.

OUTPUT

At least seven formatted output routines are needed for effective use of the program results. These are:

1. Prompts for initialization and data input.
2. Video display of menu options.
3. Video display of statistical data.
4. Video display of rectangular plot.
5. Video display of predicted data.
6. Statistical data routine for line printer.
7. Rectangular plot for line printer.

Each is designed for easy recognition of significant detail and ease of use. No other error correction procedures need be designed into the program so far as output is concerned. Any computational errors will show up as a return to the basic interpreter and require elimination.

PROCESSING

The computational algorithms for statistical data are well known and can be found in any beginning text on statistics. For my purposes, these calculations are the only direct processing of the data required. There are a few items necessary, however, for the rectangular plot routines. First of all, to make the display of the information more meaningful, provide some sort of scale for each axis of the plot. This will require calculating the range of the data from lowest to highest value of each variable. This range will then be equally divided for display next to the index marks on the plot diagrams.

One additional matter must be considered due to limitations of the line printer. When plotting on the video display screen, the cursor position in TRS-80 BASIC can be moved around. This enables you to make more than one pass from top to bottom, or even from bottom to top if that is more convenient.

With the line printer you do not have this option. Since the line printer cannot reverse it's direction of paper feed, it must print all information contained on a line at the same time. You'll have to combine the printing of the data points with the construction of the plot diagram. This requires the data pairs to be numerically ordered. This is not required for initial entry of the points. You'll have to include a sorting routine to do this before sending the data to the line printer.

Computational speed and memory requirements are not critical in a moderate-sized, self-contained program of this type. The computations themselves will probably be double precision in order to retain the single precision accuracy needed for the statistical displays. The plotted points are no problem. Even single precision data is more accurate than the resolution of the video display or line printer. The plots are useful as a guide and a picture of the general form of the plotted data but cannot be relied upon for detailed accuracy. Any processing errors, if they occur, can be handled by restarting the program.

DESIGN

The initial task in the design of the program is to divide it into logically structured units. These units can later be subdivided into still smaller units until the level of individual program instructions is reached.

The basic subdivisions of any processing task are Input, Processing, and Output. Whether or not this division is useful depends on the nature of the task the program is to perform.

The major portion of this program will be concerned with output—with how the information can be displayed in useful form for your use. You'll want to have printed as well as video displays of the information. Since a line printer cannot reverse the paper feed, it will complicate the plotting routine. It will be necessary to print all information contained on a line at one time, and in sequence from left to right, instead of skipping around as on the video display.

Perhaps the easiest way to begin is by preparing a flowchart of the main program segments. Then combine this with modular and structured programming techniques to develop the more detailed segments needed later for the actual coding.

The first flowchart, Fig. 10-1, is of the three main sections, input, processing, and output. The input section is then further subdivided into program initialization, Fig. 10-2, where the various program requirements are set up, and data entry, Fig. 10-3, where the entry options are displayed and the data routines selected.

Note that this is a combination of top-down design and modular programming. This will enable you to later test your module as you proceed rather than wait until coding is complete.

Now, you are almost at the instructional level. What needs to be done to initialize the program? In the TRS-80 Model II version of BASIC memory space is reserved for string storage and manipulation. In some versions of BASIC this is not necessary. In these BASICs it is handed automatically by the operating system. Next set up general variable type definitions. This will save program memory space as it permits omission of specific type declarations for each occurrence of each variable. Also reserve memory space for data storage. This is done by *dimensioning* the lists or arrays needed for the variables.

The next steps are to set up the variables for entry into the program. These set the program variables to their initial values and define the format variables. Here, think ahead and prepare for later output phases. You will need a structured output for the *plot* scale values. By defining these formats now, your coding task will be easier. You can also save some program memory in this way.

Finally, provide an error trap in case you run short of memory, print the display heading for the program and provide for restarting the program from this point if any other error occurs.

Now you are ready to input the data to be processed as shown in Fig. 10-4. In order to make the program more versatile, three options for data input are provided.

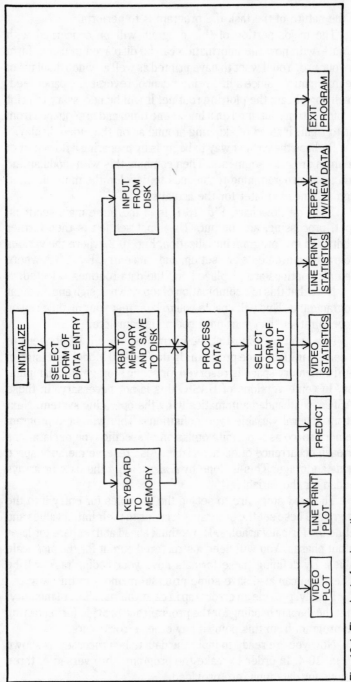

Fig. 10-1. Flowchart of main sections.

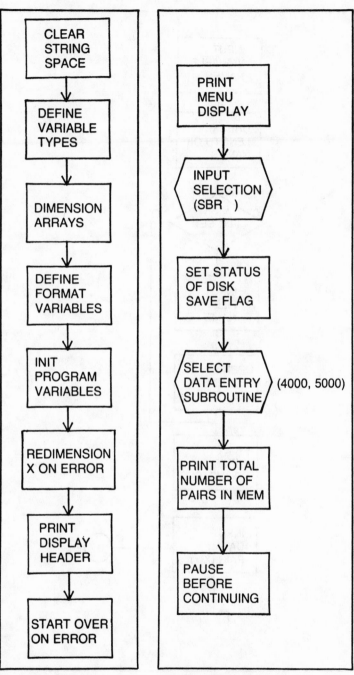

Fig. 10-2. Initialization flowchart.   Fig. 10-3. Form of data entry.

157

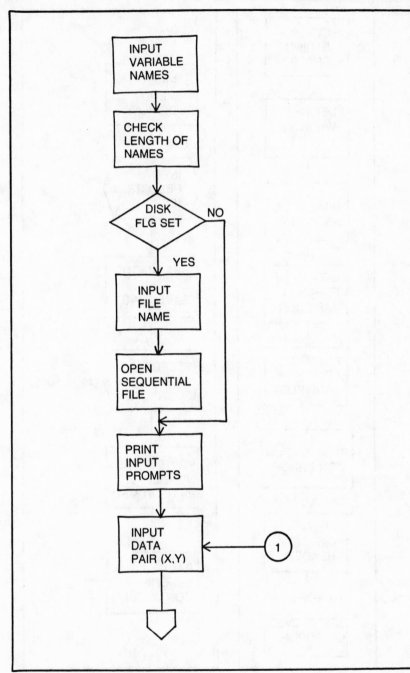

Fig. 10-4. Keyboard to memory (optional save to disk).

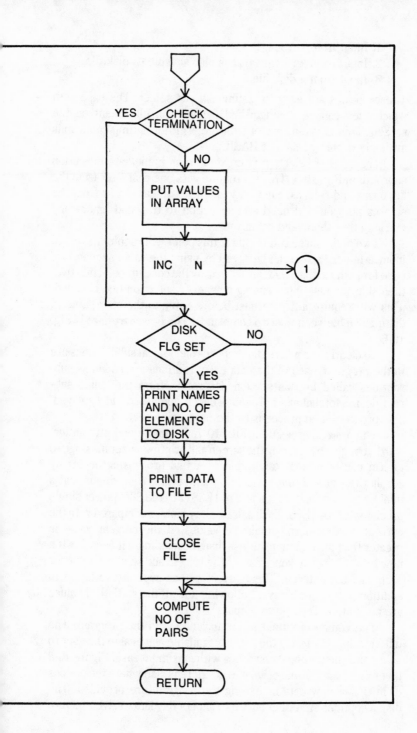

159

1. Input from keyboard.
2. Input from keyboard that is also saved to a disk file.
3. Input from a disk file.

These options are easy to distinguish and select. The ease with which they can be distinguished depends on placement on the screen. This is taken care of with the print formatting commands available in this version of BASIC.

The ease of selection is created by an immediate execution subroutine, Fig. 10-5. This subroutine gets one character from the keyboard and returns. Since any character releases you from the subroutine, you will need an instruction to trap and ignore any entries other than valid commands.

Two of the three commands at this point will require keyboard input. Memory space can be saved by using the same sequence of code for both routines. Do this by writing the code for selection two, then skip the disk input coding whenever selection one is called. This will require a flag set just before entry to the subroutine to distinguish between the two commands. The flowchart here is Fig. 10-6.

To clearly see where the branches and logical subdivisions are in the program, each of the data entry routines are coded as subroutines called by this section. On return from the called subroutine, the total number of *pairs* of data is computed and displayed. The program then proceeds to the processing section.

The *processing* section, Fig. 10-7, is simple and straightforward. It begins by clearing the screen and printing a user message to inform you of what is taking place. Actual processing begins by zeroing the processing variables, then setting a maximum and a minimum value for both X and Y of 1E38 (1 to the 38th power single precision) and $-1E38$. Each pair of data points is compared with the current maximum and minimum values. If the current value is greater than the minimum or less than the maximum it becomes the new limit. This way you arrive at the largest and smallest value for each variable entered. These are stored as separate variables in addition to the data arrays. Following this all the statistical values are computed. Then go to output.

The coding of output is the major task in the program. The initial task is to display the options available and enable the user to select the one (or ones) he wishes with maximum ease. Figure 10-8 gives us a basic outline of what to do. Here is also where the options of inputting new data or exiting the program are provided. The display options are either an X by Y plot of the data to give a picture

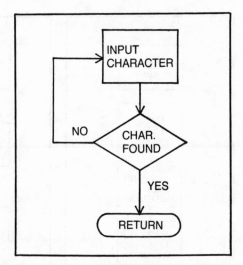

Fig. 10-5. Character input.

of its distribution; a tabular display of the appropriate statistical data; or a data prediction routine.

The program clears the screen and sets up the display for these items on the top two-thirds of the screen. Selection of the desired option is by use of the immediate subroutine again (SBR 940) with the selection character returned in II. The next two lines constitute the selection procedure. The first line sets up a case structure command for the first four options and calls them as subroutines. The second line repeats the display on any value of II except 5. This holds us in the program except for the exit option (choice 5).

The subroutines for the plot and statistics displays are two-level routines. Figures 10-9 and 10-10 are the first-level flowcharts. The first-level initializes and selects the options then calls the final routines. The predictive routine and the repeat choice need no further selection of options. They are complete within the first-level (see Fig. 10-15).

The plot point coordinates are computed according to the following algorithm where "A" and "B" are the coordinates of the origin of the graph on the display, and "C" and "D" are the appropriate scale multipliers.

$$JO = A + (X-XL)/(XH-XL)*C$$
$$JP = B - (Y-YL)/(YH-YL)*D$$

X and Y are the values of the current plot point. XH, XL, YH, and YL are the greatest and least values of the X and Y points input. Since X and Y are already used for other things in the program, the coordinate values are designated as JO for the X coordinate and JP for the Y

161

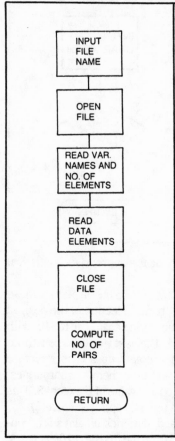

Fig. 10-6. Disk input.

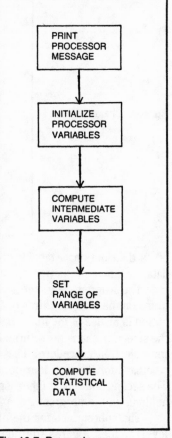

Fig. 10-7. Processing.

coordinate. These values are computed successively inside a for-next loop and stored in a list for use by the display routine. One additional set of values must be computed. These are the scale values to be printed for the X and Y axes of the diagram. These are stored in list "A". They are computed before the subroutine is called.

In setting up the X by Y plot first, you have two initial prompts. The first directs you to the desired display device (video screen or line printer) and the second flags a choice, whether a regression line shown on the display. This is your first level. Subroutine 3100 sets the flags for these options. Branching is to subroutine 1500 for the video display and to subroutine 1000 for hard copy from the line printer.

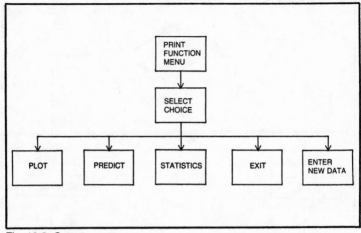

Fig. 10-8. Output.

The video display, Fig. 10-11, operates in the following manner. The plot diagram is printed first. This includes the horizontal and vertical markers, plus the scale numerals and variable names if they are present. Then the routine checks to see if a regression line is desired. If so, it inserts it and holds the display for viewing. If not, the display is held before returning to the main display option menu.

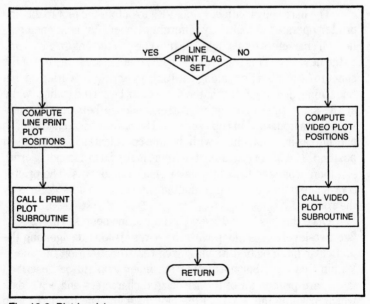

Fig. 10-9. Plot-level 1.

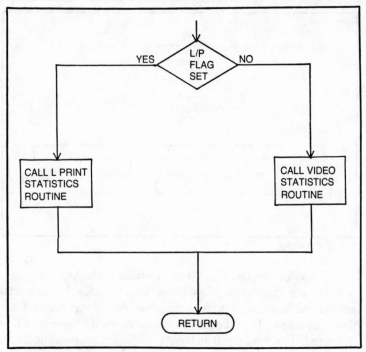

Fig. 10-10. Statistics routine.

The hard copy routine, Fig. 10-12, to output the plot to the line printer operates in a slightly different manner. As mentioned earlier, all characters on a single line must be printed before advancing to the next line. This requires the data points nearest the top of the sheet to be printed first, along with any other data appearing on that line. Doing this requires that the data points be sorted by line, while at the same time maintaining correspondence between the individual data items making up each pair. Do this by concatenating each pair into a single data item with the line coordinates in the leftmost position. The list of concatenated items is sorted in ascending order and then separated back into its original components. The printer coordinate points are then computed and stored in a list for use by the routine.

Once this has been done the print routine begins. This routine is a two-level nested loop with the outer (J) loop designating the particular line position moving from top to bottom on the sheet. Within this loop, but not within the inner loop (to be described later), are printed all of the associated characters and scale data which make up the Y axis of the plot diagram. The inner (L) loop

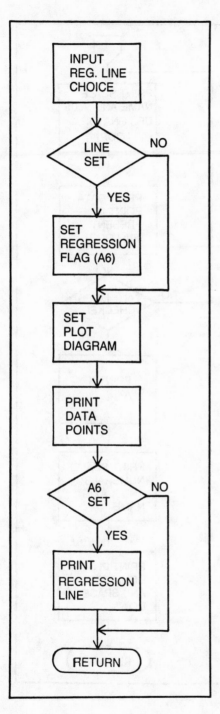

Fig. 10-11. Video plot.

165

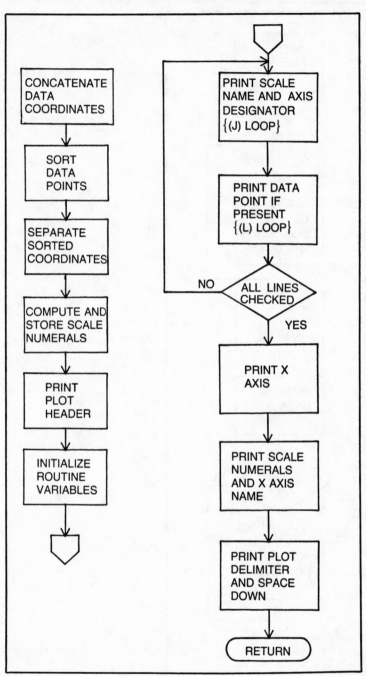

Fig. 10-12. Line printer plot routine.

designates the position on an individual line and determines the printing of the plot characters in the appropriate positions on the paper.

With both loops completed, print the X axis, its associated scale numerals, and variable name. The routine then spaces down from the variable name and prints a partial line of asterisks as a plot delimiter. Finally, the routine inserts a form feed to place the printer at the top of the next page. With this accomplished, return to the output display option menu for whatever further commands are desired.

The statistics routine, Fig. 10-13, is similar in that the first-level routine merely permits branching to either the video or line printer routines before returning. The display is formatted the same way in either case and returns to the output display option menu.

Prediction is straightforward. Figure 10-14. The prompts appear on the screen and the X coordinate is input by the user. The routine uses the equation of the line to compute the corresponding Y value appearing opposite on the screen. The routine checks to see if the input X value is within the range of values used to compute the equation. If not, an "X NOT IN RANGE" alerts the operator that this is an extrapolated value and not as reliable as one interpolated from entered data. An escape character is provided to return to the output display menu when desired.

The remaining options, Fig. 10-15, are merely graceful ways to exit or restart the program. The "ENTER NEW DATA" option executes a RUN command. This starts at the beginning of the program and automatically clears and resets all variables. The EXIT option closes all open data files and exits to the BASIC prompt.

CODING

Now that the program design is fairly well worked out, it is time to set down the actual code and check it out. As is usual in high-level programs, coding will start from the top down. The initial code sequence is shown in Fig. 10-16. This sequence initializes the program variables and sets up the data entry display. The only other sequence needed at this time is subroutine 940. This gets a single character from the keyboard and returns. The other subroutines can be represented by stubs at present. These merely indicate the proper jump and return to the main program.

Testing this sequence shows how the display appears on the screen, and whether the selection logic is working properly. There are only two questions to ask at this time. Are you satisfied with the

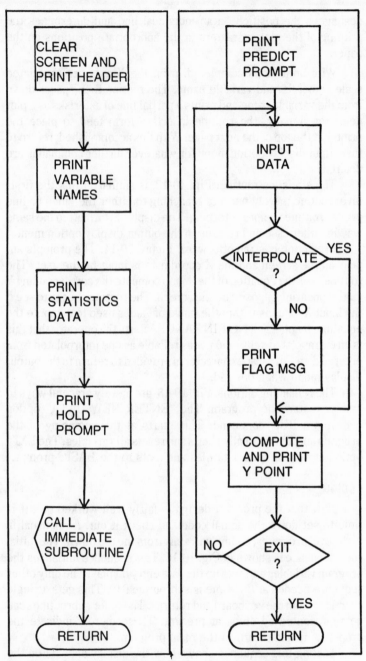

Fig. 10-13. Statistics routine (video and line printer).

Fig. 10-14. Predict routine.

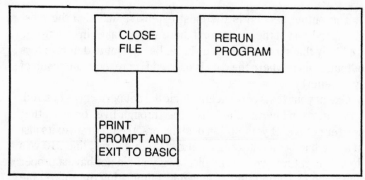

CLOSE
FILE

RERUN
PROGRAM

PRINT
PROMPT AND
EXIT TO BASIC

Fig. 10-15. Exiting and restarting the program.

appearance of the display? That is, can you easily pick out pertinent information to make your choice quickly and easily? Second, do the various selections put you at the proper lines? If the answer to both is yes, proceed to the next sequence.

The second phase, Fig. 10-17, is to enter the data entry subroutines to test completely the entry segment of the program. Enter these directly following the direct input subroutine. They start at line 980 and continue through line 1370. Space is reserved up to line 940 for the rest of the main program, to provide some logic to the way the program is laid out.

Once this new code has been entered, run the program from the start and enter new data. Since option one and option two both use the same routine for input, make sure that option two is working as planned. In this way, save the data entered for use with the third option. This is the most economical way to assure that all options are working.

If everything is working well to this point, test the processing section residing from line 400 to 750, Fig. 10-18. There are no branches in this section, so the only thing to make sure of is that the algorithms have been coded correctly. This can be done by working through some simple examples to see if they correspond to the results given by the processing code.

Now begin verification of the output section shown with the rest of the program so far in Fig. 10-19. This is done in sections, since there are so many segments making up the output code. As before, the first thing done is to code the option display. This completes the remainder of the main program. The appearance of the display seems pleasing. To check the branching logic for the output options, place stubs at the branch points until they are verified.

The output section is the most extensive and also the most complicated part of the program. If there are mistakes in coding it is more likely that they will show up here. Be vigilant to detect errors in output. This is where the data is used and represents the result of all your efforts.

One of your tests of branching logic did not perform as desired. If you enter a numeral other than one through five, or any other character not one of your option designators, the program exits just as if a five had been entered. To eliminate this error, line 910 was added. This returns you to the display if you did not have a proper input. Some execution time is saved by eliminating the subroutine for option four. This is now taken care of by line 900, which returns to the beginning of the input display.

With these corrections made, now begin the major task of the program—checkout of the individual display options. The most complex of these is the X by Y plot (option 1). This is one of your multilevel subroutines. Its coding is shown in Fig. 10-20. The first level begins at line 1380. A video display is initially assumed. The loop from 1380 through 1430 computes the X and Y screen coordinates for a video display of the data. Lines 1440 through 1490 compute the scale values for the X and Y axes. The ones used in the program are for a 24 line by 80 character video display. If you have a 16 line by 64 character display as many microcomputers do, you will have to experiment with the origin coordinates and scale multipler until you have an acceptable plot.

The next level begins at line 1380 and ends at line 1630. Set up your options for a regression line on the video plot, and the option of going to the video display or the line printer. The regression line option is activated by setting A6 equal to 1 in line 1550 if the input character is "Y". The character variable (II) is now reset and called again for the line printer option. This time the variable calls the appropriate subroutine to execute the desired command.

The video plot, executing at line 2680, has little problem except for computing the proper plot coordinates for the screen size used. These coordinates are computed before entry into the subroutine, but are necessary for its correct operation.

The X by Y plot on the line printer is next on your checklist. This one is troubling. First of all, the plot coordinates are the same as the video display. The spacing on the line printer is not the same, so the plot made no sense at all. A new coordinate algorithm had to be inserted as subroutine 3030. The general form of the algorithm did not change, but by comparing lines 3070 and 3080 with lines

1410 and 1420, the origin coordinates and the scale multipliers had to be changed. If you have trouble with either of these routines on your machine, they may have to be adjusted for the size of your video display or printer. The Line printer I am using is the Radio Shack Line Printer III. It has a 132-character line with 6 lines per inch of paper.

The next section for concatenation (lines 1650 after the subroutine through 1680) worked correctly after we made all the numerals the same number of digits by adding leading zeros where necessary. Remember that concatenation is necessary to preserve correspondence between coordinate points, while they are sorted in the next section of the routine.

The sort routine (a Shell-Metzger sort) sorts by character position. Without adding leading zeros where necessary, the numerals will not sort in numerical order. For example 10, 100, 50, 5 will sort as 10, 100, 5, 50 unless all numerals have the same number of digits. Enter the sort with the sequence 010, 100, 050, 005 to have them sort correctly. Once the sort is completed, separate the pairs into their separate variables in the TI list. This is done in the loop between 1870 and 1910.

The remainder of the routine is rather straightforward though not trivial. Most of the problems centered on syntax errors. Although they were not severe enough to halt the program, they created errors in the printout which were difficult to trace.

One example, in line 2310, prints the actual plot points on the printer display. I was having problems with the plot points occasionally printing past the point they should. This was not consistent and seemed to be random. Most of the points were at the proper places, so I knew that the coordinate algorithms were correct and the sorting and separating had to also be proceeding correctly. This left only the print statement itself. By single stepping through the two-nested loops I found that the print commands coming at the correct time, but still, the points themselves were occasionally in the wrong place. Finally the light dawned. There was a comma following the tab statement in the LPRINT command. This was causing an occasional shift to the next tab position on the printer if the carriage happened to be just past the correct spot on the paper. Removal of the comma cured the problem.

The prediction and statistics display options presented no problems except for positioning on the appropriate displays. Once they were properly formatted no other problems were present. The final corrected listing of the program appears as Fig. 10-21.

```
0 '                        *  INITIALIZATION  *
1 ' SETS NUMBER TYPES, STRING SPACE, VARIABLES,
     FORMATS, TRAPS OM ERROR
2 CLEAR 1500
4 DEFSNG A-H,O-W
6 DEFINT I-N
8 DEFDBL X,Y
10 DEFSTR Z
12 DIM A(16),JO(16),JP(16),X(50),C$(25)
14 A$="#####.##"
16 B$="######.##"
18 BB$="########.##"
20 N=0
22 J=0
24 IS=0
26 IC=0
28 ON ERROR GOTO 40
30 CLOSE:GOTO50
40 ERASE X:DIM X(MEM/8-100):RESUME 50
42 '                        *  DATA ENTRY DISPLAY  *
43 ' DISPLAYS CHOICES, GETS SELECTION & ROUTES
       TO PROPER SUBROUTINE
50 CLS
52 PRINT
54 PRINTTAB(12)"C O R R E L A T I O N   &   L I N E A R
                R E G R E S S I O N"
56 PRINT
58 ON ERROR GOTO 0
60 PRINT:II=0:ZI="N"
62 PRINT TAB(30)"SPECIFY DATA ENTRY METHOD"
64 PRINT@ 596,"<1>  KEYBOARD TO MEMORY"
66 PRINT@ 756,"<2>  KBD TO MEM & SAVE TO DISK"
68 PRINT@ 916,"<3>  INPUT FROM DISK FILE"
```

Fig. 10-16. Initial code sequence.

172

```
70 PRINT@ 1400,"ENTER CHOICE ";
72 GOSUB 2340
74 II=VAL(II$)
75 IF II=2 THEN ZI="Y"
76 ON II GOSUB 2490,2490,2780
78 PRINT
80 PRINT N;"PAIRS WERE ENTERED."
82 PRINT@ 1400,CHR$(23);
84 INPUT"PRESS ENTER TO CONTINUE";B

              IMMEDIATE INPUT SUBROUTINE

2340 II$=INKEY$
2350 IF II$="" THEN 2340
2360 RETURN
```

```
0 '                    *  INITIALIZATION *
1 ' SETS NUMBER TYPES, STRING SPACE, VARIABLES,
   FORMATS, TRAPS OM ERROR
2 CLEAR 1500
4 DEFSNG A-H,O-W
6 DEFINT I-N
8 DEFDBL X,Y
10 DEFSTR Z
12 DIM A(16),JO(16),JP(16),X(50),C$(25)
14 A$="#####.##"
16 B$="######.##"
18 BB$="########.##"
20 N=0
22 J=0
```

Fig. 10-17. Data entry added to initial sequence.

173

```
24 IS=0
26 IC=0
28 ON ERROR GOTO 40
30 CLOSE:GOTO50
40 ERASE X:DIM X(MEM/8-100):RESUME 50
42 '                  * DATA ENTRY DISPLAY *
43 ' DISPLAYS CHOICES, GETS SELECTION & ROUTES
     TO PROPER SUBROUTINE
50 CLS
52 PRINT
54 PRINTTAB(12)"C O R R E L A T I O N  &  L I N E A R
                R E G R E S S I O N"
56 PRINT
58 ON ERROR GOTO 0
60 PRINT:II=0:ZI="N"
62 PRINT TAB(30)"SPECIFY DATA ENTRY METHOD"
64 PRINT@ 596,"<1>  KEYBOARD TO MEMORY"
66 PRINT@ 756,"<2>  KBD TO MEM & SAVE TO DISK"
68 PRINT@ 916,"<3>  INPUT FROM DISK FILE"
70 PRINT@ 1400,"ENTER CHOICE ";
72 GOSUB 2340
74 II=VAL(II$)
75 IF II=2 THEN ZI="Y"
76 ON II GOSUB 2490,2490,2780
78 PRINT
80 PRINT N;"PAIRS WERE ENTERED."
82 PRINT@ 1400,CHR$(23);
84 INPUT"PRESS ENTER TO CONTINUE";B
2340 II$=INKEY$
2350 IF II$="" THEN 2340
2360 RETURN
2485 '                    * KEYBOARD INPUT ROUTINE *
```

Fig. 10-17. Data entry added to initial sequence (continued from page 173).

```
2490 PRINT @ 240,CHR$(24)
2500 PRINT@ 576,;
2510 INPUT"WHAT IS THE NAME OF VARIABLE X ";ZV
2520 PRINT@ 736,;
2530 INPUT"WHAT IS THE NAME OF VARIABLE Y ";ZU
2540 IF LEN(ZV)>14 THEN ZV=LEFT$(ZV,14)
2550 IF LEN(ZU)>14 THEN ZU=LEFT$(ZU,14)
2560 IF ZI="N" THEN 2600
2570 PRINT@ 896,;
2580 INPUT"WHAT IS THE NAME OF YOUR DATA FILE ";ZN
2590 OPEN "O",1,ZN
2600 PRINT@ 1060,"BEGIN ENTERING YOUR DATA PAIRS ( X/Y )"
2610 PRINT@ 1140,"SIGNAL END OF DATA WITH @,@"
2620 PRINT@ 1300,;
2630 PRINT TAB(20);
2640 INPUT Z,ZB
2650 IF Z="@" THEN 2700
2660 X(N+1)=VAL(Z)
2670 X(N+2)=VAL(ZB)
2680 N=N+2
2690 GOTO 2630
2700 IF ZI="N" THEN 2760
                              DATA OUTPUT TO DISK
2710 PRINT#1,ZV;CHR$(13);ZU;CHR$(13);N;
2720 FOR I= 1 TO N
2730 PRINT#1,X(I);
2740 NEXT I
2750 CLOSE
2760 N=N/2
2770 RETURN
```

175

```
0 '                          *    INITIALIZATION *

1 ' SETS NUMBER TYPES, STRING SPACE, VARIABLES,
      FORMATS, TRAPS OM ERROR

2 CLEAR 1500

4 DEFSNG A-H,O-W

6 DEFINT I-N

8 DEFDBL X,Y

10 DEFSTR Z

12 DIM A(16),JO(16),JP(16),X(50),C$(25)

14 A$="#####.##"

16 B$="######.##"

18 BB$="########.##"

20 N=0

22 J=0

24 IS=0

26 IC=0

28 ON ERROR GOTO 40

30 CLOSE:GOTO50

40 ERASE X:DIM X(MEM/8-100):RESUME 50

42 '                          *    DATA ENTRY DISPLAY *

43 ' DISPLAYS CHOICES, GETS SELECTION & ROUTES TO
       PROPER SUBROUTINE

50 CLS

52 PRINT

54 PRINTTAB(12)"C O R R E L A T I O N  &  L I N E A R
                 R E G R E S S I O N"

56 PRINT

58 ON ERROR GOTO 0

60 PRINT:II=0:ZI="N"

62 PRINT TAB(30)"SPECIFY DATA ENTRY METHOD"

64 PRINT@ 596,"<1>  KEYBOARD TO MEMORY"

66 PRINT@ 756,"<2>  KBD TO MEM & SAVE TO DISK"

68 PRINT@ 916,"<3>  INPUT FROM DISK FILE"
```

Fig. 10-18. Initial sequence plus data entry and processing.

176

```
70 PRINT@ 1400,"ENTER CHOICE ";
72 GOSUB 2340
74 II=VAL(II$)
75 IF II=2 THEN ZI="Y"
76 ON II GOSUB 2490,2490,2780
78 PRINT
80 PRINT N;"PAIRS WERE ENTERED."
82 PRINT@ 1400,CHR$(23);
84 INPUT"PRESS ENTER TO CONTINUE";B
85 '                    *    PROCESSING   *
86 CLS
88 PRINT@ 1072,"PROCESSING DATA"
90 X1=0
91 X2=0
93 Y1=0
94 Y2=0
95 XY=0
96 TZ=0
97 YL=1E38
98 YH=-1E38
99 XH=-1E38
100 XL=1E38
102 FOR J=1 TO 2*N STEP 2
104 X1=X1+X(J)
106 Y1=Y1+X(J+1)
108 X2=X2+X(J)^2
110 Y2=Y2+X(J+1)^2
112 XY=XY+X(J)*X(J+1)
114 IF X(J)>XH THEN XH=X(J)
116 IF X(J)<XL THEN XL=X(J)
118 IF X(J+1)>YH THEN YH=X(J+1)
120 IF X(J+1)<YL THEN YL=X(J+1)
```

177

```
122 NEXT J
124 TM=(XY*N-Y1*X1)/(X2*N-X1*X1)
126 TD=(Y1*X2-XY*X1)/(X2*N-X1*X1)
128 TA=XY-(X1*Y1)/N
130 TB=X2-X1*X1/N
132 TC=Y2-Y1^2/N
134 TS=SQR(TB/N)
136 TE=X1/N
138 TH=Y1/N
140 TT=SQR(TC/N)
142 TB=SQR(TB)
144 TC=SQR(TC)


        IMMEDIATE SUBROUTINE


2340 II$=INKEY$
2350 IF II$="" THEN 2340
2360 RETURN
2485 '                    * KEYBOARD INPUT ROUTINE *
2490 PRINT @ 240,CHR$(24)
2500 PRINT@ 576,;
2510 INPUT"WHAT IS THE NAME OF VARIABLE X ";ZV
2520 PRINT@ 736,;
2530 INPUT"WHAT IS THE NAME OF VARIABLE Y ";ZU
2540 IF LEN(ZV)>14 THEN ZV=LEFT$(ZV,14)
2550 IF LEN(ZU)>14 THEN ZU=LEFT$(ZU,14)
2560 IF ZI="N" THEN 2600
2570 PRINT@ 896,;
2580 INPUT"WHAT IS THE NAME OF YOUR DATA FILE ";ZN
2590 OPEN "O",1,ZN
2600 PRINT@ 1060,"BEGIN ENTERING YOUR DATA PAIRS ( X/Y )"
2610 PRINT@ 1140,"SIGNAL END OF DATA WITH @,@"
```

Fig. 10-18. Initial sequence plus data entry and processing (continued from page 177).

178

```
2620 PRINT@ 1300,;
2630 PRINT TAB(20);
2640 INPUT Z,ZB
2650 IF Z="@" THEN 2700
2660 X(N+1)=VAL(Z)
2670 X(N+2)=VAL(ZB)
2680 N=N+2
2690 GOTO 2630
2700 IF ZI="N" THEN 2760

          DISK OUTPUT ROUTINE

2710 PRINT#1,ZV;CHR$(13);ZU;CHR$(13);N;
2720 FOR I= 1 TO N
2730 PRINT#1,X(I);
2740 NEXT I
2750 CLOSE
2760 N=N/2
2770 RETURN
```

```
0 '                    *  INITIALIZATION *
1 ' SETS NUMBER TYPES, STRING SPACE, VARIABLES,
  FORMATS, TRAPS OM ERROR
2 CLEAR 1500
4 DEFSNG A-H,O-W
6 DEFINT I-N
8 DEFDBL X,Y
10 DEFSTR Z
12 DIM A(16),JO(16),JP(16),X(50),C$(25)
14 A$="#####.##"
16 B$="######.##"
```

Fig. 10-19. Initialization, data entry, processing, and output display.

```
18 BB$="########.##"
20 N=0
22 J=0
24 IS=0
26 IC=0
28 ON ERROR GOTO 40
30 CLOSE:GOTO50
40 ERASE X:DIM X(MEM/8-100):RESUME 50
42 '                          *    DATA ENTRY DISPLAY    *
43 ' DISPLAYS CHOICES, GETS SELECTION & ROUTES TO
       PROPER SUBROUTINE
50 CLS
52 PRINT
54 PRINTTAB(12)"C O R R E L A T I O N  &  L I N E A R
                R E G R E S S I O N"
56 PRINT
58 ON ERROR GOTO 0
60 PRINT:II=0:ZI="N"
62 PRINT TAB(30)"SPECIFY DATA ENTRY METHOD"
64 PRINT@ 596,"<1>  KEYBOARD TO MEMORY"
66 PRINT@ 756,"<2>  KBD TO MEM & SAVE TO DISK"
68 PRINT@ 916,"<3>  INPUT FROM DISK FILE"
70 PRINT@ 1400,"ENTER CHOICE ";
72 GOSUB 2340
74 II=VAL(II$)
75 IF II=2 THEN ZI="Y"
76 ON II GOSUB 2490,2490,2780
78 PRINT
80 PRINT N;"PAIRS WERE ENTERED."
82 PRINT@ 1400,CHR$(23);
84 INPUT"PRESS ENTER TO CONTINUE";B
85 '                          *    PROCESSING    *
86 CLS
```

Fig. 10-19. Initialization, data entry, processing, and output display (continued
from page 179).

```
88 PRINT@ 1072,"PROCESSING DATA"
90 X1=0
91 X2=0
93 Y1=0
94 Y2=0
95 XY=0
96 TZ=0
97 YL=1E38
98 YH=-1E38
99 XH=-1E38
100 XL=1E38
102 FOR J=1 TO 2*N STEP 2
104 X1=X1+X(J)
106 Y1=Y1+X(J+1)
108 X2=X2+X(J)^2
110 Y2=Y2+X(J+1)^2
112 XY=XY+X(J)*X(J+1)
114 IF X(J)>XH THEN XH=X(J)
116 IF X(J)<XL THEN XL=X(J)
118 IF X(J+1)>YH THEN YH=X(J+1)
120 IF X(J+1)<YL THEN YL=X(J+1)
122 NEXT J
124 TM=(XY*N-Y1*X1)/(X2*N-X1*X1)
126 TD=(Y1*X2-XY*X1)/(X2*N-X1*X1)
128 TA=XY-(X1*Y1)/N
130 TB=X2-X1*X1/N
132 TC=Y2-Y1^2/N
134 TS=SQR(TB/N)
136 TE=X1/N
138 TH=Y1/N
140 TT=SQR(TC/N)
142 TB=SQR(TB)
```

```
144 TC=SQR(TC)
145 '                        *  OUTPUT DISPLAY  *
146 ' SHOWS OUTPUT OPTIONS, GETS CHOICE, & ROUTES PGM
      TO PROPER SBR
150 CLS
155 PRINT@ 92,"C O R R E L A T I O N  &  L I N E A R
               R E G R E S S I O N"
160 PRINT
165 PRINTTAB(30)"DISPLAY OPTIONS"
170 PRINT@ 512,"<1>  X BY Y PLOT"
175 PRINT@ 592,"<2>  PREDICT VALUES"
180 PRINT@ 672,"<3>  DISPLAY STATISTICS"
185 PRINT@ 752,"<4>  ENTER NEW VALUES"
190 PRINT@ 832,"<5>  END PROGRAM"
195 PRINT@ 1400,"ENTER CHOICE";
200 GOSUB 2340
210 II=VAL(II$)
220 ON II GOSUB 240,300,320
221 IF II=4 THEN 50
222 IF II <>5 THEN 150
225 CLOSE
230 END
          IMMEDIATE SUBROUTINE
2340 II$=INKEY$
2350 IF II$="" THEN 2340
2360 RETURN
2485 '                      *  KEYBOARD INPUT ROUTINE  *
2490 PRINT @ 240,CHR$(24)
2500 PRINT@ 576,;
2510 INPUT"WHAT IS THE NAME OF VARIABLE X ";ZV
2520 PRINT@ 736,;
2530 INPUT"WHAT IS THE NAME OF VARIABLE Y ";ZU
```

Fig. 10-19. Initialization, data entry, processing and output display (continued from page 181).

182

```
2540 IF LEN(ZV)>14 THEN ZV=LEFT$(ZV,14)
2550 IF LEN(ZU)>14 THEN ZU=LEFT$(ZU,14)
2560 IF ZI="N" THEN 2600
2570 PRINT@ 896,;
2580 INPUT"WHAT IS THE NAME OF YOUR DATA FILE ";ZN
2590 OPEN "O",1,ZN
2600 PRINT@ 1060,"BEGIN ENTERING YOUR DATA PAIRS ( X/Y )"
2610 PRINT@ 1140,"SIGNAL END OF DATA WITH @,@"
2620 PRINT@ 1300,;
2630 PRINT TAB(20);
2640 INPUT Z,ZB
2650 IF Z="@" THEN 2700
2660 X(N+1)=VAL(Z)
2670 X(N+2)=VAL(ZB)
2680 N=N+2
2690 GOTO 2630
2700 IF ZI="N" THEN 2760
                 DISK OUTPUT ROUTINE
2710 PRINT#1,ZV;CHR$(13);ZU;CHR$(13);N;
2720 FOR I= 1 TO N
2730 PRINT#1,X(I);
2740 NEXT I
2750 CLOSE
2760 N=N/2
2770 RETURN
```

```
0 '                        *   INITIALIZATION  *
1 ' SETS NUMBER TYPES, STRING SPACE, VARIABLES,
     FORMATS, TRAPS OM ERROR
2 CLEAR 1500
4 DEFSNG A-H,O-W
```

Fig. 10-20. All plot coding added to Fig. 10-19.

183

```
6 DEFINT I-N
8 DEFDBL X,Y
10 DEFSTR Z
12 DIM A(16),JO(16),JP(16),X(50),C$(25)
14 A$="#####.##"
16 B$="######.##"
18 BB$="########.##"
20 N=0
22 J=0
24 IS=0
26 IC=0
28 ON ERROR GOTO 40
30 CLOSE:GOTO50
40 ERASE X:DIM X(MEM/8-100):RESUME 50
42 '                        *    DATA ENTRY DISPLAY   *
43 ' DISPLAYS CHOICES, GETS SELECTION & ROUTES TO
     PROPER SUBROUTINE
50 CLS
52 PRINT
54 PRINTTAB(12)"C O R R E L A T I O N   &   L I N E A R
                R E G R E S S I O N"
56 PRINT
58 ON ERROR GOTO 0
60 PRINT:II=0:ZI="N"
62 PRINT TAB(30)"SPECIFY DATA ENTRY METHOD"
64 PRINT@ 596,"<1>  KEYBOARD TO MEMORY"
66 PRINT@ 756,"<2>  KBD TO MEM & SAVE TO DISK"
68 PRINT@ 916,"<3>  INPUT FROM DISK FILE"
70 PRINT@ 1400,"ENTER CHOICE ";
72 GOSUB 2340
74 II=VAL(II$)
75 IF II=2 THEN ZI="Y"
76 ON II GOSUB 2490,2490,2780
```

Fig. 10-20. All plot coding (continued from page 183).

```
78 PRINT
80 PRINT N;"PAIRS WERE ENTERED."
82 PRINT@ 1400,CHR$(23);
84 INPUT"PRESS ENTER TO CONTINUE";B
85 '                          *  PROCESSING  *
86 CLS
88 PRINT@ 1072,"PROCESSING DATA"
90 X1=0
91 X2=0
93 Y1=0
94 Y2=0
95 XY=0
96 TZ=0
97 YL=1E38
98 YH=-1E38
99 XH=-1E38
100 XL=1E38
102 FOR J=1 TO 2*N STEP 2
104 X1=X1+X(J)
106 Y1=Y1+X(J+1)
108 X2=X2+X(J)^2
110 Y2=Y2+X(J+1)^2
112 XY=XY+X(J)*X(J+1)
114 IF X(J)>XH THEN XH=X(J)
116 IF X(J)<XL THEN XL=X(J)
118 IF X(J+1)>YH THEN YH=X(J+1)
120 IF X(J+1)<YL THEN YL=X(J+1)
122 NEXT J
124 TM=(XY*N-Y1*X1)/(X2*N-X1*X1)
126 TD=(Y1*X2-XY*X1)/(X2*N-X1*X1)
128 TA=XY-(X1*Y1)/N
130 TB=X2-X1*X1/N
```

```
132 TC=Y2-Y1^2/N
134 TS=SQR(TB/N)
136 TE=X1/N
138 TH=Y1/N
140 TT=SQR(TC/N)
142 TB=SQR(TB)
144 TC=SQR(TC)
145 '                    *  OUTPUT DISPLAY  *
146 ' SHOWS OUTPUT OPTIONS, GETS CHOICE, & ROUTES PGM
      TO PROPER SBR
150 CLS
155 PRINT@ 92,"C O R R E L A T I O N  &  L I N E A R
                R E G R E S S I O N"
160 PRINT
165 PRINTTAB(30)"DISPLAY OPTIONS"
170 PRINT@ 512,"<1>  X BY Y PLOT"
175 PRINT@ 592,"<2>  PREDICT VALUES"
180 PRINT@ 672,"<3>  DISPLAY STATISTICS"
185 PRINT@ 752,"<4>  ENTER NEW VALUES"
190 PRINT@ 832,"<5>  END PROGRAM"
195 PRINT@ 1400,"ENTER CHOICE";
200 GOSUB 2340
210 II=VAL(II$)
220 ON II GOSUB 240,300,320
221 IF II=4 THEN 50
222 IF II <>5 THEN 150
225 CLOSE
230 END
235 '              *  X BY Y PLOT LEVEL ONE  *
240 FOR J=1 TO 2*N-1 STEP 2
242 X=X(J)
244 Y=X(J+1)
```

Fig. 10-20. All plot coding (continued from page 185).

```
246 JO(J)=11+(X-XL)/(XH-XL)*45
248 JP(J+1)=22-(Y-YL)/(YH-YL)*16
250 NEXT J
255 FOR I=0 TO 8
258 A(I+1)=YL+I*(YH-YL)/8
260 NEXT I
262 FOR I=0 TO 5
264 A(I+10)=XL+I*(XH-XL)/5
266 NEXT I
268 PRINT
269 GOSUB 2370
270 RETURN
900 '                    * X BY Y PLOT - LINE PRINT LEVEL 2 *
991 '
992 '                          * CONCATENATION *
993 '
1000 GOSUB 8000:FOR TI=1 TO 2*N STEP 2
1010 IF JP(TI+1)<10 THEN C$(TI)=" 0"+MID$(STR$(JP(TI+1))
     ,2,1)+STR$(JO(TI)):GOTO 1030
1020 C$(TI)=STR$(JP(TI+1))+STR$(JO(TI))
1030 NEXT TI
1031 '
1032'                          * SHELL-METZGER SORT*
1033 '
1040 TI=N*2
1050 N=N*2
1060 M=N
1070 M=INT(M/2)
1080 IF M=0 THEN .210
1090 J=1
1100 K=N-M
1110 I=J
```

```
1120 L=I+M
1130 IF C$(I)< C$(L) THEN 1180
1140 SWAP C$(I),C$(L)
1150 I=I-M
1160 IF I<1 THEN 1180
1170 GOTO 1120
1180 J=J+1
1190 IF J>K THEN 1070
1200 GOTO 1110
1210 TI=1  ' END OF SORT. SEPARATE SORTED VARIABLES
1220 FOR I=N/2+1 TO N
1230 JP(TI+1)=VAL(LEFT$(C$(I),4))
1240 JO(TI)=VAL(RIGHT$(C$(I),2))
1250 TI=TI+2
1260 NEXT I
1270 N=N/2
1274 '
1275 '     * COMPUTE & STORE SCALE VALUES *
1276 '
1280 FOR I=0 TO 6
1290 A(I+1)=YL+I*(YH-YL)/6
1300 NEXT I
1310 FOR I=0 TO 5
1320 A(I+8)=XL+I*(XH-XL)/5
1330 NEXT I
1331 '
1332 '                    * START OF PLOT *
1333 '
1340 LPRINTTAB(51)"X  BY  Y  PLOT"
1350 LPRINTTAB(48)"--------------------"
1360 LPRINT
1370 LC=7
```

Fig. 10-20. All plot coding (continued from page 187).

188

```
1380 LR=0
1390 LZ=4
1400 LP=(39-LEN(ZU)*2)/2
1410 LJ=0
1420 K= -1
1430 TI=1
1440 FOR J=3 TO 41
1450 LI=15
1460 LJ=LJ+1
1470 LZ=LZ+1
1480 K=-K
1490 IF LJ=>LP AND LR<LEN(ZU) AND SGN(K)=1
     THEN 1500 ELSE 1530
1500 LR=LR+1
1510 LPRINTTAB(4)MID$(ZU,LR,1);
1520 GOTO 1540
1530 LPRINT" ";
1540 IF LZ<>6 THEN 1610
1550 LPRINTTAB(5);
1560 LPRINT USING A$;A(LC);
1570 LPRINT" +";
1580 LC=LC-1
1590 LZ=0
1600 GOTO 1620
1610 LPRINTTAB(15)"I";
1620 FOR L=15 TO 70
1630 LI=LI+1
1640 IFLI=JO(TI) AND J=JP(TI+1) THEN LPRINT
     TAB(LI)"*":TI=TI+2:GOTO 1680
1650 NEXT L
1660 IF LC=0 THEN 1690
1670 LPRINT" "
1680 NEXT J
```

```
1690 LPRINT TAB(15)"----------+----------+----------+
                 ----------+ ----------+----"
1700 LPRINT" "
1710 LPRINT TAB(6)" ";
1720 FOR J=8 TO 13
1730 LPRINT USING BB$;A(J);
1740 NEXT J
1750 LPRINT
1760 LPRINT
1770 LL=LEN(ZV)
1780 LPRINT TAB(12+(64-2*LL)/2);
1790 FOR J=1 TO LL
1800 LPRINT MID$(ZV,J,1);
1810 LPRINT" "
1820 NEXT J
1830 FOR J=1 TO 3
1840 GOSUB 1900
1850 NEXT J
1860 LPRINT" "
1870 LPRINT" "
1880 GOSUB 1940
1885 SYSTEM "FORMS {T}
1890 RETURN
1900 FOR JF=1 TO 3
1910 LPRINT" "
1920 NEXT JF
1930 RETURN
1940 FOR L=1 TO 13
1950 LPRINT"*****";
1960 NEXT L
1970 LPRINT" "
1980 RETURN
```

Fig. 10-20. All plot coding (continued from page 189).

```
1985 '                * X BY Y PLOT  VIDEO ROUTINE LEVEL 2 *
1990 CLS
2000 PRINT STRING$(4,CHR$(13))
2010 FOR I=9 TO 1 STEP -1
2020 PRINT
2030 PRINT USING A$;A(I)
2040 NEXT I
2050 PRINT@ 1844," ";
2060 FOR I= 10 TO 15
2070 PRINT USING B$;A(I);
2080 NEXT I
2090 FOR I=11 TO 60
2100 PRINT@ (22,I),"-";
2110 NEXT I
2120 FOR I=6 TO 22
2130 PRINT@ (I,11),"!";
2140 NEXT I
2150 FOR J=6 TO 22 STEP 2
2160 PRINT@ (J,10),"-";
2170 NEXT J
2180 FOR J=1 TO 2*N-1 STEP 2
2190 PRINT@ (JP(J+1),JO(J)),"*";
2200 NEXT J
2210 TJ=XL
2220 TQ=(XH-XL)/100
2230 ON A6 GOTO 2240,2310
2240 JO=11+(TJ-XL)/(XH-XL)*45
2250 JP=22-(TM*TJ+TD-YL)/(YH-YL)*16
2260 IF JP>60 OR JP<11 THEN 2280
2270 PRINT@ (JP,JO),"*"
2280 TJ=TJ+TQ
2290 IF TJ>XH THEN 2310
```

191

```
2300 GOTO 2240
2310 PRINT@ 15,"PRESS ENTER TO CONTINUE ";
2320 INPUTZI
2330 RETURN

                    IMMEDIATE ENTRY SUBROUTINE

2340 II$=INKEY$
2350 IF II$="" THEN 2340
2360 RETURN
2365 '            * X BY Y PLOT - DEVICE SELECTION SBR *
2370 PRINTTAB(30)"WANT REGRESSION LINE SHOWN  ( Y/N ) ";
2380 II$=""
2390 GOSUB 2340
2400 IFII$="Y" THEN A6=1
2410 IFII$="N" THEN A6=2
2420 PRINT
2430 PRINTTAB(30)" IS OUTPUT TO LINE PRINTER  ( Y/N ) ";
2440 II$=""
2450 GOSUB 2340
2460 IF II$="Y" THEN GOSUB 1000
2470 IF II$="N" THEN GOSUB 1990
2480 RETURN
2485 '                    * KEYBOARD INPUT ROUTINE *
2490 PRINT @ 240,CHR$(24)
2500 PRINT@ 576,;
2510 INPUT"WHAT IS THE NAME OF VARIABLE X ";ZV
2520 PRINT@ 736,;
2530 INPUT"WHAT IS THE NAME OF VARIABLE Y ";ZU
2540 IF LEN(ZV)>14 THEN ZV=LEFT$(ZV,14)
2550 IF LEN(ZU)>14 THEN ZU=LEFT$(ZU,14)
2560 IF ZI="N" THEN 2600
```

Fig. 10-20. All plot coding (continued from page 191).

```
2570 PRINT@ 896,;
2580 INPUT"WHAT IS THE NAME OF YOUR DATA FILE ";ZN
2590 OPEN "O",1,ZN
2600 PRINT@ 1060,"BEGIN ENTERING YOUR DATA PAIRS ( X/Y )"
2610 PRINT@ 1140,"SIGNAL END OF DATA WITH @,@"
2620 PRINT@ 1300,;
2630 PRINT TAB(20);
2640 INPUT Z,ZB
2650 IF Z="@" THEN 2700
2660 X(N+1)=VAL(Z)
2670 X(N+2)=VAL(ZB)
2680 N=N+2
2690 GOTO 2630
2700 IF ZI="N" THEN 2760
2710 PRINT#1,ZV;CHR$(13);ZU;CHR$(13);N;
2720 FOR I= 1 TO N
2730 PRINT#1,X(I);
2740 NEXT I
2750 CLOSE
2760 N=N/2
2770 RETURN
7000 '                    *    LINE PRINT COORDINATE ROUTINE  *
8000 FOR J=1 TO 2*N-1 STEP2
8010 X=X(J)
8020 Y=X(J+1)
8030 JO(J)=15+((X-XL)/(XH-XL))*51
8040 JP(J+1)=41-((Y-YL)/(YH-YL))*38
8050 NEXT J
8060 RETURN
```

193

```
0 '                        *  INITIALIZATION *
1 ' SETS NUMBER TYPES, STRING SPACE, VARIABLES,
     FORMATS, TRAPS OM ERROR
2 CLEAR 1500
4 DEFSNG A-H,O-W
6 DEFINT I-N
8 DEFDBL X,Y
10 DEFSTR Z
12 DIM A(16),JO(16),JP(16),X(50),C$(25)
14 A$="#####.##"
16 B$="######.##"
18 BB$="#########.##"
20 N=0
22 J=0
24 IS=0
26 IC=0
28 ON ERROR GOTO 40
30 CLOSE:GOTO50
40 ERASE X:DIM X(MEM/8-100):RESUME 50
41'
42'                          *  DATA ENTRY DISPLAY
43' DISPLAYS CHOICES, GETS SELECTION & ROUTES
     TO PROPER SUBROUTINE
44'
50 CLS
52 PRINT
54 PRINTTAB(12)"C O R R E L A T I O N  &  L I N E A R
              R E G R E S S I O N"
56 PRINT
58 ON ERROR GOTO 0
60 PRINT:II=0:ZI="N"
62 PRINT TAB(30)"SPECIFY DATA ENTRY METHOD"
64 PRINT@ 596,"<1>  KEYBOARD TO MEMORY"
```

Fig. 10-21. Final program listing.

194

```
66 PRINT@ 756,"<2>  KBD TO MEM & SAVE TO DISK"
68 PRINT@ 916,"<3>  INPUT FROM DISK FILE"
70 PRINT@ 1400,"ENTER CHOICE ";
72 GOSUB 2340
74 II=VAL(II$)
75 IF II=2 THEN ZI="Y"
76 ON II GOSUB 2490,2490,2780
78 PRINT
80 PRINT N;"PAIRS WERE ENTERED."
82 PRINT@ 1400,CHR$(23);
84 INPUT"PRESS ENTER TO CONTINUE";B

85 '                          *  PROCESSING  *
86 CLS
88 PRINT@ 1072,"PROCESSING DATA"
90 X1=0
91 X2=0
93 Y1=0
94 Y2=0
95 XY=0
96 TZ=0
97 YL=1E38
98 YH=-1E38
99 XH=-1E38
100 XL=1E38
102 FOR J=1 TO 2*N STEP 2
104 X1=X1+X(J)
106 Y1=Y1+X(J+1)
108 X2=X2+X(J)^2
110 Y2=Y2+X(J+1)^2
112 XY=XY+X(J)*X(J+1)
114 IF X(J)>XH THEN XH=X(J)
```

195

```
116 IF X(J)<XL THEN XL=X(J)
118 IF X(J+1)>YH THEN YH=X(J+1)
120 IF X(J+1)<YL THEN YL=X(J+1)
122 NEXT J
124 TM=(XY*N-Y1*X1)/(X2*N-X1*X1)
126 TD=(Y1*X2-XY*X1)/(X2*N-X1*X1)
128 TA=XY-(X1*Y1)/N
130 TB=X2-X1*X1/N
132 TC=Y2-Y1^2/N
134 TS=SQR(TB/N)
136 TE=X1/N
138 TH=Y1/N
140 TT=SQR(TC/N)
142 TB=SQR(TB)
144 TC=SQR(TC)
145 '                          *  OUTPUT DISPLAY  *
146 ' SHOWS OUTPUT OPTIONS, GETS CHOICE, & ROUTES PGM
       TO PROPER SBR
150 CLS
155 PRINT@ 92,"C O R R E L A T I O N  &  L I N E A R
                R E G R E S S I O N"
160 PRINT
165 PRINTTAB(30)"DISPLAY OPTIONS"
170 PRINT@ 512,"<1>  X BY Y PLOT"
175 PRINT@ 592,"<2>  PREDICT VALUES"
180 PRINT@ 672,"<3>  DISPLAY STATISTICS"
185 PRINT@ 752,"<4>  ENTER NEW VALUES"
190 PRINT@ 832,"<5>  END PROGRAM"
195 PRINT@ 1400,"ENTER CHOICE";
200 GOSUB 2340
210 II=VAL(II$)
220 ON II GOSUB 240,300,320
```

Fig. 10-21. Final program listing (continued from page 195).

196

```
221 IF II=4 THEN 50
222 IF II <>5 THEN 150
225 CLOSE
230 END
235 '             *  X BY Y PLOT LEVEL ONE  *
240 FOR J=1 TO 2*N-1 STEP 2
242 X=X(J)
244 Y=X(J+1)
246 JO(J)=11+(X-XL)/(XH-XL)*45
248 JP(J+1)=22-(Y-YL)/(YH-YL)*16
250 NEXT J
255 FOR I=0 TO 8
258 A(I+1)=YL+I*(YH-YL)/8
260 NEXT I
262 FOR I=0 TO 5
264 A(I+10)=XL+I*(XH-XL)/5
266 NEXT I
268 PRINT
269 GOSUB 2370
270 RETURN
300 CLS:PRINTTAB(33)"* DATA INTERPOLATION *"
301 PRINT:PRINT" ENTER @ TO STOP PREDICTING"
302 PRINT:PRINT" X        PREDICTED Y":PRINTSTRING$(26,"-")
303 INPUT ZO:IFZO="@"THEN310
304 X=VAL(ZO):R=0:C=0:C=POS(0):R=ROW(0):R=R-1:
    C=C+10:PRINT@(R,C),;
305 AY=TM*X+TD
306 IFX<XL OR X>XH THEN 308
307 PRINTTAB(14)AY:GOTO 303
308 PRINTTAB(14)AY;"  (X NOT IN RANGE)":GOTO 303
310 RETURN
315 '                  * STATISTICS ROUTINE LEVEL ONE  *
```

```
320 PRINT

322 PRINT TAB(30)"IS OUTPUT TO LINE PRINTER  ( Y/N )"

324 II$=""

326 GOSUB 2340

328 IF II$="Y" THEN GOSUB 340

330 IF II$="N" THEN GOSUB 400

332 RETURN

335 '                        * STATISTICS LINE PRINT ROUTINE *

340 LPRINTTAB(12)"C O R R E L A T I O N  &  L I N E A R
    R E G R E S S I O N"

345 LPRINT:LPRINT:LPRINT:LPRINTTAB(10)"VARIABLE X:
    ";ZV;TAB(48)"VARIABLE Y: ";ZU

350 LPRINT:LPRINTTAB(14)"MEAN OF X = ";TE,"
    MEAN OF Y = ";TH

355 LPRINT TAB(14)"S.D. OF X.= ";TS,"
    S.D. OF Y = ";TT:LPRINT

360 LPRINT:LPRINTTAB(12)"NUMBER OF PAIRS (N)
    = ";N:LPRINT

365 LPRINTTAB(12)"CORRELATION COEFFICIENT (R)        = ";R

370 LPRINTTAB(12)"DEGREES OF FREEDOM (DF)
    = ";N-2:LPRINT

380 LPRINTTAB(12)"SLOPE OF REGRESSION LINE          = ";TM

385 LPRINTTAB(12)"Y INTERCEPT FOR THE LINE (B)      = ";TD

387 FORJ=1TO2:GOSUB1900:NEXTJ:GOSUB1940:SYSTEM"FORMS {T}"

390 LPRINT:LPRINT:PRINTTAB(40)"PRESS ENTER TO
    CONTINUE ";:GOSUB 2340

395 RETURN

398 '                            * STATISTICS VIDEO ROUTINE  *

400 CLS:PRINTTAB(12)"C O R R E L A T I O N  &  L I N E A R
                    R E G R E S S I O N"

401 PRINT:PRINTTAB(10)"VARIABLE X: ";ZV;TAB(48)
    "VARIABLE Y: ";ZU

402 PRINT:PRINTTAB(14)"MEAN OF X  = ";TE,"
    MEAN OF Y  = ";TH
```

Fig. 10-21. Final program listing (continued from page 197).

```
403 PRINT TAB(14)"S.D. OF X =  ";TS,"
    S.D. OF Y = ";TT:PRINT
404 PRINT:PRINTTAB(12)"NUMBER OF PAIRS (N)
    = ";N:PRINT
405 PRINTTAB(12)"CORRELATION COEFFICIENT (R)      = ";R
406 PRINTTAB(12)"DEGREES OF FREEDOM (DF)
    = ";N-2:PRINT
407 PRINTTAB(12)"SLOPE OF REGRESSION LINE         = ";TM
408 PRINTTAB(12)"Y INTERCEPT FOR THE LINE (B)     = ";TD
409 PRINT:PRINT:PRINTTAB(40)"PRESS ENTER TO
    CONTINUE ";:GOSUB 2340
410 RETURN
900 '                  * X BY Y PLOT - LINE PRINT LEVEL 2 *
991 '
992 '                      * CONCATENATION *
993 '
1000 GOSUB 8000:FOR TI=1 TO 2*N STEP 2
1010 IF JP(TI+1)<10 THEN C$(TI)=" 0"+MID$(STR$(JP(TI+1)),
     2,1)+STR$(JO(TI)):GOTO 1030
1020 C$(TI)=STR$(JP(TI+1))+STR$(JO(TI))
1030 NEXT TI
1032                      * SHELL-METZGER SORT*
1033 '
1040 TI=N*2
1050 N=N*2
1060 M=N
1070 M=INT(M/2)
1080 IF M=0 THEN 1210
1090 J=1
1100 K=N-M
1110 I=J
1120 L=I+M
1130 IF C$(I)< C$(L) THEN 1180
```

199

```
1140 SWAP C$(I),C$(L)
1150 I=I-M
1160 IF I<1 THEN 1180
1170 GOTO 1120
1180 J=J+1
1190 IF J>K THEN 1070
1200 GOTO 1110
1210 TI=1 ' END OF SORT. SEPARATE SORTED VARIABLES
1220 FOR I=N/2+1 TO N
1230 JP(TI+1)=VAL(LEFT$(C$(I),4))
1240 JO(TI)=VAL(RIGHT$(C$(I),2))
1250 TI=TI+2
1260 NEXT I
1460 LJ=LJ+1
1470 LZ=LZ+1
1480 K=-K
1490 IF LJ=>LP AND LR<LEN(ZU) AND SGN(K)=1
     THEN 1500ELSE 1530
1500 LR=LR+1
1510 LPRINTTAB(4)MID$(ZU,LR,1);
1520 GOTO 1540
1530 LPRINT" ";
1540 IF LZ<>6 THEN 1610
1550 LPRINTTAB(5);
1560 LPRINT USING A$;A(LC);
1570 LPRINT" +";
1580 LC=LC-1
1590 LZ=0
1600 GOTO 1620
1610 LPRINTTAB(15)"I";
1620 FOR L=15 TO 70
1630 LI=LI+1
```

Fig. 10-21. Final program listing (continued from page 199).

200

```
1640 IFLI=JO(TI) AND J=JP(TI+1) THEN LPRINT TAB(LI)"*":
     TI=TI+2:GOTO 1680
1650 NEXT L
1660 IF LC=0 THEN 1690
1670 LPRINT" "
1680 NEXT J
1690 LPRINT TAB(15)"----------+----------+----------+
               ----------+----------+----"
1700 LPRINT" "
1710 LPRINT TAB(6)" ";
1720 FOR J=8 TO 13
1730 LPRINT USING BB$;A(J);
1740 NEXT J
1750 LPRINT
1760 LPRINT
1770 LL=LEN(ZV)
1780 LPRINT TAB(12+(64-2*LL)/2);
1790 FOR J=1 TO LL
1800 LPRINT MID$(ZV,J,1);
1810 LPRINT" ";
1820 NEXT J
1830 FOR J=1 TO 3
1840 GOSUB 1900
1850 NEXT J
1860 LPRINT" "
1870 LPRINT" "
1880 GOSUB 1940
1885 SYSTEM "FORMS {T}
1890 RETURN
1900 FOR JF=1 TO 3
1910 LPRINT" "
1920 NEXT JF
```

```
1930 RETURN
1940 FOR L=1 TO 13
1950 LPRINT"*****";
1960 NEXT L
1970 LPRINT" "
1980 RETURN
1985 '          * X BY Y PLOT  VIDEO ROUTINE LEVEL 2 *
1990 CLS
2000 PRINT STRING$(4,CHR$(13))
2010 FOR I=9 TO 1 STEP -1
2020 PRINT
2030 PRINT USING A$;A(I)
2040 NEXT I
2050 PRINT@ 1844," ";
2060 FOR I= 10 TO 15
2070 PRINT USING B$;A(I);
2080 NEXT I
2090 FOR I=11 TO 60
2100 PRINT@ (22,I),"-";
2110 NEXT I
2120 FOR I=6 TO 22
2130 PRINT@ (I,11),"!";
2140 NEXT I
2150 FOR J=6 TO 22 STEP 2
2160 PRINT@ (J,10),"-";
2170 NEXT J
2180 FOR J=1 TO 2*N-1 STEP 2
2190 PRINT@ (JP(J+1),JO(J)),"*";
2200 NEXT J
2210 TJ=XL
2220 TQ=(XH-XL)/100
2230 ON A6 GOTO 2240,2310
```

Fig. 10-21. Final program listing (continued from page 201).

```
2240  JO=11+(TJ-XL)/(XH-XL)*45
2250  JP=22-(TM*TJ+TD-YL)/(YH-YL)*16
2260  IF JP>60 OR JP<11 THEN 2280
2270  PRINT@ (JP,JO),"*"
2280  TJ=TJ+TQ
2290  IF TJ>XH THEN 2310
2300  GOTO 2240
2310  PRINT@ 15,"PRESS ENTER TO CONTINUE ";
2320  INPUTZI
2330  RETURN
2340  II$=INKEY$
2350  IF II$="" THEN 2340
2360  RETURN
2365  '              * X BY Y PLOT - DEVICE SELECTION SBR *
2370  PRINTTAB(30)"WANT REGRESSION LINE SHOWN  ( Y/N ) ";
2380  II$=""
2390  GOSUB 2340
2400  IFII$="Y" THEN A6=1
2410  IFII$="N" THEN A6=2
2420  PRINT
2430  PRINTTAB(30)" IS OUTPUT TO LINE PRINTER   ( Y/N ) ";
2440  II$=""
2450  GOSUB 2340
2460  IF II$="Y" THEN GOSUB 1000
2470  IF II$="N" THEN GOSUB 1990
2480  RETURN
2485  '                    * KEYBOARD INPUT ROUTINE *
2490  PRINT @ 240,CHR$(24)
2500  PRINT@ 576,;
2510  INPUT"WHAT IS THE NAME OF VARIABLE X ";ZV
2520  PRINT@ 736,;
2530  INPUT"WHAT IS THE NAME OF VARIABLE Y ";ZU
```

203

```
2540 IF LEN(ZV)>14 THEN ZV=LEFT$(ZV,14)
2550 IF LEN(ZU)>14 THEN ZU=LEFT$(ZU,14)
2560 IF ZI="N" THEN 2600
2570 PRINT@ 896,;
2580 INPUT"WHAT IS THE NAME OF YOUR DATA FILE ";ZN
2590 OPEN "O",1,ZN
2600 PRINT@ 1060,"BEGIN ENTERING YOUR DATA PAIRS ( X/Y )"
2610 PRINT@ 1140,"SIGNAL END OF DATA WITH @,@"
2620 PRINT@ 1300,;
2630 PRINT TAB(20);
2640 INPUT Z,ZB
2650 IF Z="@" THEN 2700
2660 X(N+1)=VAL(Z)
2670 X(N+2)=VAL(ZB)
2680 N=N+2
2690 GOTO 2630
2700 IF ZI="N" THEN 2760
2710 PRINT#1,ZV;CHR$(13);ZU;CHR$(13);N;
2720 FOR I= 1 TO N
2730 PRINT#1,X(I);
2740 NEXT I
2750 CLOSE
2760 N=N/2
2770 RETURN
2775 '                     * DISK INPUT ROUTINE  *
2780 PRINT@ 270,CHR$(24);:PRINT:PRINT:PRINT:PRINT
2790 INPUT"ENTER NAME OF DISK FILE ";ZN
2800 OPEN "I",1,ZN
2810 INPUT#1,ZV,ZU,N
2820 FOR I=1 TO N
2830 INPUT#1,X(I)
2840 NEXT I
```

Fig. 10-21. Final program listing (continued from page 203).

```
2850 CLOSE
2860 N=N/2
2870 RETURN
7000 '                    *    LINE PRINT COORDINATE ROUTINE    *
8000 FOR J=1 TO 2*N-1 STEP2
```

DOCUMENTATION

Program documentation, except for the User's Guide and the Program Maintenance Manual, is scattered through the preceeding pages. The Program Logic Manual contains the material found on pages 154 through 167 plus material from the program design section describing the data structure and how the program handles it.

A complete User's Guide follows as an example of what is included.

A Program Maintenance Manual follows the User's Guide. This provides the programmer with information necessary to modify the program for specific purposes, or to include it as a part of a more comprehensive package of statistical analysis functions.

User's Guide

This program enables you to compute and display statistical information for variable numbers of pairs of data. The information to be computed and displayed includes the mean and standard deviation of each variable, the correlation coefficient and degrees of freedom between them, and the slope and Y intercept of the line on which they fall. You can specify the form of the display, either a video display or a printout, and repeat the calculations with new data if desired. Given one value of a coordinate you can predict the corresponding value and exit the program to the Basic Interpreter.

Startup

When the system is on line and you have your operating system READY prompt, Fig. 10-22, type DO STATS and then press the <ENTER> key. In most cases, <ENTER> tells the computer when you are finished entering commands or data, but now it acts on what you have typed.

This command line will automatically initialize the printer, and load and execute the program. If your printer was on line and initialized during startup, then pressing the Q option in the FORMS

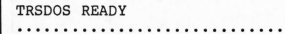

```
TRSDOS READY
··································
```

Fig. 10-22. Operating system command prompt.

command will enable you to skip this portion of the initialization process. The screen is cleared and the DATA ENTRY display appears as shown in Fig. 10-23.

Data Entry

You have three options in the data entry section, selected by pressing either <1>, <2>, or <3>. For example, if you want to enter data from the keyboard and create a disk file of that data, press <2>. The program automatically sets up the proper display and waits for you to type in the appropriate information. If you only want to enter data into memory then <1> is pressed. If the data is to be entered from a disk file then press <3>. If option <3> is desired make sure that the data file is created with this program originally, or that the format of the file is the same as one created by the program.

You may continue entering data until a total of 24 pairs of data have been entered. If you have less data there does not have to be 2 pairs of entrys. When all desired data has been entered, then press

```
         C O R R E L A T I O N   &
     L I N E A R   R E G R E S S I O N
SPECIFY DATA ENTRY METHOD


        <1> KEYBOARD TO MEMORY

        <2> KBD TO MEM & SAVE TO DISK

        <3> INPUT FROM DISK FILE



            ENTER CHOICE
```

Fig. 10-23. Data entry display screen.

$< @ , @ >$. This informs the program that all data has been entered and it is now time to proceed with the remainder of the program. Before leaving this section, a message informs you of how many pairs of data were entered. The display is held until ready to proceed.

Display

Once your data has been entered, no matter what its source, a prompt tells you that the data is being processed. After this the screen lists five display options available in the program, Fig. 10-24. This is automatic once the option selections are made. If any entry is made except numerals from 1 through 5, the program ignores it and permits you to try again.

Option <1> X by Y Plot

When selecting this option, notice a slight pause and then two additional prompts that appear in sequence. The first permits you to superimpose a regression line on the video plot. The second routes the data to the video display or to the line printer. These prompts appear just below Enter Choice on the output display. They are:

    WANT REGRESSION LINE SHOWN (Y/N)

and

    IS OUTPUT TO LINE PRINTER (Y/N)

```
          C O R R E L A T I O N   &
     L I N E A R   R E G R E S S I O N
        DISPLAY OPTIONS


            <1>   X BY Y PLOT
            <2>   PREDICT VALUES
            <3>   DISPLAY STATISTICS
            <4>   ENTER NEW VALUES
            <5>   END PROGRAM




                ENTER CHOICE
```

Fig. 10-24. Display option display screen.

Option <2> Predict Values

The prediction routine sets up an instructional display at the top of the screen, Fig. 10-25. When an X value is entered the corresponding Y value is computed and displayed in the next column. If the entered value is greater than the largest data item or less than the smallest one, an additional prompt (X NOT IN RANGE) is printed to inform you that this value is extrapolated and not as reliable as other data. The option will continue to compute Y values as long as additional X values are entered. To return to display selection enter @ for the X value and then press <ENTER>.

Option <3> Display Statistics

When <3> is pressed an additional prompt appears: IS OUTPUT TO LINE PRINTER (Y/N) Once an option is selected the remainder of the routine is automatic. The display is cleared and the information is printed on the screen or line printer, Fig. 10-26.

Option <4> Enter New Values

This option returns you to the initial data entry routine for entry of another set of values.

Option <5> End Program

This option ends the program and takes you back to the BASIC Ready prompt.

Maintenance Manual

The maintenance manual is an aid to modifying the program. Effective addition of modifications requires understanding of how the program is organized and how it achieves results. The latter is covered in the program logic manual, included in this chapter. The program is organized into a series of operational levels. This is done by setting up each level beyond the first as a subroutine, which in turn calls other lower level subroutines and so on.

Additions to Program

The easiest way to modify the program is to work within the existing structure and add new material as subroutines. Two examples of this are (1) adding data to an existing body of data in memory and then saving it to disk, (2) the ability to change or correct erroneous data in memory and save to a disk file.

The first requires an update option in the data entry section.

```
+---------------------------------------+
|                                       |
|     *  DATA INTERPOLATION  *          |
|                                       |
|   ENTER @ TO STOP PREDICTING          |
|                                       |
|     X              PREDICTED Y         |
|   -----------------------------        |
|   ?                                    |
|                                       |
+---------------------------------------+
```

Fig. 10-25. Predict display screen.

The option reads in data from a file by calling the disk input routine as a subroutine. After clearing the screen it calls the data entry subroutine beginning at line 1080. This requires a minimum amount of new code—perhaps as little as two or three lines excluding the necessary additions to the data entry display module.

The second example requires some thought. The problem is where to place this function for maximum effectiveness. Logically, it is placed with the data entry options as you enter or replace data items. With this scheme what if you decided that values needed correction after reaching the display option display? The only way to get back to data entry would be to use the Enter New Values option, but this would destroy the data.

What is needed is a way to move around in the program without destroying the data. There are advantages in having it in either data entry or display options. Another solution might be to set up a very general function menu to route the program to the various submenus as desired.

This function menu has three options; Enter Data, Display, and Correct Data. With this, any option could be selected. By providing a return to this menu for each section you could move around freely within the program. It might be more logical to place the End Program option here as a fourth choice.

The Change Data module might then be written in accordance with whatever requirements you set up. Options within this module can include direct or sequential display of data items or pairs of items and scale names; the change sequence itself; saving data to disk; merging disk data files; return to main menu; etc. The placement of an option when modifying programs involves careful consideration of the purpose of the option and where that purpose can most effectively be served.

Plot Algorithms

Modification of the plot algorithms as mentioned in the user's guide is straightforward. The initial constants in the algorithms are the coordinates of the plot origin either on the screen or on paper. You merely decide what they are and insert them.

The scale multipliers were developed by trial and error. A simple way to proceed is to select a maximum value for the X and Y coordinates in your test data. Print out the plot diagram and adjust the scale multipliers to place the largest data item at the intersection of the horizontal and vertical imaginary lines through this point. This will give you correct placement at all points on the plot. Do not expect perfect placement for all points, most video displays and line printers do not have good enough resolution for this. So long as you are close, the plot points will give you a general picture of what the line looks like.

Integration Into Larger Program

Integration of this program as a module in a larger program can be done in a number of ways. If specific functions are desired, such as a printout of the statistical data as a part of a larger report, it might be feasible to use only those portions of the coding necessary to the task. If you wish to retain the generality of the program and include it as a part of an overall package of general statistical functions, then perhaps the program might be stored on a disk and called from a menu of similar programs. Such a grouping, of any size, will almost surely be too large to remain in memory all at the same time. There might be an executive program in memory to initialize the computer and call the various functions as needed from a menu. Such a method would conserve memory space. The disadvantage, at least under TRSDOS 1.2 would be to save the data whenever a different module is loaded. Other operating systems may permit the merging of programs without loss of data.

Other Modifications

A few other modifications also suggest themselves. First of all, there is no way to ignore incorrect choice designations in the data entry section. No matter what is entered as a choice the program will act on it. If you make a mistake in entry there is no way to correct it except to start over.

Next, lines 1380 through 1490 belong with the video plot subroutine instead of where they are. Moving them speeds up operation, since they would be active only if the video plot was called.

210

Lastly, by changing the sorting algorithm to the one used in Chapters 7 and 8 you can eliminate the time and coding required to concatenate the variables and separate them after sorting. Some code is required to get the data into the correct variables, but in the long run it might be quicker and less of a bother.

Chapter 11
A Program in Z-80 Assembler

Advanced planning is desirable in programming a task in any language. I've stressed the importance of planning the procedures and then examining them to eliminate ambiguities and errors throughout the first seven chapters of the book. Programming in assembly language compounds the need for all phases of the program development sequence.

In assembler the interpreter function routines are not already worked out for us. In assembly language you cannot write A times B equals C. Instead you must specify where each number is to be found in memory; specify in exact detail how you arrive at an answer; and finally, specify where in memory it is to be stored.

Complete program design is even more essential in assembler. Because of the detail required, you must carry the breakdown of logical units into smaller ones much farther than in high-level languages. The logic must be subdivided into the smallest possible blocks so that each one can be implemented with a single instruction or just a few assembler instructions.

PROBLEM DEFINITION

Let's design a program that will accept input from the keyboard and use it to execute one of several program modules we might want to include as functions of this main program. The program must be a general one so that the numbers and types of functions can vary. It must accept command strings of up to four data items to input either in hexadecimal or decimal notation. Predesignate this to avoid extra complication in the program design.

Some of the functions to include will be (:) an output module to file with specified structures either the video display or the line printer; modules to zero blocks of memory; move blocks of memory in any direction; exit the program to the operating system; and activate the break key to abort module execution.

In addition, because of the nature of the Radio Shack Model II TRSDOS 2.0 operating system, you can provide a number of operating system commands called from within this program. Other commands or modules can be written and added as desired. This will be explained later in this chapter.

What is needed before beginning design of your program? Let's refer to Chapters 3 and 4 to assure inclusion of all necessary information. The information needed to execute the various modules is input as ASCII-coded decimal characters from the keyboard. The computer requires all data to be in binary, so you will have to convert it before processing.

In this program, processing consists of separating the command string into its component parts, identifying the various data items, converting them to binary, and placing them into their predesignated locations where the function modules can find them. This is called *parsing*. Neither speed nor precision will be a major consideration in this application.

First, set up a memory map to allocate areas of memory for the various uses. Memory is needed for the ASCII-coded information to be output to the video display as command prompt information and error messages. Space is needed for a function lookup table of module addresses. Space is needed for nonlookup functions such as the operating system commands called from the program. In addition, reserve areas for the stack, initial input of information from the keyboard, space for the conversion of our initial data to binary, and storage space for the various flags and counters necessary during program operation.

The most likely errors to input are entering a nonexistent command, entering a command with the wrong syntax, entering data in incorrect form or incorrect order, or not entering data at all. Any of these require reentry of the correct command string or data. Also provide descriptive error messages for them to aid the operator in determining what is wrong with the original input.

To summarize the problem:

1. The program is an executive type program which manages command input and output permitting function calls both to the operating system and to specially written function modules.

2. Output, exit, zero memory, and move memory modules are included as examples of function modules in addition to certain operating system function calls.

3. Error messages are provided for incorrect responses.

4. Data must be parsed, converted to binary, and placed in predesignated locations for use by the various modules.

5. Memory allocations are made for the following purposes.

A. AscII prompts and error messages
B. Function lookup table
C. Operating system command table
D. Stack
E. Keyboard input
F. Scratchpad memory for processing
G. Function module data input
H. Processing flags and counters

PROGRAM DESIGN

Again, start with the three basic program elements input, processing, and output. Let's start with top-down modular design and continue subdividing each element as much as possible. Figure 11-1 is the initial breakdown of the program. By continuing to break down each of the subdivisions into smaller units you will eventually reach the goal.

Figure 11-2 reveals the next step in the process. Here take each of the main divisions of Fig. 11-1 and break them into their component steps. Some of these may require further subdivision.

```
INPUT
    INITIALIZE PROGRAM
    GET COMMAND
PROCESSING
    PARSE COMMAND STRING
    TRANSFER DATA TO MODULE INPUT LOCATIONS
OUTPUT
    EXECUTE COMMAND
    RETURN TO PROMPT
```

Fig. 11-1. Initial structure of assembly-language program.

```
INPUT
    INITIALIZE PROGRAM
        Point to Top of Stack
        Set Break Interrupt Address
        Set Hold Interrupt Routine
        Zero User Memory
        Clear Video Display
        Clear Keyboard
        Zero Program Scratchpad Memory
    GET COMMAND
        Put Prompt on Screen
        Input Command String
PROCESSING
    PARSE COMMAND STRING
        Zero Routine Flag Locations
        Parse the String
OUTPUT
    EXECUTE COMMAND
    RETURN TO PROMPT
```

Fig. 11-2. Expanded structure of assembly-language program.

You can see from this how to create an outline of program operation. You may deviate slightly from this when coding in order to save memory space but follow it closely as a general rule.

Before proceeding, let me pause to explain some things about this Radio Shack Model II TRSDOS 2.0 operating system. Within the operating system there are a number of special-purpose routines called *SVC routines* which can be used within any machine-language program. They cannot be examined to see exactly how they accomplish their various tasks. They are essentially a "black box" for you to set up the input conditions and then invoke them. The results appear, and you may use them in your program. These routines are called *primitive routines*. They are mainly concerned with various types of input/output functions, though a number of others provide math functions, data conversion, sorts, table lookup, string comparison, and other utilities.

Figure 11-3 is a list of all SVC functions provided under TRSDOS 2.0. You can write your own special-purpose routines and designate them as SVC calls. The figure lists the decimal and equivalent hexadecimal code for each SVC as well as its mnemonic designation. In calling an SVC, the specified input data listed for each in the technical information chapter of the operating system manual must be placed in the designated registers. Then the A register is loaded with the SVC code (in hexadecimal) and a RST 8 is executed. If you wish to use an SVC call as a subroutine, then RET is placed immediately following the RST 8. I will use a number of these later in the chapter. If you are using other operating systems, there may be near equivalent primitive functions available. If not, write your own routines. In some of the smaller computers these may be available in ROM if the function addresses are known. I will explain in as much detail as possible what each use of an SVC is intended to accomplish.

Now back to the program itself. Figure 11-4 goes one step further in the breakdown process. Some of the simpler items are almost at the individual instruction level. As you can see, a listing such as this for a program of any size or complexity would be a book in itself.

INPUT

I'll go through the logic so far. The first task is to set up all the program locations needed so you can start out in the program without having to worry about unpleasant surprises due to left over data or program instructions from previous use of the memory. This is also one of the reasons why you designate your stack area within the program you are writing. In this way you should have no trouble with corruption of stack data either from your own program or from the operating system.

The next item is to reset the *break* processing routine so that it returns to the program rather than to the operating system. This is done by using the SETBRK SVC. In looking at the instructions for its use, notice that it must be called twice to set a new break processing routine. When it is executed the first time it removes the present break address from the system. It must be used again to put the desired address into operation. You only want to make this change while your program is active, so place the old address into your exit routine so that it is replaced whenever you are through using your program.

You would also like to be able to hold or temporarily halt operation of the program under certain conditions, especially when outputting information on the video display. This will enable you to examine it at your leisure without having to worry about it scrolling off the screen before you can see what it is. The HOLDKY SVC will enable this. This and the previous SETBRK routines are really interrupt service routines. There is no control over their operation

Code		Name	Code		Name
DEC	**HEX**		**DEC**	**HEX**	
0	0	INITIO	23	17	MPYDIV
1	1	KBINIT	24	18	BINHEX
2	2	SETUSR	25	19	TIMER
3	3	SETBRK	26	1A	CURSOR
4	4	KBCHAR	27	1B	SCROLL
5	5	KBLINE	28	1C	LOOKUP
6	6	DELAY	29	1D	HOLDKY
7	7	VDINIT	33	21	LOCATE
8	8	VDCHAR	34	22	RDNXT
9	9	VDLINE	35	23	DIRRD
10	0A	VDGRAF	36	24	JP2DOS
11	0B	VDREAD	37	25	DOSCMD
12	0C	VIDKEY	38	26	RTNCMD
15	0F	DISKID	39	27	ERROR
17	11	PRINIT	40	28	OPEN
18	12	PRCHAR	41	29	KILL
19	13	PRLINE	42	2A	CLOSE
20	14	RANDOM	43	2B	WRITNX
21	15	BINDEC	44	2C	DIRWR
22	16	STCOMP	45	2D	DATE
46	2E	PARSER	56	38	SORT
47	2F	RENAME	57	39	CLRXIT
49	31	STSCAN	58	3A	FILPTR
51	33	WILD	94	5E	VIDRAM
52	34	ERRMSG	95	5F	PRCTRL
53	35	RAMDIR			

Fig. 11-3. TRSDOS 2.0 SVC calls available.

except as provided in the SVC instructions, so try to determine their exact mode of operation.

The last four items in initialization are merely a matter of prudent programming. You want to insure that nothing left over

INPUT
  INITIALIZE PROGRAM
    Point to Top of Stack
    Set Break Interrupt address
      point to present break address
      call SETBRK SVC
      store current breakpoint address for exit to TRSDOS
      point to desired break address
      call SETBRK again to enable new ADDR
    Set Hold Interrupt Routine
      set function switch
      call HOLDKY subroutine
    Zero User Memory
      point to start of user memory with BC
      point to end of user memory with HL
      call zero memory subroutine
    Call Clear Video Display Subroutine
    Clear Keyboard
      load function code
      call KBINIT SVC
    Zero Scratchpad Memory
      point to start of scratchpad with BC
      point to end of scratchpad with HL
      call zero memory subroutine
  GET COMMAND
    Put Prompt on Screen
      point to ASCII prompt to be displayed
      put first character (data) in B
      go to beginning of message
      designate max. number of characters input
      point to input buffer
    Input Command String
      call VIDKEY subroutine

PARSE COMMAND STRING
  INITIALIZE ROUTINE
    Zero F030
      put 0 in A
      load in memory location
    Zero F046 through F04F
      point to start with BC
      point to end with HL
      call zero subroutine

Fig. 11-4. Structured outline of program.

Initialize Converted Data Storage
  put data in HL
  load into F04D
Initialize data Designator List
  point to start of list
  load into F048
PARSE INPUT STRING
  Count Number of Characters Input
    point to beginning of string
    load max number of characters
    load terminator
    call search and computer subroutine
    put length of string in F030
  Check for No Command
    get start of string
    put in B
    put carriage return in A
    compare with first character of string
    abort processing if match is found
  Determine Number of Data Items Required
    point to first command character
    put in A
    put in F046
    compare with B, if match goto prompt
    compare with Q, if match goto quit
    compare with A, if match load 2 in F04B
  Set up for STSCAN
    put number of characters in reg. B
    put character pointer in DE
    put start of compare string in HL
    call STSCAN subroutine
  If Match Found Put 3 in F04B
  Compare with V, If Match Put 4 in F04B
  Compare with X, If Match Put 4 in F04B
  DETERMINE IF IT IS DOS COMMAND
    Point to Start of String
    Put Number of Characters in B
    Call STSCAN SVC
    If Match goto RETCMD Routine
  SEPARATE DATA ITEMS AND IDENTIFY
    Search for either Carriage Return or = Sign
      put start of string in HL
      put equal sign in EE45 (SEARCH CHAR)
      call search subroutine

    adjust pointers
    put new pointer in storage
    compare value in HL with value in DE (designator)
    if not equal call ERRMSG
Store Number of Characters Left in String
    put original total in A
    subtract current total in L
    put result in BC
    save current pointers in stack
Search for Carriage Return or Comma
    put comma in place of previous = sign
    zero return flag
    call search routine
    get flag
    compare for carriage return
    get pointers back
    send ERRMSG if no comma
Determine Number of Characters between = and Comma
    load comma in a (SEARCH CHAR)
    search for comma and compute number of characters searched
    reduce count to eliminate comma
    put count in A
    is it 4?
    if less than 4 goto ERRMSG
Check for Hex Conversion on 2 Data Item Commands
    get value from F04A
    put 2 in C
    compare the two
    if equal convert to hex
Check for H or P Command
    get initial of command to A
    compare with H, if equal convert to decimal
    compare with P, if equal convert to decimal
Convert from Hexadecimal
    move data to scratchpad area
    convert hex to binary
    goto transfer module
Convert from Decimal
    transfer data to scratchpad
    add leading zeros if necessary
    convert decimal to binary
Transfer Converted Data to Perm. Loc.
    set up pointer to correct LOC.
    compute correct pointer

Fig. 11-4. Structured outline of program (continued from page 218).

>>>>>>>> move pointer to HL
>>>>>>>> transfer data
>>>> Record Transfer of Data in Flag Loc. and Check if All Data Processed
>>>>>>>> get current count from memory
>>>>>>>> add 1
>>>>>>>> store count
>>>>>>>> save count in stack
>>>>>>>> get maximum count
>>>>>>>> put in B
>>>>>>>> restore current count
>>>>>>>> compare current with max.
>>>>>>>> restore data pointer
>>>>>>>> repeat processing if not complete
>>>> Transfer Switches if Present
>>>>>>>> set up pointers for search
>>>>>>>> search for/and compute count
>>>>>>>> get max. count
>>>>>>>> compare the two
>>>>>>>> if equal put carriage return in switch location
>>>>>>>> compute number of characters to move
>>>>>>>> move to new location

OUTPUT

EXECUTE COMMAND

Check for Operating System Command Word

- get start of string
- compute length of command word
- put in B
- point to operating system key words
- call STSCAN subroutine
- if present execute RETCMD SVC and goto prompt

Check for Function Module in Lookup Table

- put character in B
- point to start of table
- call lookup SVC
- go to address of module

RETURN TO PROMPT

Zero Hex Data Buffer

- put start in BC
- put end in HL
- call zero subroutine

Reset Stack Pointer

Point to Prompt

- point to location
- load number of characters

Go to VIDKEY routine

from previous use of memory will interfere with proper operation of the program. All of them serve this same purpose.

First clear all user memory by filling it with zeros. A zero is the machine-language code for the NOP instruction in Z80 assembler. A NOP instruction does nothing but use up a microsecond in execution time. It has no effect on registers or memory. Therefore no data or program instructions are affected if the program counter is accidentally sent into this memory and begins executing these instructions.

In a similar manner you want no data from previous programs or operations to interfere with proper display of data on the video display or the input of data from the keyboard. Initializing the video display and keyboard sets up the conditions and clears any stored characters or keystrokes from the local memory of these devices.

Finally you want to make sure that old data from your own program will not interfere with or corrupt new data being entered. For this reason zero your scratchpad memory area where temporary processing is carried out during program execution.

Once you have cleared all our memory locations and have the computer set up for your program, input your desired command. Ordinarily this is a fairly complicated task. Your job is simplified considerably because of your SVCS included with the operating system. Figure 11-5 is a simplified outline of what an input routine such as our SVC can do. If you were to write such a routine yourself it would probably occupy 80 to 100 bytes of memory or more. By using the SVC you obtain the same results with only 17 bytes of code. Don't be misled. The rest of the code is still there somewhere, but it is not in user memory.

To set up the SVC, merely follow the instructions. Simplify matters by supplying the number of characters (including control characters) to be output as a data item at the beginning of the message. This is placed in the proper register and the pointer moved to the beginning of the message. Then set the maximum number of characters the routine will accept and point to the beginning of the buffer. This will hold your keyboard input. Once this is done, call the routine and the rest is automatic.

PROCESSING

When input is complete and the data is in the input buffer, it must be converted to a form usable by the computer. Input from the keyboard is ASCII-coded hexadecimal input. Each byte represents one character (letter, numeral, or punctuation mark). In addition, have several types of data input together one after the other on a

```
Put Prompt on Screen
    point to ASCII message
    load number of characters (or count and load)
    check character for ASCII
    point to video memory
    output character
    check number of characters to load
    if not equal repeat from "CHECK CHARACTER"
Get Input
    point to input buffer
    get character from keyboard
    check for control codes
    check for ASCII
    put character in input buffer
    add one to character count input
    check for carriage return
    go to next location
    repeat from "GET CHARACTER"
```

Fig. 11-5. Outline of input routine replaced by SVC.

single line. There must be some way for the computer to recognize more than one data item, and you must also provide a way to separate them into individual items that can be dealt with and used in the correct manner.

During program operation the command prompt will surely be used a number of times. This requires that certain memory locations used by the program be cleared each time a new command is entered. This gives interference and undesired results.

Your next task is to separate or "parse" the command string into its separate data items, identify these items, convert them to binary format and store them in the locations where the computer program expects to find them when executing a function module. The first thing to do is determine the length or number of characters in the complete input string for use as a comparison. Don't attempt to place any characters not input with this command into program locations. After this the program checks to make sure that a command was really entered. If not the command prompt reappears.

Next, the program must check to see what type of command has been entered. This could be a function command executed by your program code or it could be a command to execute an operating system function. Commands to the operating system need no processing. The SVC processing routine for these commands merely requires that the start of the command string be identified for the routine and that it be in the correct format as required by the operating system.

Once a command is there and is not an operating system instruction, determine how many data items are required for that command, that is how many items the program needs to execute it. Do this by grouping the commands by the number of items they require. By proper coding you can select and designate how many data items are expected with any command, and use that number to test completion of the conversion loop.

This requires advance planning in deciding what form your data will take for the program. If the program is to distinguish data items and identify them, set up a precise format for each item which the program can identify and deal with. In your present program choose the following format for an individual datum.

1. A letter identifying it to the program.

2. An equal sign (=) to designate the beginning of a numerical value.

3. The datum itself (either in hexadecimal or decimal as required by the function).

4. A comma to signal the end of that particular datum.

When processing the input data it might be possible for the program to find the end of the command string, designated by a carriage return (ENTER), before finding either of the search characters. This happens at the end of the command string. Therefore if the carriage return is found before either of the others the search is terminated and a flag is set to signal a carriage return.

Several things need to be checked. The data must be in a specified order to be processed correctly. This can be checked by the identifying letter preceding the equal sign. If there is a match between this letter and the correct one in memory, separate the data.

To separate the data items, first count the number of characters between the equal sign and the comma. This cannot be more than five characters in length. Next, determine if the data should be converted from decimal to binary or from hexdecimal to binary. This is done in two stages. First, check to see which datum you are working with. Only the first two values ever get converted from decimal. The third value, if there, is always converted to hexadecimal. Second, check to see if you are calling either the print or hard copy functions. If so, automatically go to decimal conversion.

The two conversion routines follow with the program routing

data through either one as appropriate. Initially, transfer the characters to the temporary buffer for processing. In the case of the decimal routine, pad the numeral with leading zeros if it is not five characters long. Once in the temporary buffer and in correct format the data is converted using the appropriate SVC.

After the datum is converted it is transferred to the permanent storage location for use by the program. Then the counter is moved to the next location and the program checks to see if all expected data has been processed. If not the parsing sequence is repeated.

Once the data items are converted make one final check. It is possible that optional alternative routines have been designated to modify the processing of the particular function called. If the total length of the command string is longer than what has been used, then the remainder is assumed to be optional routines and is transferred in its entirety to the proper location. With this done parsing is complete.

OUTPUT

Now that all the data is in place, identify and then execute the command in the proper manner. Assume that any commands so far will be for function modules. This accounts for the two-stage routine.

The first stage determines if the command word, which is all characters from the beginning of the line up to the first blank space, is one of a list of operating system command words supplied in memory. If so, the entire line is executed via the RETCMD SVC as explained earlier.

If your command word is not one of these, assume it is a function module and go to the lookup table to find its starting address. The table itself must be set up so that a single character, designating the function, is followed by the two-byte address of that function. When a match is found with the character, the LOOKUP SVC returns the address of that function in the HL register. Then execute the function with a single instruction, i.e., JP (HL).

After the function has executed, reinitialize the data buffer, reset the stack to its initial position, reprint the prompt, and wait for additional input.

I have alluded from time to time to the need for allocating portions of memory for various purposes. The specific locations must be chosen before coding can begin. Figure 11-6 is a memory map showing the final locations decided upon for all functions. This is another of the essential documents before coding.

C600-EBFF	OVERLAY PROGRAM AREA
EC00-EDD2	MAIN INPUT AND PARSING CODE
EDD5-EE3C	HARDCOPY/PRINT MODULE
EE3F-EE51	SEARCH DIVIDE SUBROUTINE FOR PARSER
EE85-EE99	MOVE FUNCTION MODULE
EE9C-EEA9	ZERO FUNCTION MODULE
EEAF-EEBC	OPERATING SYSTEM COMMAND FUNCTION MODULE
EEE1-EEFA	QUIT FUNCTION MODULE
EEFD-EF16	ERROR SUBROUTINE - REVERSES 1ST 2 PARAMETERS IF IN INCORRECT ORDER
EF17-EF29	ERROR SUBROUTINE - CHECKS FOR DATA IN 3RD DATA LOCATION
EF2A-EF3F	PRINTS ONE LINE ON VIDEO DISPLAY
EF40-EF4A	PRINTS ERROR MESSAGE ON VIDEO DISPLAY
EF4B-EF4E	BIN/DEC SVC SUBROUTINE
EF70-EF7A	COUNTS NUMBER OF CHARACTERS TO A SEARCH CHARACTER IN A STRING
EF7B-EF7E	STSCAN SVC
EF7F-EF82	ERRMSG SVC
EF83-EF86	ERROR SVC
EF87-EF8A	WRITENX SVC
EF8B-EF8E	READNX SVC
EF8F-EF92	CLOSE SVC
EF93-EF96	OPEN SVC
EF97-EF9B	RETCMD SVC

Fig. 11-6. Memory map for Z80 program.

CODING

When coding programs in high-level languages, you usually begin coding with the main command level and work out the subprogram modules later after the command logic has been verified. In coding assembly-language programs, however, it is easier to code and verify the simplest subroutines needed and then incorporate them into larger structures after they have been verified. This sequence is one of the reasons why the entire program logic is

EF9C-EFAD	PROCESSING COMPLETE MSG SUBROUTINE
EFAE-EFC0	BUFFER FULL MSG SUBROUTINE
EFC1-EFC4	VIDLINE SVC
EFC5-EFCB	VIDINIT SVC
EFCC-EFCF	VIDKEY SVC
EFD0-EFD3	HOLDKY SVC
EFD4-EFD7	LOOKUP SVC
EFD8-EFF1	MOVE DATA IN MEMORY SUBROUTINE
EFF2-EFFF	ZERO MEMORY SUBROUTINE
F000-F028	INPUT BUFFER
F030	STORAGE LOCATION FOR NUMBER OF CHARACTERS INPUT IN COMMAND STRING
F040-F045	TEMPORARY STORAGE FOR DATA WHILE BEING CONVERTED FROM EITHER HEX OR DECIMAL TO BINARY
F046-F04F	FLAGS AND TEMPORARY STORAGE BY PARSER
F080-F08F	PERMANENT STORAGE FOR MODULE PARAMETERS AND SWITCHES
F090-F0FA	RESERVED FOR STACK
F2A9-F2AF	OPERATING SYSTEM COMMAND INDEX TABLE
F2B0-F2B6	FUNCTION MODULE COMMAND INDEX TABLE
F2B8-F2BB	PARAMETER DESIGNATOR TABLE
F2C0-F2D8	ASCII COMMANDS
F2E9-F31A	MODULE JUMP TABLE
F31B-F3FF	ASCII MESSAGE AREA

worked out before coding begins. You want to know which of the simple routines will be needed as the program develops.

By reserving 1023 bytes of memory beginning at F000 for program workspace and ASCII messages, place the subroutines immediately preceding F000 in memory. In other words put them at the end of program memory.

One of the first things necessary is a subroutine to zero a block of memory. A function module is planned to do this, and such a routine is also needed at several places in the program. An elegant way to do this is provided in the Z80 LDIR instruction which automatically transfers the contents of the memory location designated by the HL register pair to the contents of the memory location designated by the DE register pair. The number of transfers is determined by the value in the BC register pair.

To implement this scheme, you will need code to place the number of bytes to transfer in BC, the beginning address in HL, and the destination address in DE. If possible, have the program compute the number of transfers to be made. How is this done?

To compute the number of bytes transferred, subtract the beginning address from the ending address. Also save the beginning address for use by the routine. Note on examining the subtract instructions available for register pairs that both BC and DE can be subtracted from HL with the difference remaining in HL. To put your beginning address in BC and the ending address in HL, you can subtract and have the difference in HL. The ending address is not needed after this so it does not matter that the ending address is destroyed in the process.

You will have to transfer the two-byte beginning address to the HL register as well as get the difference to BC. The easiest and most economical way to transfer two-byte values between register pairs is by use of the *PUSH* and *POP* instructions. These transfer the data to the stack from one register pair and then transfer it back to another when the POP is executed. Remember that PUSHes only copy data and do not destroy it in the original register pair. Now let's see what to do with the routine.

Assume that when the routine is called the beginning address is in the BC register pair and the ending address is in the HL register pair. Since the beginning address is in the HL register pair, save it in the stack for the transfer. Then subtract leaving the difference in HL. The difference must be transferred to BC and the saved beginning address put in HL and DE. Then move DE (our destination pointer) one byte and put a zero in the location pointed to by HL. Now you're ready to execute the LDIR instruction.

A commented mnemonics listing of this subroutine as described above follows.

PUSH	BC	Save beginning address for transfer to HL.
SBC	HL,BC	Compute number of bytes to zero.
PUSH	HL	Transfer number of bytes to BC.

```
POP    BC
POP    HL        Put beginning address
                 in H.
PUSH   HL        Put beginning address
                 also in DE.
POP    DE
INC    DE        Go to second byte
                 of block.
LD     (HL),0    Put zero in first
                 byte of block.
LDIR             Zero the entire block.
RET              Exit to the main
                 program.
```

If you have an assembler available, entering these mnemonics will produce your assembly-language instructions. If not, you will have to look up the machine code for each instruction.

This is a fairly straightforward, self-contained routine. If you tested it, you know it works. It uses a total of 14 bytes of code. You will notice that in the entire subroutine the only instruction which actually performs the action desired is the LDIR. All the instructions preceding it are for the purpose of setting up the various registers with the values they will need when the LDIR actually executes. This is typical of assembly-language programming. Most of the code is for the purpose of setting up registers, clearing flag bits, placing data in the proper places, and so on. Only a small proportion of the code actually carries out any particular procedure.

The next routine is actually shorter, but this is because it makes use of one of the built in service routines from the Model II operating system. This one prints a display prompt on the screen and then waits for input in response. The set up required to use this SVC is as follows. The routine is designated as the VIDKEY SVC.

1. HL   Points to the start of the text to be displayed.

2. DE   Points to the start of the input buffer. (the area where input will be stored)

3. B   Contains the number of characters (including control codes) to be printed.

4. C   Contains the maximum number of characters accepted for input.

Since this routine will be used by other modules designed, the SVC call is the only part of the routine to be made a subroutine.

Let's assume that your ASCII message is located at F340, well within the reserved workspace. Designate the start of the input storage area as F000. One way to save a bit of memory is to place the number of characters in a message in the byte immediately preceding the start of the text. This can be read as data and placed in the B register before going to the start of the actual message. The only other thing to be decided is the maximum number of characters to accept. In this case let's make it 72 as you then will have room for any command string you might wish to designate.

With these things in mind design your segment as follows:

LD	HL,F340	Point to start of message
LD	B,(HL)	Put number of charac-ters to send in B
INC	HL	Point to first message character
LD	C,48H	Put max input in C (in hex)
LD	DE,F000	Point to start of input buffer
CALL	VIDKEY	Call routine and execute

Another of the routines, while straightforward in design, uses a clever device to make it usable for two different purposes in the program. With proper coding it can serve any number of similar purposes within a program. This is the routine which is used to search for either an equal sign or a comma and a carriage return. Let's look at the operation of the routine in general to see how the switch is made to enable a single routine to do multiple duty.

The routine compares the contents of the A register with the contents of the address contained in the HL register pair. The A register is first loaded with a carriage return. If the comparison is true, the routine puts a 1 in location F04C to indicate this fact and returns to the calling program. If the character is not a carriage return, the routine loads either an equal sign or a comma into the A register depending on which part of the parsing routine of the main program we are in.

If the character is present, return to the main program. If not, go to the next memory location and repeat from the beginning of the subroutine. Now comes the trick. As the program is now set up, the instruction that loads either the equal sign or the comma is located at memory locations EE44 and EE45. Before calling the subroutine, place the appropriate character into location EE45 so that the routine is looking for the proper thing. By doing this create a routine to search for whatever combination of characters desired. This makes this routine more versatile than might otherwise be expected.

These three examples give some idea of the thought processes in designing assembly-language code. In many instances examining available source listings of assembly-language programs or utility routines reveals segments which can either be used as is or modified to be used in your programs. The main thing to keep in mind is what is to be accomplished by a particular routine or segment of code. What task is it to perform and how can code be written to most efficiently perform that task.

Designing and coding assembly-language programs is such a meticulous task that once you have a working program, no matter how inefficient, there is the temptation to say, "It's working now, let's leave well enough alone." If you later find a better way to code a segment, by all means, try it out. Perhaps the improvement is in performance, perhaps in ease of understanding, or perhaps it uses less memory. In any case you can be proud of the improvements made. Remember that most programs are improved only after a little use reveals their imperfections and inconveniences.

Figure 11-7 is a complete assembly-language source listing of this program including the function modules. A careful study of their design may prove useful in understanding more about the design of assembly-language programs. Note carefully how the logical structures are implemented in the code; where and why certain combinations are used; and what advantages this confers in the module. Such careful analysis will help you become a better programmer than all the instructions I could give.

Lines 100 through 280 set up the conditions necessary for proper operation of the program by clearing various areas of memory and setting up the stack and interrupt processing routines. These subroutine calls are

```
VIDINIT   EFC5
HOLDKY    EFD0
ZERO      EFF2
```

Lines 290 through 340 prints the command prompt and obtains the command input. It uses the VIDKEY SVC.

```
100   EC00   31 FA F0     LD     SP,F0FA: SET STACK
110   EC03   21 00 00     LD     HL,0000: REMOVE DOS BRK
120   EC06   3E 03        LD     A,03   : ADDRESS
130   EC08   CF           RST    8
140   EC09   22 ED EE     LD     (EEED),HL: SAVE ADDR
150   EC0C   21 F5 EE     LD     HL,EEF5: SET PGM BRK
160   EC0F   3E 03        LD     A,03   : ADDRESS
170   EC11   CF           RST    8
180   EC12   06 01        LD     B,01   : ENABLE HOLDKY
190   EC14   CD D0 EF     CALL   HOLDKY
200   EC17   01 00 28     LD     BC,2800: ZERO USER MEMORY
210   EC1A   21 00 C6     LD     HL,C600
220   EC1D   CD F2 EF     CALL   ZERO
230   EC20   CD C5 EF     CALL   VIDINIT: CLEAR SCREEN
240   EC23   3E 01        LD     A,01   : CLEAR KEYBOARD
250   EC25   CF           RST    8
260   EC26   01 00 F0     LD     BC,F000: ZERO SCRATCHPAD
270   EC29   21 A0 F0     LD     HL,F0A0
280   EC2C   CD F2 EF     CALL   ZERO
290   EC2F   21 40 F3     LD     HL,MSG PTR
300   EC32   46           LD     B,(HL)   : GET MSG COUNT
310   EC33   23           INC    HL       : POINT TO MSG
320   EC34   0E 48        LD     C,48     : LOAD MAX ENTRY
330   EC36   11 00 F0     LD     DE,INP BUF
340   EC39   CD CC EF     CALL   VIDKEY
350   EC3C   3E 00        LD     A,00
360   EC3E   32 30 F0     LD     (F030),A
370   EC41   01 46 F0     LD     BC,F046
380   EC44   21 4F F0     LD     HL,F04F
390   EC47   CD F2 EF     CALL   ZERO
400   EC4A   21 7E F0     LD     HL,F07E
410   EC4D   22 4D F0     LD     (F04D),HL
420   EC50   21 B7 F2     LD     HL,F2B7
430   EC53   22 48 F0     LD     (F048),HL
440   EC56   21 00 F0     LD     HL,INP BUF
450   EC59   01 40 00     LD     BC,0040
460   EC5C   3E 0D        LD     A,0D
470   EC5E   CD 70 EF     CALL   SRCH & COUNT
480   EC61   22 30 F0     LD     (F030),HL
490   EC64   EB           EX     DE,HL
500   EC65   46           LD     B,(HL)
510   EC66   3E 0D        LD     A,0D
520   EC68   B8           CP     B
530   EC69   CA B1 ED     JP     Z,WARM START
540   EC6C   21 00 F0     LD     HL,INP BUF
550   EC6F   7E           LD     A,(HL)
560   EC70   32 46 F0     LD     (F046),A
570   EC73   FE 42        CP     B
580   EC75   CA B1 ED     JP     Z,WARM START
590   EC78   FE 51        CP     Q
600   EC7A   CA E1 EE     JP     Z,QUIT
610   EC7D   FE 41        CP     A
620   EC7F   28 04        JR     Z,EC85
630   EC81   FE 5A        CP     Z
640   EC83   20 05        JR     NZ,EC8A
650   EC85   3E 02        LD     A,02
660   EC87   32 4B F0     LD     (F04B),A
670   EC8A   06 01        LD     B,01
680   EC8C   EB           EX     DE,HL
690   EC8D   21 B0 F2     LD     HL,F2B0
700   EC90   CD 7B EF     CALL   STSCAN
710   EC93   20 05        JR     NZ,EC9A
720   EC95   3E 03        LD     A,03
```

Fig. 11-7. Assembly-language source listing.

730	EC97	32 4B F0	LD	(F04B),A
740	EC9A	FE 56	CP	V
750	EC9C	28 04	JR	Z,ECA2
760	EC9E	FE 58	CP	X
770	ECA0	20 05	JR	NZ,ECA7
780	ECA2	3E 04	LD	A,04
790	ECA4	32 4B F0	LD	(F04B),A
800	ECA7	21 A9 F2	LD	HL,F2A9
810	ECAA	06 01	LD	B,01
820	ECAC	CD 7B EF	CALL	STSCAN
830	ECAF	CA AF EE	JP	Z,RETCMD SBR
840	ECB2	EB	EX	DE,HL
850	ECB3	3E 3D	LD	A,"="
860	ECB5	32 45 EE	LD	(EE45),A
870	ECB8	CD 3F EE	CALL	SRCH DELIMIT
880	ECBB	ED 5B 48 F0	LD	DE,(F04B)
890	ECBF	2B	DEC	HL
900	ECC0	13	INC	DE
910	ECC1	1A	LD	A,(DE)
920	ECC2	ED 53 48 F0	LD	(F048),DE
930	ECC6	BE	CP	(HL)
940	ECC7	28 06	JR	Z,ECCF
950	ECC9	CD 40 EF	CALL	ERRMSG
960	ECCC	C3 B1 ED	JP	WARM START
970	ECCF	23	INC	HL
980	ECD0	3A 30 F0	LD	A,(F030)
990	ECD3	95	SUB	L
1000	ECD4	06 00	LD	B,00
1010	ECD6	4F	LD	C,A
1020	ECD7	E5	PUSH	HL
1030	ECD8	D5	PUSH	DE
1040	ECD9	3E 2C	LD	A,2C
1050	ECDB	32 45 EE	LD	(EE45),A
1060	ECDE	3E 00	LD	A,00
1070	ECE0	32 4C F0	LD	(F04C),A
1080	ECE3	CD 3F EE	CALL	SRCH DELIMIT
1090	ECE6	3A 4C F0	LD	A,(F04C)
1100	ECE9	FE 01	CP	01	;FLAG SET ?
1110	ECEB	D1	POP	DE	;RESTORE PTRS
1120	ECEC	E1	POP	HL	
1130	ECED	28 DA	JR	Z,ERRMSG	;ABORT IF SET
1140	ECEF	3E 2C	LD	A,COMMA	;LD SRCH CHR
1150	ECF1	CD 70 EF	CALL	SRCH & COUNT	
1160	ECF4	2B	DEC	HL	;ADJ COUNT
1170	ECF5	7D	LD	A,L	;PUT IN A
1180	ECF6	FE 04	CP	04	
1190	ECF8	38 CF	JR	C,ERRMSG	;ABORT IF COUNT
					;MORE THAN FOUR
1200	ECFA	3A 4A F0	LD	A,(F04A)	;GET #
1210	ECFD	0E 02	LD	C,02	;COMPARE
1220	ECFF	B9	CP	C	;WITH 2
1230	ED00	28 0B	JR	Z,HEX	;IF YES,GO
1240	ED02	3A 46 F0	LD	A,(F046)	;GET INIT
					;CHARACTER
1250	ED05	FE 48	CP	H	;COMPARE
1260	ED07	28 1A	JR	Z,DECIMAL	
1270	ED09	FE 50	CP	P	
1280	ED0B	28 16	JR	Z,DECIMAL	
1290	ED0D	EB	HEX EX	DE,HL	;PUT POINTER
					;BACK IN HL
1300	ED0E	23	INC	HL	;GO TO NXT LOC
1310	ED0F	01 04 00	LD	BC,0004	;SET UP XFER
1320	ED12	11 40 F0	LD	DE,F040	;TO F040

```
1330  ED15  E5              PUSH   HL          ;SAVE BFFR PTR
1340  ED16  DD E1           POP    IX          ;IN IX
1350  ED18  D5              PUSH   DE          ;SAVE DEST PTR
1360  ED19  ED B0           LDIR               ;MOVE DATUM
1370  ED1B  E1              POP    HL          ;GET DEST PTR
                                               ;TO HL FOR SVC
1380  ED1C  06 01           LD     B,01        ;DESIG CONVERT
1390  ED1E  3E 18           LD     A,18        ;EXECUTE SVC
1400  ED20  CF              RST    8
1410  ED21  18 24           JR     TRANSFER    ;SKIP DECIMAL
1420  ED23  2B     DECIMAL  DEC    HL          ;ADJ COUNT
1430  ED24  E5              PUSH   HL          ;PUT COUNT IN
1440  ED25  C1              POP    BC          ;BC & SAVE IN
1450  ED26  C5              PUSH   BC          ;STACK
1460  ED27  AF              XOR    A           ;CLR A & CARRY
1470  ED28  ED 5A           ADC    HL,DE       ;GT END OF DTA
1480  ED2A  D5              PUSH   DE          ;SAVE PTR IN IX
1490  ED2B  DD E1           POP    IX
1500  ED2D  11 44 F0        LD     DE,F044     ;SET UP DEST
                                               ;FOR TRANSFER
1510  ED30  ED B8           LDDR               ;MOVE DATA
1520  ED32  C1              POP    BC          ;RESTORE COUNT
1530  ED33  3E 05           LD     A,05        ;SUBTRACT FM 5
1540  ED35  91              SUB    C
1550  ED36  47              LD     B,A         ;PUT DIFF IN B
1560  ED37  EB              EX     DE,HL       ;PUT PTR IN HL
1570  ED38  FE 00           CP     00          ;IF EQUAL SKIP
1580  ED3A  28 05           JR     Z,ED41      ;LEADING ZEROS
1590  ED3C  36 30           LD     (HL),30     ;ADD LEADING
1600  ED3E  2B              DEC    HL          ;ZEROS
1610  ED3F  10 FB           DJNZ   ED3C
1620  ED41  06 01           LD     B,01        ;SET UP FOR
1630  ED43  23              INC    HL          ;DECIMAL
1640  ED44  3E 15           LD     A,15        ;CONVERSION &
1650  ED46  CF              RST    8           ;EXECUTE
1660  ED47  3A 4F F0  TRANSFER  LD  A,(F04F)   ;GET OFFSET
                                               ;FM F04F
1670  ED4A  3C              INC    A           ;ADD 2
1680  ED4B  3C              INC    A
1690  ED4C  ED 4B 4D F0     LD     BC,(F04D)   ;LD BASE
                                               ;ADDRESS
1700  ED50  32 4F F0        LD     (F04F),A    ;STORE NEW
                                               ;OFFSET
1710  ED53  81              ADD    A,C         ;ADD BASE +
1720  ED54  4F              LD     C,A         ;OFFSET &
1730  ED55  C5              PUSH   BC          ;PUT IN HL
1740  ED56  E1              POP    HL
1750  ED57  73              LD     (HL),E      ;XFER VAL FM
1760  ED58  23              INC    HL          ;DE TO LOC
1770  ED59  72              LD     (HL),D
1780  ED5A  3A 4A F0        LD     A,(F04A)    ;UPDATE DATA
1790  ED5D  3C              INC    A           ;COUNTER
1800  ED5E  32 4A F0        LD     (F04A),A
1810  ED61  F5              PUSH   AF          ;SAVE DTA CT
1820  ED62  3A 4B F0        LD     A,(F04B)    ;PUT ITEMS
1830  ED65  47              LD     B,A         ;TO LD IN B
1840  ED66  F1              POP    AF          ;RESTORE DTA
                                               ;COUNT
1850  ED67  DD E5           PUSH   IX          ;GET PTR BACK
1860  ED69  E1              POP    HL          ;TO HL
1870  ED6A  B8              CP     B           ;CMPARE DATA
1880  ED6B  23              INC    HL          ;GTO NXT LOC
1890  ED6C  C2 B3 EC        JP     NZ,ECB3     ;RPT IF MORE
                                               ;DATA NEEDED
```

Fig. 11-7. Assembly language source listing (continued from page 232).

234

```
1900  ED6F  21 00 F0        LD    HL,INP BUF    ;PT TO BUF
1910  ED72  ED 4B 30 F0     LD    BC,(F030)     ;LD MAX CT
1920  ED76  3E 2F           LD    A,"/"         ;LD SRCH
                                                ;CHAR
1930  ED78  CD 70 EF        CALL  SRCH & COUNT
1940  ED7B  3A 30 F0        LD    A,(F030)      ;LD MAX CT
1950  ED7E  BD              CP    L             ;CMPARE
1960  ED7F  28 09           JR    Z,ED8A        ;IF MAX CT
                                                ;SKIP XFER
1970  ED81  ED 5A           ADC   HL,DE         ;GET START
                                                ;OF DATA
1980  ED83  11 88 F0        LD    DE,F088       ;PT TO DEST
1990  ED86  ED B0           LDIR                ;MOVE IT
2000  ED88  18 05           JR    ED8F          ;SKIP CR
2010  ED8A  21 88 F0        LD    HL,F088       ;PUT CR
2020  ED8D  36 0D           LD    (HL),0D       ;IN F088
2030  ED8F  21 00 F0        LD    HL,INP BUF    ;PT TO BUFF
2040  ED92  3E 20           LD    A,SPACE
2050  ED94  CD 70 EF        CALL  SRCH & COUNT
2060  ED97  45              LD    B,L           ;PUT CT IN
2070  ED98  05              DEC   B             ;B
2080  ED99  21 C0 F2        LD    HL,F2C0       ;PT TO TBL
2090  ED9C  CD 7B EF        CALL  STSCAN
2100  ED9F  20 06           JR    NZ,LOOKUP     ;GO IF NOT
                                                ;IN TABLE
2110  EDA1  EB              EX    DE,HL         ;PUT BFR PTR
                                                ;IN HL
2120  EDA2  CD 97 EF        CALL  RETCMD
2130  EDA5  18 0A           JR    WARM START
2140  EDA7  EB        LOOKUP EX   DE,HL         ;PUT PTR IN HL
2150  EDA8  46              LD    B,(HL)        ;GET CHAR
2160  EDA9  EB              EX    DE,HL         ;SAVE PTR
2170  EDAA  21 EA F2        LD    HL,F2EA       ;LOAD TBL
2180  EDAD  3E 1C           LD    A,1C          ;EXECUTE
2190  EDAF  CF              RST   8             ;LOOKUP
2200  EDB0  E9              JP    (HL)          ;GTO ADDR
2210  EDB1  01 80 F0   WARM START  LD  BC,F080 ;ZEROMODULE
2220  EDB4  21 8F F0        LD    HL,F08F       ;DATA BFFR
2230  EDB7  CD F2 EF        CALL  ZERO
2240  EDBA  31 FA F0        LD    SP,F0FA       ;RESET STACK
2250  EDBD  21 9E F3        LD    HL,PROMPT     ;PRINT CMD
2260  EDC0  06 03           LD    B,03          ;PROMPT
2270  EDC2  C3 34 EC        JP    EC34
2280  EDC5  21 00 F0        LD    HL,INP BUF
2290  EDC8  3E 20           LD    A,20          ;LD CHAR
2300  EDCA  CD 70 EF        CALL  SRCH & COUNT
2310  EDCD  45              LD    B,L           ;PUT CT
                                                ;IN B
2320  EDCE  EB              EX    DE,HL         ;PTR TO HL
2330  EDCF  CD 97 EF        CALL  RETCMD
2340  EDD2  C3 B1 ED        JP    WARM START
2350  EDD5  06 0E           LD    B,0E
2360  EDD7  3E 08           LD    A,08
2370  EDD9  CF              RST   8
2380  EDDA  CD FD EE        CALL  REVERSE       ;CHECK FOR
                                                ;REVERSED
                                                ;PARAMETERS
2390  EDDD  2A 82 F0        LD    HL,(F082)     ;LOAD
2400  EDE0  ED 5B 80 F0     LD    DE,(F080)     ;PARAMETERS
2410  EDE4  ED 52           SBC   HL,DE         ;GET DIFF
2420  EDE6  01 0A 01        LD    BC,010A       ;DIVIDE
2430  EDE9  3E 17           LD    A,17          ;BY 10
```

235

2440	EDEB	CF		RST	8	
2450	EDEC	23		INC	HL	;ADD 2 TO
2460	EDED	23		INC	HL	;ADJ FOR SUB
2470	EDEE	E5		PUSH	HL	
2480	EDEF	EB		EX	DE,HL	;GET BEG NBR
2490	EDF0	0E 0A		LD	C,0A	;DIVIDE
2500	EDF2	3E 17		LD	A,17	;BY 10
2510	EDF4	CF		RST	8	
2520	EDF5	11 09 00		LD	DE,0009	;SUBTRACT
2530	EDF8	ED 52		SBC	HL,DE	;NINE
2540	EDFA	EB		EX	DE,HL	;SAVE IN DE
2550	EDFB	2A 84 F0		LD	HL,(F084)	;GET START
2560	EDFE	2B		DEC	HL	;MINUS 1
2570	EDFF	01 FF B7		LD	BC,B7FF	;LIMIT SRC
2580	EE02	3E 0D		LD	A,0D	;GET SRCH
						;CHAR
2590	EE04	ED B1		CPIR		;SEARCH
2600	EE06	1B		DEC	DE	;SUB 1 FM
2610	EE07	3E 00		LD	A,00	;DE & EXIT
2620	EE09	BB		CP	E	;WHEN DE
2630	EE0A	20 03		JR	NZ,EE0F	;EQUALS
2640	EE0C	BA		CP	D	;ZERO
2650	EE0D	28 03		JR	Z,EE12	
2660	EE0F	23		INC	HL	;GTO NXT
2670	EE10	18 F0		JR	EE02	;LOC & RPT
2680	EE12	D1		POP	DE	;RESTORE
						;COUNT
2690	EE13	43		LD	B,E	;PUT IN B
2700	EE14	D5		PUSH	DE	;SAVE
2710	EE15	C5		PUSH	BC	;DATA
2720	EE16	CD 2A EF		CALL	PRINT LINE	
2730	EE19	ED 5A		ADC	HL,DE	;GTO END
						;OF LINE
2740	EE1B	79		LD	A,C	
2750	EE1C	F5		PUSH	AF	;SAVE FLG
2760	EE1D	01 00 20		LD	BC,2000	;EXECUTE
2770	EE20	3E 06		LD	A,06	;DELAY
2780	EE22	CF		RST	8	
2790	EE23	06 02		LD	B,02	
2800	EE25	CD D0 EF		CALL	HOLDKY	
2810	EE28	F1		POP	AF	;RESTORE
2820	EE29	C1		POP	BC	;DATA
2830	EE2A	10 E9		DJNZ	EE15	;RPT UNTIL
						;B=0
2840	EE2C	D1		POP	DE	;GET TOTAL
2850	EE2D	3E 00		LD	A,00	;EXIT IF
2860	EE2F	BA		CP	D	;D = 0
2870	EE30	28 04		JR	Z,EE36	
2880	EE32	15		DEC	D	;CT -1
2890	EE33	D5		PUSH	DE	;SAVE
2900	EE34	18 DF		JR	EE15	;REPEAT
2910	EE36	01 00 0F		LD	BC,0F00	
2920	EE39	3E 08		LD	A,08	
2930	EE3B	CF		RST	8	
2940	EE3C	C3 B1 ED		JP	EDB1	
2950	EE3F	3E 0D		LD	A,0D	
2960	EE41	BE		CP	(HL)	
2970	EE42	28 08		JR	Z,EE4C	
2980	EE44	3E 2C		LD	A,2C	
2990	EE46	BE		CP	(HL)	
3000	EE47	28 08		JR	Z,EE51	
3010	EE49	23		INC	HL	
3020	EE4A	18 F3		JR	EE3F	
3030	EE4C	3E 01		LD	A,01	

Fig. 11-7. Assembly-language source listing (continued from page 235).

3040	EE4E	32 4C F0	LD	(F04C),A
3050	EE51	C9	RET	
3570	EE85	CD FD EE	CALL	REVERSE
3580	EE88	CD 17 EF	CALL	ABORT
3590	EE8B	ED 4B 80 F0	LD	BC,(F080) ;LOAD
3600	EE8F	ED 5B 84 F0	LD	DE,(F084) ;PARAMETERS
3610	EE93	2A 82 F0	LD	HL,(F082)
3620	EE96	CD D8 EF	CALL	MOVE
3630	EE99	C3 B1 ED	JP	WARM START
3640	EE9C	CD FD EE	CALL	REVERSE
3650	EE9F	ED 4B 80 F0	LD	BC,(F080) ;LOAD
3660	EEA3	2A 82 F0	LD	HL,(F082) ;PARAMETERS
3670	EEA6	CD F2 EF	CALL	ZERO
3680	EEA9	C3 B1 ED	JP	WARM START
3720	EEAF	21 00 F0	LD	HL,F000 ;PT TO BFR
3730	EEB2	3E 0D	LD	A,0D
3740	EEB4	CD 70 EF	CALL	SRCH & COUNT
3750	EEB7	45	LD	B,L ;CT TO B
3760	EEB8	EB	EX	DE,HL ;PTR TO HL
3770	EEB9	CD 97 EF	CALL	RETCMD
3780	EEBC	C3 B1 ED	JP	WARM START
4130	EEE1	06 0F	LD	B,0F ;TURN OFF
4140	EEE3	3E 08	LD	A,08 ;DUAL
4150	EEE5	CF	RST	8
4160	EEE6	21 00 00	LD	HL,0000 ;REPLACE
4170	EEE9	3E 03	LD	A,03 ;ORIGINAL
4180	EEEB	CF	RST	8 ;BREAK ADDR
4190	EEEC	21 02 00	LD	HL,0002
4200	EEEF	3E 03	LD	A,03
4210	EEF1	CF	RST	8
4220	EEF2	3E 24	LD	A,24 ;JP2DOS
4230	EEF4	CF	RST	8
4240	EEF5	06 0F	LD	B,0F ;TURN OFF
4250	EEF7	3E 08	LD	A,08 ;DUAL
4260	EEF9	CF	RST	8
4270	EEFA	C3 BA ED	JP	EDBA
4280	EEFD	2A 80 F0	LD	HL,(F080) ;LOAD
4290	EF00	ED 5B 82 F0	LD	DE,(F082) ;DATA
4300	EF04	E5	PUSH	HL
4310	EF05	ED 52	SBC	HL,DE ;GET DIFF
4320	EF07	38 05	JR	C,EF0E ;GO IF CY
4330	EF09	D5	PUSH	DE ;REVERSE
4340	EF0A	E1	POP	HL ;ORDER OF
4350	EF0B	D1	POP	DE ;OPERANDS
4360	EF0C	18 01	JR	EF0F ;SKIP RSTOR
4370	EF0E	E1	POP	HL ;RESTORE
4380	EF0F	22 80 F0	LD	(F080),HL ;STORE
4390	EF12	ED 53 82 F0	LD	(F082),DE ;DATA
4400	EF16	C9	RET	
4410	EF17	ED 4B 84 F0	LD	BC,(F084) ;LD DATA
4420	EF1B	3E 00	LD	A,00 ;IF THERE
4430	EF1D	B9	CP	C ;RETURN
4440	EF1E	20 09	JR	NZ,EF29
4450	EF20	B8	CP	B
4460	EF21	20 06	JR	NZ,EF29
4470	EF23	CD 40 EF	CALL	ERRMSG
4480	EF26	C3 B1 ED	JP	WARM START
4490	EF29	C9	RET	
4500	EF2A	3E 0D	LD	A,0D ;LD SRCH CHAR
4510	EF2C	CD 70 EF	CALL	SRCH & COUNT
4520	EF2F	45	LD	B,L ;PUT CT -1
4530	EF30	05	DEC	B ;IN B
4540	EF31	0E 0D	LD	C,0D ;ADD EOL CHAR

```
4550  EF33  EB         EX    DE,HL       ;PTR TO HL
4560  EF34  CD C1 EF   CALL  VDLINE
4570  EF37  F5         PUSH  AF          ;SAVE FLG
4580  EF38  C4 40 EF   CALL  NZ,ERRMSG
4590  EF3B  F1         POP   AF          ;RSTORE FLG
4600  EF3C  C2 B1 ED   JP    NZ,WARM START
4610  EF3F  C9         RET
4620  EF40  21 1B F3   LD    HL,F31B     ;PT TO BUF
4630  EF43  46         LD    B,(HL)      ;GET # CHAR
                                         ;TO PRINT
4640  EF44  0E 0D      LD    C,0D        ;EOL CHAR
4650  EF46  23         INC   HL          ;PT TO MSG
4660  EF47  CD C1 EF   CALL  VDLINE
4670  EF4A  C9         RET
4680  EF4B  3E 15      LD    A,15
4690  EF4D  CF         RST   8
4700  EF4E  C9         RET
4910  EF70  11 00 00   LD    DE,0000
4920  EF73  E5         PUSH  HL
4930  EF74  D1         POP   DE
4940  EF75  ED B1      CPIR
4950  EF77  AF         XOR   A
4960  EF78  ED 52      SBC   HL,DE
4970  EF7A  C9         RET
4980  EF7B  3E 31      LD    A,31
4990  EF7D  CF         RST   8           (STSCAN)
5000  EF7E  C9         RET
5010  EF7F  3E 34      LD    A,34
5020  EF81  CF         RST   8           (DOS ERRMSG)
5030  EF82  C9         RET
5040  EF83  3E 27      LD    A,27
5050  EF85  CF         RST   8           (DOS ERROR)
5060  EF86  C9         RET
5070  EF87  3E 2B      LD    A,2B
5080  EF89  CF         RST   8           (WRITENX)
5090  EF8A  C9         RET
5100  EF8B  3E 22      LD    A,22
5110  EF8D  CF         RST   8           (READNX)
5120  EF8E  C9         RET
5130  EF8F  3E 2A      LD    A,2A
5140  EF91  CF         RST   8           (CLOSE)
5150  EF92  C9         RET
5160  EF93  3E 28      LD    A,28
5170  EF95  CF         RST   8           (OPEN)
5180  EF96  C9         RET
5190  EF97  3E 26      LD    A,26
5200  EF99  CF         RST   8           (RETCMD)
5210  EF9A  C9         RET
5220  EF9B  E5         PUSH  HL          ;SAVE ALL
5230  EF9C  C5         PUSH  BC          ;REGISTERS
5240  EF9D  D5         PUSH  DE
5250  EF9E  F5         PUSH  AF
5260  EF9F  21 A2 F3   LD    HL,F3A2     ;PT TO BFR
5270  EFA2  46         LD    B,(HL)      ;GET # CHAR
5280  EFA3  23         INC   HL          ;PT TO MSG
5290  EFA4  0E 0D      LD    C,0D        ;EOL CHAR
5300  EFA6  CD C1 EF   CALL  VDLINE
5310  EFA9  F1         POP   AF          ;RESTORE
5320  EFAA  D1         POP   DE          ;ALL REGS
5330  EFAB  C1         POP   BC
5340  EFAC  E1         POP   HL
5350  EFAD  C9         RET
```

Fig. 11-7. Assembly-language source listing (continued from page 237).

```
5360   EFAE   E5            PUSH   HL
5370   EFAF   C5            PUSH   BC
5380   EFB0   D5            PUSH   DE
5390   EFB1   F5            PUSH   AF
5400   EFB2   21 C7 F3      LD     HL,F3C7
5410   EFB5   46            LD     B,(HL)
5420   EFB6   23            INC    HL

5430   EFB7   0E 20         LD     C,20
5440   EFB9   CD C1 EF      CALL   VDLINE
5450   EFBC   F1            POP    AF
5460   EFBD   D1            POP    DE
5470   EFBE   C1            POP    BC
5480   EFBF   E1            POP    HL
5490   EFC0   C9            RET

5500   EFC1   3E 09         LD     A,09
5510   EFC3   CF            RST    8            (VDLINE)
5520   EFC4   C9            RET

5530   EFC5   01 01 01      LD     BC,0101
5540   EFC8   3E 07         LD     A,07
5550   EFCA   CF            RST    8            (VIDINIT)
5560   EFCB   C9            RET

5570   EFCC   3E 0C         LD     A,0C
5580   EFCE   CF            RST    8            (VIDKEY)
5590   EFCF   C9            RET

5600   EFD0   3E 1D         LD     A,1D
5610   EFD2   CF            RST    8            (HOLDKY)
5620   EFD3   C9            RET

5630   EFD4   3E 1C         LD     A,1C
5640   EFD6   CF            RST    8            (LOOKUP)
5650   EFD7   C9            RET

5660   EFD8   C5            PUSH   BC           ;SAVE BEG ADDR
5670   EFD9   ED 42         SBC    HL,BC        ;CMPUTE DIFF
5680   EFDB   E5            PUSH   HL           ;DIFF TO BC
5690   EFDC   C1            POP    BC
5700   EFDD   E1            POP    HL           ;BEG ADR TO HL
5710   EFDE   E5            PUSH   HL           ;SAVE ADDR
5720   EFDF   B7            OR     A            ;CLR CARRY
5730   EFE0   ED 52         SBC    HL,DE        ;IS THERE
                                                ;OVERLAP
5740   EFE2   E1            POP    HL           ;RESTORE ADDR
5750   EFE3   38 05         JR     C,EFEA       ;GO IF YES
5760   EFE5   03            INC    BC           ;ADJ COUNT
5770   EFE6   ED B0         LDIR                ;MOVE IT
5780   EFE8   18 07         JR     EFF1         ;RETURN
5790   EFEA   09            ADD    HL,BC        ;GTO END OF BLK
5800   EFEB   EB            EX     DE,HL        ;& END OF
5810   EFEC   09            ADD    HL,BC        ;DESTINATION
5820   EFED   EB            EX     DE,HL        ;BLOCK
5830   EFEE   03            INC    BC           ;ADJ COUNT
5840   EFEF   ED B8         LDDR                ;MOVE IT
5850   EFF1   C9            RET

5860   EFF2   C5            PUSH   BC           ;SAVE BEG ADDR
5870   EFF3   ED 42         SBC    HL,BC        ;GET COUNT
5880   EFF5   E5            PUSH   HL           ;MOVE CT TO BC
5890   EFF6   C1            POP    BC
5900   EFF7   E1            POP    HL           ;BEG ADDR TO HL
5910   EFF8   E5            PUSH   HL           ;ALSO TO DE
5920   EFF9   D1            POP    DE
5930   EFFA   13            INC    DE           ;DE = HL + 1
5940   EFFB   36 00         LD     (HL),00      ;LD CHAR
5950   EFFD   ED B0         LDIR                ;MOVE IT
5960   EFFF   C9            RET
```

Lines 1100 through 1130 check the status of the carriage return flag in the just completed subroutine. If set, we go to an error message and abort the input.

Lines 1140 through 1190 check the length of the data item we have just delimited. If it is more than four characters long, we have bad data and the routine is aborted.

Lines 1200 through 1230 check to see if only two data items are required for operation. If this is so, then the module requires conversion from hexadecimal to binary, and we go directly to the hex conversion routine. As the program is now configured, the only decimal conversion routines are HARDCOPY and PRINT. These both require three items for proper functioning.

If two items are not present, the routine, lines 1240 through 1280 then check specifically for H (hardcopy) or P (print) and go to decimal conversion if either is present.

Lines 1290 through 1410 present one of two alternate routes through the program. They set up the proper register values and convert an ASCII-coded hexadecimal input to binary.

The alternate decimal-to-binary conversion routine is found in lines 1420 through 1650. Both the HEX and this routine go to TRANSFER on completion of processing.

The transfer section, lines 1660 through 1890, moves the converted data from the temporary locations starting at F040 to the permanent locations beginning with F080. This is done using a type of indexing to move the address pointers each time another datum is to be loaded.

Lines 1900 through 2020 check the command string for the presence of optional switches, which may be designed into any of the function modules. If present, they are transferred to their designated locations; if not, a carriage return is placed there instead to signify that none were present.

Lines 2030 through 2130 identify the type of command input and route the program to the proper processing routine.

Lines 2140 through 2200 process function module commands and transfer control to the proper program address.

Lines 2210 through 2270 begin the restart of the program. It is labeled WARM START because this is where we reenter the program on completion of any function module or DOS command. It is also where we reenter from DEBUG if we do not wish to destroy our programs or data in user memory.

Lines 2280 through 2340 is the module that processes functions using overlay programs from the disk. Its purpose is to set up registers for the RETCMD SVC in order to load and execute the program desired.

The following sections are the function routines and the various utility routines used by the program. The first of these is the HARDCOPY/PRINT routine, which outputs a buffer of information either to the video display or a printer of some sort. This routine saves memory and programming time by making use of a feature of the TRSDOS 2.0 operating system called DUAL. This feature, when activated, outputs to a printer whatever is being sent to the video display by the program.

Lines 2350 through 2370 activate DUAL to provide a HARDCOPY function. Lines 2380 through 2540 begin the PRINT function processing.

The portion of PRINT in lines 2550 through 2670 starts at the designated buffer address and counts carriage returns until it has counted the number contained in the DE register which was computed above. This is the beginning of the first line to be printed. The portion in lines 2680 through 2900 prints the line on the screen. It also provides bookkeeping functions for the program in determining how many lines are yet to be printed, a delay function to slow down the printing rate slightly, and polling of the holdkey interrupt routine to permit halting of the display at any time.

Lines 2910 through 2940 end the routine by turning off the DUAL function and returning control to WARM START.

The portion of the code in lines 2950 through 3050 is the SEARCH DELIMITER subroutine called in the parsing routine earlier. This routine searches for a carriage return or either an equal sign or a comma, depending on the contents of memory location EE45. A flag is set at F04C by this routine. A 1 is loaded for a carriage return and a 0 for either of the other two.

Lines 3570 through 3630 are the MOVE function module. The two subroutines at the beginning check for error conditions.

Lines 3640 through 3680 are the ZERO function, which is similar to MOVE in structure. Lines 3720 through 3780 are the RETCMD module used to process all DOS commands. It searches for a carriage return, which is the end of the command string. The entire string is then transferred to the operating system where the command is executed.

Lines 4130 through 4230 process the QUIT command, which returns us to the operating system.

The BREAK processing routine is given in lines 4240 through 4270. It turns off DUAL routing, then goes to WARM START without destroying data in the parameter storage locations.

The subroutine in lines 4280 through 4400 reverses data in the first two storage locations if in the wrong order. The first should be less than the second.

The subroutine in lines 4410 through 4490 prints an error message and aborts processing if no data is present in the third data location.

The subroutine in lines 4500 through 4610 prints one line of data on the screen. It also traps any attempt to print non-ASCII characters in the string being printed. If such an attempt is made, the routine aborts the print, prints an error message, and returns to the command prompt.

The subroutine in lines 4620 through 4070 prints the ILLEGAL PARAMETERS error message used in the previous subroutine and elsewhere in the program.

Lines 4680 through 4700 is the BIN/DEC SVC subroutine.

The subroutine in lines 4910 through 4970 is SEARCH & COUNT, referenced throughout the program. It searches for a designated character in a string and then computes the number of characters searched in order to find the character. The beginning of the string is shifted to DE during execution and the number of characters is placed in HL.

SVC routines coded as subroutines are given in lines 4980 through 5210. In the listing, each is identified as a comment.

The subroutine in lines 5220 through 5350 prints the PRO-CESSING COMPLETE message on the screen. All registers are unaffected by the routine.

The subroutine in lines 5360 through 5490 prints the BUFFER FULL message on the screen. All registers are unaffected by the routine. Comments are the same as in the previous subroutine.

Lines 5500 through 5650, five subroutines, are SVC calls as designated as comments in the listing.

Lines 5660 through 5850 is the MOVE subroutine for the MOVE function module. It computes the number of characters to move and can move them either forward or back including overlapping blocks without destroying data. On entry, the beginning address of the block to be moved is in BC; the ending address is in HL; and the destination address is in the DE register.

The final subroutine, lines 5860 through 5960, is the ZERO MEMORY subroutine used throughout the program. The beginning address of the block to be zeroed is in BC and the end address is in HL as the routine begins.

TESTING AND DEBUGGING

These topics have been covered in Chapter 6 and so need not be rediscussed here. The same things mentioned there apply to any assembly-language program. The main point to be made is that segments being tested should be kept small. When they are thoroughly reliable, they can be incorporated into larger segments. Any new code tested will never be such a large chunk that debugging becomes difficult. If the amount of new code in a segment is kept to a minimum, both testing and debugging are made easier. The errors, where they occur, are easier to detect and, in consequence, take less time to correct. As an additional benefit you will not be discouraged when they are encountered.

DOCUMENTATION AND REDESIGN

This portion of the design process is especially important in assembly-language programming. Rather than discussing what to include, I shall merely provide documentation for the program. It will be easier to see how the program fits together, and what provisions for change and expansion have been designed into it.

Program Description

This program is designed as an executive program to input commands, parse them into appropriate data forms and call subprograms to execute the various functions available. Commands are entered as a command string along with required data which is separated by various delimiting characters. Function modules presently available are *zero* a block of memory, *move* a block of memory in any direction (including overlapping blocks); *exit* to the operating system; output previously created files to either the video display or line printer; and execute any of the following operating system commands: CLS, DATE, DEBUG (if debug is active), DIR, DUMP, FORMS, FREE, KILL, LIB, LIST, LOAD, and TIME.

This is achieved in the following manner. The program, after initialization of necessary locations, prints a prompt on the screen asking for command input. Only active commands will cause obvious program execution. Nonvalid commands are either ignored and the program returns to the prompt, or an error message ILLEGAL COMMAND appears, followed by a return to the prompt. This also happens if a command is entered incorrectly, such as a misspelled word or incorrect punctuation.

The only error tolerated by the program is reversal of starting and ending addresses or line numbers. In this case the program puts the lesser of the two in the first location and the larger in the second, no matter what their original position as one of the first two inputs. If data is omitted or other types of errors occur, the program will display one of two error messages: ILLEGAL PARAMETERS or ILLEGAL COMMAND.

Once the command has been input in the proper form, the program separates the command string into its component parts, converts them to the proper format, transfers them to the module execution locations, and recognizes and executes the proper command. Each module looks for its data in the same locations. The first data item is always in locations F080 and F081, the second in F082 and F083 and so on. In this way any module desired can be incorporated just so long as its initial data are obtained from these locations.

Room has been left for a few short routines, or one or two medium-sized ones within the program area. If desired this area can be used for routines frequently used in your application. Longer modules or those less frequently used can be written as separate programs called and executed with operating system commands. Fairly long function programs can be included to overlay one another in the area immediately preceding the start of your executive program.

Memory allocations for the program appear below in generalized form. The program logic manual contains more detailed memory allocation data.

C6000-EBFF	Overlay module area
EC00-EFFF	Main program and short modules
F000-F028	Program input buffer
F030-F07F	Flags, variable storage and temporary processing
F080-F08F	Converted data input locations for all modules
F090-F0FA	Stack
F2A8-F31A	Lookup tables and command jump table
F31B-F3FF	ASCII message area

244

Program Logic Manual

This manual gives a step-by-step explanation of all program instructions. It is designed to accompany Fig. 11-7, the commented source listing of the program.

Initialization

Line 100 initializes the stack to its designated program location. Lines 110, 120, and 130 remove the current *break key* processing address and place it in the HL register via the SETBRK SVC. Line 140 places the original break address in location EEED. This provides replacement of this address whenever the program is exited to the operating system. Line 150 places the new break key processing address in HL prior to execution of the SETBRK SVC again in lines 160 and 170.

The next step is to activate the HOLD KEY processor. This is done in lines 180 and 190. Subroutine EFD0 executes the HOLDKY SVC. Following this, clear user memory with your ZERO subroutine. Lines 200 and 210 load the beginning and ending addresses of the block to be cleared. Line 220 calls the zero subroutine itself.

Now initialize the input and output functions. Line 230 calls the video initialization subroutine. This routine sets the video output parameters (character size and line width) and clears any output previously stored in video memory. This is done by use of the VIDINIT (video initialization) SVC. Then call the KBINIT SVC to clear any previously stored characters in keyboard memory.

The final act before printing the prompt is to clear the scratch-pad buffer before starting input. This is done in lines 260, 270, and 280. Again, use the ZERO memory subroutine. Lines 260 and 270 load the starting and ending addresses of the block to be cleared.

Command Input

Now let's set up for input of the user commands. Line 290 points to the beginning of the ASCII message. 300 loads the number of characters to be printed which is included as the first byte of the ASCII message. 310 points to the beginning of the actual text. Line 320 indicates the maximum number of characters the routine will accept as input, 330 points to the start of the input buffer where the command will initially be stored, and 340 calls the VIDKEY SVC which prints the prompt and accepts the input. At this point the program waits until input has been completed. Completion is indicated whenever either the maximum number of characters designated has been input or when a carriage return is entered.

Command Processing

Initialize Processing Buffers. Once a command has been input prepare for parsing the command string. The first of these is to zero a number of memory locations used within the parsing portion of the program. Lines 350 and 360 zero location F030 used later to store the total number of characters input in the command. Then zero F046 thru F04F using the zero subroutine in lines 370, 380, and 390. Lines 400 and 410 put the beginning address of the module data storage area into locations F04D and F04E for use later in the program. In a similar manner the next two lines (420 and 430) put the beginning address of the parameter designators into F048 and F049.

Identify Command. Now begin the actual processing. Count the number of characters actually input and store this figure in F030. This is done in lines 440 through 480. Line 440 points to the start of the input buffer; 450 loads the maximum number of characters to search; 460 loads the terminating character; and 470 calls the search subroutine. Upon return from the subroutine, the beginning address is in DE and the number of characters counted is in HL. Line 480 puts this value in F030. Then put the starting address back in HL with line 490, load the first character of the command into the B register and compare it with a carriage return via lines 500, 510, and 520.

If the test is true, that is if a carriage return is the first character, then no command has been entered and the program goes back to the command prompt in line 530. If it is not true and a command is present, the program continues.

The program again loads the start of the command string into HL, but this time it also puts the first character in the A register. This is done in lines 540 and 550. Then store that character in location F046 before comparing it with a number of possible ASCII command characters. It is compared with B in line 570, with Q in 590, with A in 610, and with Z in line 630. Each of these is followed by an address to which the program goes if the characters are the same. If B is entered, the program returns to the command prompt via line 530 since there is no B command active at this time. If a module were written and designated as B it could be included by changing the jump address in this line to the starting address of the new module.

If Q(uit) is entered, go immediately to the beginning of the exit routine via line 600. If A or Z is the first character, then the value 2 is placed in location F04B by 650 and 660. This indicates to the program that two values must be present in the command string and must be transferred to the module storage locations for valid input and processing.

Following this, and starting at line 670, use the STSCAN SVC to compare the input character with a number of command characters. Line 670 designates how many characters are to be compared; 680 puts the start of the command string in DE where it must be at the start of the SVC routine; 690 points to the string to be compared; and 700 calls the SVC itself. If a match is found the zero flag is set on exit. Test for this in line 710, skipping to line 740 if no match is found. If the input was one of the characters in the string a 3 is entered in F04B with lines 720 and 730. Lines 740 through 790 do the same thing with V and X, putting 4 in F04B if true.

Lines 800 through 830 use the STSCAN SVC again to test for operating system commands. If the command is an operating system command, control transfers to EEAF. This is the beginning of the RETCMD SVC routine, which executes these commands.

Parse Data String. Line 840 begins the actual parsing of the command data. Begin by setting up the subroutine as described on page 239 to search for either a carriage return or an equal sign. 840 places the address of the command string back in HL. 850 and 860 place the equal sign in the subroutine. Line 870 calls the subroutine. On return put the address of the last data identifier into DE. Since the subroutine finds the equal sign, which is the character immediately following the data identifier, go to the identifier itself by decreasing the value of the pointer by one in line 890. 900 increases DE by one to point to the current identifier. This character is then put in the A register and also in F048 for use during the next repetition of the loop. This is done with lines 910 and 920. Then check HL with A in line 930. If the character is correct continue with line 970. If not, lines 950 and 960 give an ILLEGAL PARAMETERS message and returns to the command prompt.

At this point the number of characters to the equal sign is in HL. Add one to the count in 970, get the total length of the string in 980, compute the difference in 990, and transfer this value to BC in lines 1000 and 1010. Then save the count in HL and the data identifier pointer in DE in lines 1020 and 1030.

The next step is to find comma in the string, which is the terminator for this value. Use your subroutine at EE3F again. The comma is put in place via lines 1040 and 1050. Lines 1060 and 1070 reinitialize the carriage return flag before calling the subroutine. The routine itself is called in 1080. Lines 1090 and 1100 test for a carriage return found during the search. If so, go to the illegal parameter error message again in line 1130. Lines 1110 and 1120 restore the data previously saved in the stack.

Now let's compute the number of characters between the equal sign and the comma. This is done by placing a comma (the search character) in A and calling subroutine EF70 in line 1150. This subroutine searches until it finds the search character, or until the search runs out, and then computes the number of characters searched. The elapsed character count is returned in HL. This count must be reduced by one to get the actual number inbetween the two. This is done in line 1160. Then put the count in A with line 1170 and see if there are 4 characters. Test in 1190. If the count is less than 4 there is an illegal input and the error message illegal parameters is displayed.

Hexadecimal or Decimal Conversion. Lines 1200 through 1280 provide routing for conversion of either hexadecimal or decimal input to binary. 1200, 1210, and 1220 provide a comparison for the number of parameters entered. If only two are needed, the values must be in hexadecimal since the only decimal input routines have three data items to be entered. Then go to 1290. If not, check to see if you are parsing data for either the print or hardcopy routines in lines 1240, 1250, and 1270. If either of these are active, the routine goes to line 1420 and begins the decimal conversion routine. The two conversion routines begin at lines 1290 and 1420.

Hexadecimal Conversion. Hexadecimal conversion begins by putting the data pointer back in HL. Go to the first data character in line 1300. The data is then transferred to the temporary processing location beginning at F040. Lines 1310 and 1320 initialize this transfer by placing the number of characters to be transferred in BC and the beginning of the temporary buffer in DE. Lines 1330, 1340, and 1350 save the initial addresses of the buffer and temporary storage location for later use. Then make the transfer in line 1360. Lines 1370, 1380, 1390, and 1400 set up and call the SVC. 1370 retrieves the beginning address of the temporary buffer, 1380 and 1390 set up the switch in B for conversion to binary and place the SVC code in A. Line 1400 is the call itself. Line 1410 then jumps past the decimal conversion routine to line 1660.

Decimal Conversion. Decimal conversion, beginning at line 1420, is slightly different. The SVC assumes a five-byte area to convert; therefore, if the decimal input is less than five bytes, add leading zeros to complete the filling of the conversion buffer. Line 1420 puts you at the first data character, which is then transferred to

248

BC and saved. This is done in the next three lines, 1430, 1440, and 1450. Clear A and the carry in line 1460 to prepare for the next instruction. Line 1470 adds the number of characters to the start address to compute the location of the last character. This is necessary since this routine loads the data into the temporary buffer starting with the last character. The start address remains intact here since it is in DE and the result of the add is placed in HL. This address is saved in IX for later use by lines 1480 and 1490. The end address of the temporary buffer is then loaded into DE as the destination pointer in line 1500 and the data is transferred in line 1510 by the LDDR instruction.

Once the data is transferred, the next task is to pad the beginning of the conversion buffer with enough zeros to make the data five characters in length. Begin by computing how many zeros are necessary. Line 1520 begins this process by restoring the number of characters loaded back into BC. Put your maximum number of characters in A with line 1530, subtract the two in 1540, and put the difference in B with 1550 in preparation for an automatic loop to load the zeros. Line 1560 puts the current destination address back in HL. In 1570 compare the difference (in A) between the number left and zero. When the count reaches zero, activate the conversion controlled by line 1580. Line 1590 puts an ASCII 0 in the current buffer location, and line 1600 points to the next previous location. Line 1610 controls the loop and terminates it when the value in B reaches 0. Finally lines 1620, 1630, 1640, and 1650 set up and activate the decimal to binary conversion routine.

Transfer to Permanent Location. Lines 1660 through 1740 compute the current locations to which the converted values are transferred. This is done in the following manner. In line 1660, get the latest offset used by this routine from F04F. It is put in A in line 1660 and increased by two in lines 1670 and 1680. The original pointer is loaded from F04D into BC in line 1690 and the new increment is stored in F04F. The increment and the original address are then added together with the result being transferred into BC. This is done in lines 1710, 1720, and 1730. The new transfer location is now put in HL via lines 1730 and 1740. 1750, 1760, and 1770 make the actual transfer of the two bytes of data.

Check for Completion. Lines 1780, 1790, and 1800 increment the data counter in F04A which keeps track of how many data items have been processed to date. Line 1810 saves the count in the stack, and lines 1820 and 1830 get the total count to B from F04B. Line 1840 then restores the current count to A. Then bring back the buffer pointer stored in IX in lines 1850 and 1860. Finally, compare the current count with the total number required in 1870, go to the next input buffer location in 1880, and test your comparison in 1890. If the values are not equal, then more data exists and the routine loops back to line 850 where the entire sequence repeats.

Transfer Option Switches. Now that the data has been converted and stored in the correct locations, make sure that all of the command has been processed. Do this by searching the entire command string again looking for a slash (/) character. Line 1900 reloads the start of the input buffer, and 1910 puts the number of characters to search in BC. This is obtained from F030 where the total length of the command string is stored. Line 1920 puts the slash in A for the comparison, and 1930 calls the search and count subroutine. Remember that the number of characters counted appears in HL on exit from the routine. In line 1940 put the total length of the string in A and compare it with the counted value in line 1950. If the two are equal then there are no more characters to transfer and your program goes to line 2010 where a terminating carriage return is placed in location F088 by 2010 and 2020.

If the two are not equal there is more data to transfer. In this case add the number of characters counted to the original starting address shifted to DE by the subroutine. Line 1970 does this. Then all remaining data including slashes is transferred to location F088 and following locations. Line 1980 loads the destination address and 1990 makes the transfer with the automated LDIR instruction. Line 2000 then skips the next two lines which are activated if no data is to be transferred.

Identify Command

The command format was set up so that the command name is followed by a space before inputting any additional data required by the routine in question. Begin this section by pointing to the beginning of the input buffer in line 2030. To isolate the command from the rest of the data, use the blank as your terminating character in the search routine. Line 2040 puts this blank in A for the search. Line 2050 calls the search and count routine. On return, the number of characters up to the blank is transferred to B by line 2060. Since this count includes the final blank, reduce the count by one in line 2070.

Now set up for use of the STSCAN SVC. The number of characters to compare is in B and the beginning of the compare string in DE due to the transfer during the search and count subroutine. Now point to the beginning of the area to be searched and call the SVC. Line 2080 takes care of the first part and line 2090 calls the SVC. Line 2100 makes the test to find out if the command is present, since the zero flag is set on exit if the command string is found.

If the command is present, then it is an operating system command and executes by placing the pointer for the beginning of the string in HL via line 2110 and calling the RETCMD SVC in line 2120. Finally, return to the command prompt from line 2130.

If the command is not present, go directly to line 2140. This sequence is slightly different since it uses the lookup table starting at F2EA for special commands representing your own written modules. Begin by placing the first character of the command in B with lines 2140 and 2150. Then put the pointer back in DE since the HL register must be used to point to the start of the lookup table. This happens in line 2160. Line 2170 loads the start of the lookup table into HL, and lines 2180 and 2190 execute the LOOKUP SVC itself. Assume here that since all other possibilities have been eliminated, the command must be one of those in the table. Due to this the starting address of your routine will appear in HL on exit from the SVC and can be called with the single instruction in line 2200.

This completes the main part of the processor. However, there are a few things to go over to fully understand the program operation.

Warm Start

Lines 2210 through 2270 are the portion of the program which reinitializes certain areas of memory and returns to the command prompt. Lines 2210, 2220, and 2230 rezero the permanent data buffer before going to the command prompt for new data. This is done again with the zero memory subroutine. Line 2240 resets the stack pointer to its original location, 2250 points to the restart prompt, 2260 loads the number of characters to be displayed and line 2270 takes you to line 320 where the remainder of the VIDKEY SVC is set up and called for input.

Lines 2280 through 2340 provide a function call routine for overlay modules called from the operating system. This address is included in the lookup table for any overlay function modules written. Begin in a similar manner to the other RETCMD modules. Line 2280 loads the start of the buffer, 2290 loads the search character, and 2300 calls the search and count subroutine. Line 2310 puts the number of characters in the command name into B, 2320 replaces the pointer in HL, and 2330 calls the RETCMD SVC. The command name entered is really the file name of the overlay module from the disk. Finally, in 2340, return to the command prompt via the restart or warm start address in line 2210.

Print and Hardcopy

The *print* and *hardcopy* routines are located from line 2350 to line 2940. They use the same code. The hardcopy routine outputs to the line printer as well as the video display. It does so by calling an SVC, which outputs to the printer, whatever goes to the video display. This SVC is called *dual* and is turned on in lines 2350, 2360, and 2370 if the HARDCOPY routine is called by the program. Processing of the data for both begins at line 2380. This is the starting address for the PRINT function module.

The subroutine called in line 2380 is an error correction subroutine. It checks the two values in the first and second function storage locations to make sure that the first is less than the second. This is the only check of this nature made in the program. It is necessary since the beginning number is in the first location and the ending number in the second. If the two numbers are not in this order, the subroutine reverses them in the storage locations.

Lines 2390 and 2400 then load the data for the module into DE and HL. 2410 computes the difference which remains in HL. Lines 2420, 2430, and 2440 set up and call an SVC which divides the difference by 10. This allows the number of lines to print and line numbers in the file are in increments of 10. 2420 sets up the parameters for the SVC. Placing a 1 in B sets the division and C contains the divisor in hexdecimal. 2430 loads the function code and 2440 calls the SVC.

The quotient appears in HL on exit and is then increased by 2 in lines 2460 and 2470.

The pointer for the first value in then moved back to HL in line 2480. 2490 through 2540 divides the beginning line number by 10 and then subtracts 9 in order to compute the value of the first line number you want to print. Lines 2490, 2500, and 2510 divide your value by 10; 2520 and 2530 subtract 9 from the quotient which is then switched to DE by line 2540.

The next segment finds the beginning of the storage buffer in memory. This occurs in lines 2550 through 2670. The segment begins by loading the starting address of the buffer designated in the command string. This value is put into HL and then reduced by one in order to start the search with a carriage return. 2550 loads the value. 2560 reduces it by one. Line 2570 puts the end of user memory into the BC register to terminate the search if nothing is found. Line 2580 loads the search character into the A register and 2590 conducts the search with the automated CPIR search.

The search stops when the first carriage return is found. You only want it to stop when a designated number of them has been reached. The remainder of the code in this segment make this possible. The segment of code from line 2600 through 2670 executes each time a carriage return is found by the search.

Terminate the loop here when the line count in DE, computed in the previous section, goes to zero. Line 2600 subtracts one from the line count each time a carriage return is found and the code is activated. To test the count, put 0 in the A register with line 2610 and then set up a 16 bit comparison with the value in DE. This requires a bit of logic since only eight bits can be compared at a time. Line 2620 compares the 0 with the value in E, the least significant byte. If E is not zero the search must continue. Line 2630 goes to 2660 which takes you to the next memory location to repeat the search by returning to line 2580 via line 2670.

If the value in E is zero, you may still have a nonzero value in D. Check for this with lines 2640 and 2650. If the value in both D and E is zero, then the test in line 2650 will be true; exit the segment and continue with the processing. If not, repeat as described above.

Now begin printing the lines. This requires some extra code to keep track of how many lines have been printed. There is also code to check on some of your interrupt functions. Begin by placing the total number of lines to be printed back in DE with line 2680. Use the DJNZ instruction to control the loop and transfer the value in E to B in line 2690. The DE register is used for other things before the end of the loop, so save this value in the stack with line 2700. Also save the value in B. This is done with 2710.

Line 2720 calls the subroutine which actually prints the line on the screen. This subroutine will be explained in detail later but it does contain error traps in addition to the actual printing commands. On exit from this subroutine start address of the line has just been printed in HL, and the number of characters printed including the ending carriage return in DE. These are added in line 2730 to produce the starting address of the next line.

Lines 2740 and 2750 put the value of C in A and save it in the stack while two other segments operate in the sequence. These are a delay SVC from lines 2760 through 2780 and the HOLD function

SVC in 2790 and 2800. Then the two registers (AF and BC) are restored to their state before these functions are called in lines 2810 and 2820. 2830 activates the automatic loop until B reaches zero.

This much of the code will print lines until B reaches zero, but this limits you to a maximum of 256 lines. To give us a reasonable number continue with the following code. The last time you go through the DJNZ instruction when B is zero, the register will decrement to FF (hex) even though the loop is not repeated. Because of this, start the loop over again for another 256 lines if you want to.

The total number of lines is in DE. Therefore, whenever B goes past zero reduce D by one and exit when D goes to zero. This is the purpose of the code from line 2840 through 2900. 2840 restores the current value of DE. The comparison value of zero is placed in A with line 2850 and the comparison is made in 2860. If D is zero you are finished, and line 2870 goes to line 2910 for the final exit coding. If not, then D is reduced by one in 2880 and saved for the next check in 2890. Then go back to the beginning of the original loop in line 2710 and repeat the entire sequence.

There is one more thing to do before returning to the command prompt. In the middle of the print module there is no way of knowing whether or not the hardcopy code has been activated. To make certain it is deactivated at the end of the module, lines 2910, 2920, and 2930 have been added. This turns the DUAL SVC off if it was on. Otherwise it has no effect. The final instruction in line 2940 returns us to the command prompt for further commands.

Additional Modules and Subroutines

Lines 2950 through 3050 need no further explanation. This is the subroutine used in the parsing section to find the delimiters for the entered data and is explained on pages 230 and 231. Since the routine is short and uncomplicated, there is little problem in understanding it. Remember to place the second search character in the proper location and have the beginning of the search area in HL before calling the routine. The carriage return is searched for first, and a flag is set if it is found. If not, then the code in lines 2980 through 3020 is executed with a jump to line 3050 if the delimiter is found. If the delimiter is not found, then go to the next memory location and repeat the entire subroutine. The flag location used here is F04C. A one is entered if a carriage return is found.

Move Module

The *move* function is found in lines 3570 through 3630. This is an example of how a function can be designed from smaller function modules. Line 3570 checks the first two values in the module storage buffer to make sure that they are in correct order. If not it reverses them. Line 3580 checks to make sure that there is data in the third location. If not an error message is printed and execution is aborted. Lines 3590, 3600, and 3610 load the data into the proper registers for execution. 3620 executes the processing subroutine and 3630 returns us to the command prompt.

Zero Memory

The *zero* function is similar in design. Check for parameter reversal in line 3640, load the data in lines 3650 and 3660, process the data in the subroutine called by line 3670, and return to the command prompt in line 3680.

Operating System Commands

This module is similar to the one in lines 2280 through 2340. The only difference is that there you want only the file name (the characters up to the space), while in this module you want the entire command string. To do this you need to change only one instruction. The beginning of the command string is designated in line 3720. The next line is the different one. The search character you want is the carriage return at the end of the command, instead of the space separating the command from its associated parameters. This is because the operating system command processor has its own built in parsing routine. This character (carriage return) is loaded in line 3730. Line 3740 calls the search and count routine, which puts the start address in DE and the number of characters in HL on exit. 3750 puts the count in B and 3760, shifts the starting address back to HL in preparation for the RETCMD SVC subroutine called in 3770. 3780 then returns to the command prompt again once the command has been executed.

Notice that you skip a number of lines throughout the explanation of program logic. These lines have no function at present and have only NOPs as code.

Quit

The *quit* processor has three functions which operate in sequence. First, turn off the DUAL SVC in case it has been activated by the previous routine or module. This takes place in lines 4130, 4140, and 4150. Lines 4160 through 4210 replaces the program break processing address with that found in the operating system at the beginning of the program. As in the previous use of SETBRK at the start of the program, it must be called twice. The first time it removes the break address currently in the system and the second time it places the new one in the system. The first call is performed in lines 4160, 4170, and 4180. The second is in the next three lines, 4190, 4200, and 4210. Following that, use the JMP TO DOS SVC to return to the operating system.

Break

The break processor begins with line 4240. The first thing to do is turn off the DUAL SVC. Lines 4240, 4250, and 4260 handle this task. Following this line, 4270 takes us to line 2240 where the stack is reset and the command prompt is loaded in preparation for printing.

Reverse

This segment is the reverse data subroutine used in the PRINT and HARDCOPY modules. It is also the one used in MOVE and ZERO. It begins by loading the two values to be compared into HL and DE in lines 4280 and 4290. Save the first value in the stack in line 4300. Line 4310 subtracts the two. If a carry is generated by the subtraction, then the first was less than the second and the data is placed back in the locations unchanged. This takes place in lines 4370, 4380, and 4390.

If the first value is larger than the second no carry will be generated. In this case the lines from 4330 through 4360 will be executed. Here, transfer the second value from DE to HL in lines 4330 and 4340. Then the first value previously saved in the stack is placed in DE by line 4350. Then skip the next instruction in line 4370 which executes if a carry is generated. The skip is executed by line 4360.

The final two lines replace the current values in HL and DE in the first and second locations. After this return from the subroutine in line 4400.

Check for Data

This subroutine is an error-checking subroutine. It aborts processing if required data is not present in the third parameter location at F084. I mentioned it in the MOVE and ZERO modules. It begins at line 4410. Since the program zeros these locations after each command, you will find either the correctly entered data or zeros.

256

The contents of the data location is put into BC by line 4410. The search character (0) is placed in A with 4420 and is compared with C in 4430. If the character in C is not zero, then there is data in the location and you exit the subroutine by going from 4440 to 4490 where you return. If the contents of C is zero, check B to be sure that no data exists. Line 4450 makes the comparison with B. 4460 takes you to the return at 4490 if B is not zero. In any other case an error message is printed by line 4470 and you return to the command prompt via line 4480.

Print Line

This subroutine uses lines 4500 through 4610. It prints a single line of ASCII characters on the screen. It also returns an error message and aborts printing if a nonprintable character is in the string.

It starts by computing the length of the line to be printed. This is done by counting characters until a carriage return is found. The search character is loaded in line 4500 and the search and count subroutine is executed by line 4510. On return, the count is loaded into B and reduced by one to adjust for the carriage return printed separately. This takes place in lines 4520 and 4530. The carriage return is then placed in C and the VIDLINE SVC is called in line 4560.

If a nonprintable character is found in the string by the routine, the zero flag is reset before exit. The zero flag is always set on exit from a successful execution of the SVC. The error trap takes advantage of this fact to activate the error message and the return to the command prompt. The flag registers may be changed by the error message subroutine, so save the flags in the stack with line 4570 before calling them. The error message subroutine is activated only if the zero flag is not set on exit from the SVC. This takes place in the conditional call in line 4580. Then restore the original flags before calling the conditional jump to the command prompt in lines 4590 and 4600. There is no apparent effect to the execution of the program if the zero flag is set. Return is normal from line 4610.

Illegal Parameters Error Message

The error message subroutine mentioned in the last section starts at line 4620 and continues through line 4670. It is simple and straightforward. Line 4620 points to the ASCII message, 4630 loads the number of characters to print into the correct register, 4640 loads the terminating character, 4650 points to the beginning of the actual text printed with the VIDLINE SVC called in 4660. Line 4670 returns to the calling program from the subroutine.

Lines 4680, 4690, and 4700 are respectively the function code, the call, and return from the BIN/DEC SVC. All function codes for SVC calls must be in hexadecimal.

Search and Count Subroutine

This subroutine is used extensively throughout the program. See how simple it really is? It starts at line 4910 where DE is zeroed. Then transfer the start address (HL) to DE with lines 4920 and 4930, and use the automated CPIR compare instruction in 4940 to look for whatever search character was placed in A before the routine was called. Next clear A and the carry flag with line 4950 to prepare for the subtraction of the beginning and ending addresses in the registers. This computes the number of characters counted, then the subroutine returns to the calling program via line 4970.

SVC Routines

A number of SVC codes and calls are set up as three line subroutines between 4980 and 5210, and from 5500 through 5650. These are all similar and details of the various routines can be obtained from the TRS-80 Model II owners' manual. Not all of them are used in the program. They are included to make it easier to modify or write additional modules for inclusion in the program.

Move Subroutine

The move subroutine is a major subroutine of the program, since one of the modules is based around it. As mentioned when discussing the MOVE module, after the error checks have been completed the starting address of the block to be moved is put in BC. The ending address of the block of memory is placed in HL and the destination address in DE.

The subroutine begins by saving the starting address in the stack with line 5660. The length of the block is then computed in 5670 and placed in BC with lines 5680 and 5690. The beginning address is then placed in HL from the stack in 5700.

Now determine whether to start at the beginning or at the end of the block in order to avoid destroying some of our data. This is done by subtracting the beginning address of the destination from the beginning address of the block in order to see if a carry is generated or not. After the subtraction is complete, replace the beginning address of the block in HL. This is carried out in lines 5710, 5720, 5730, and 5740.

Line 5750 checks the status of the carry. If there was no carry go ahead and transfer with the LDIR instruction using lines 5760 and 5770. Then skip the remaining code and return to the calling module.

If the carry was set by the subtraction, then start at the end of the block and work backward toward the beginning. Do this by adding the number of characters to be transferred to both the beginning address of the block to be transferred and to the destination address as well. This is done in lines 5790 through 5820. Then move the block with the LDDR instruction in 5840 and return.

User's Manual

This manual is written for use with the TRS-80 Model II and assumes familiarity with the operating system and command structure of this microcomputer. Begin by turning on all associated peripheral devices connected to the computer—the printer, the auxiliary disk drive controller, and so on. Then turn on the computer and wait for the built-in disk drive to come up to speed. When you have a white screen with an "insert diskette" message in the center, release the latch on the door of the built-in drive unit and gently but firmly slide the diskette into the unit on the main console. When the diskette is seated in the slot close the door. The drive will come on and load the operating system.

During this initial startup period two prompts appear on the screen which require input from you. The first asks you to enter the current date as specified in the owner's manual.

MM/DD/YYYY <ENTER>

This must be done to continue. The next prompt to enter the time is optional. If you do not want this merely press "ENTER". With this done the TRSDOS READY prompt will appear on the left side of the screen followed by a row of dots. This lets you know that the operating system is ready to accept commands.

You are now ready to load and execute the program unless you want to use the debug monitor program while running your program. If you do this, turn it on from the operating system before calling the program. To do this type; DEBUG ON <ENTER> in capital letters. The screen will clear and a message says; DEBUG IS NOW ON. If you have not activated DEBUG then to get into the program type; Z80 <ENTER> and you will find the program at the command prompt waiting for you to enter.

If you do turn on the debug monitor remember that even the program you want to run will be intercepted by the monitor. You will see the debug display with the starting address of your program in the program counter register (PC) on the display. To run the program merely type C (for continue) to execute the program.

Commands Available

Operating System Commands. All operating system commands executed from the program require the same format and parameters as listed in the TRS-80 Model II owners manual. The following commands are executed from the program:

Cls—Clears the screen of all data displayed there.

Date—Returns the current date as entered when the system was turned on.

Debug—Permits examination of all areas of user memory and use of all subcommands normally executable under Debug. To return to the program from debug, enter EDB1 into the program counter (PC) and then execute. Typing S (System) or Q (Quit) from Debug will return you to the operating system.

Dir—Gives the normal directory display.

Dump—When used with correct parameters permits saving a machine-language program to a disk file while remaining in the program.

Forms—Permits initializing the line printer from the program and also advancing the paper to the top of the next page.

Free—Permits viewing the free space map of the current disk.

Kill—Permits deleting a file from the disk while still in the program.

Lib—Permits viewing of library commands from the program.

List—Permits listing a disk file for viewing from the program.

Load—Permits loading a file from disk to memory from the program.

Time—Returns the time entered at the beginning of the program. If it has not been entered then this command returns elapsed time since the computer has been turned on.

Program Commands. The following program commands are available with this version of the program.

Move—Move relocates a block of memory to any location desired. It will handle overlapping blocks as well as simpler cases. The command format is

MOVE S=nnnn,E=nnnn,D=nnnn,

All entries must be in hexadecimal. The first value is the starting address of the block to be moved. The second value is the ending address of the block. The final value is the beginning address of the destination block. There are no options with this command. No visible output is displayed. To verify operation of the command enter the debug monitor and examine the memory locations in question.

Zero—Zero fills a specified block of memory with 0 (hex). There are no options with the command and no display output. The command format is:

ZERO S=nnnn,E=nnnn,

The first value is the beginning address of the block, the second value is the ending address. Both must be in hexadecimal.

Print—Print displays the contents of an ASCII file on the video display. The file, created with any program, must be in the following format to be displayed by this module.

Each line to be displayed must have an ASCII line number as the first data item of the line. These numbers must be between 100 and 65535 in increments of 10. Following the number is the actual text of the line whatever it may be. Finally, the line must be terminated with a carriage return. In addition, the first line number must be preceeded by a carriage return.

The module will not load a file for display. This must be done with the LOAD command described earlier. Once the file is in user memory it can be output by the PRINT module. Command format for PRINT is

PRINT S=dddd,E=dddd,D=nnnn,

The first value is the beginning line number you wish displayed in decimal. It can be up to five characters long, but must have a value of at least 100. Leading zeros are not required. The second value is the last line number you wish displayed, also in decimal. The final value is the memory address which the module begins searching for your text. This address must be entered in hexadecimal.

Hardcopy—This has exactly the same requirements as PRINT. Command format is the same except for the substitution of the word HARDCOPY for the word PRINT. File format requirements are the same. Neither command has options.

Quit—This has no parameters and no options. This command returns control to TRSDOS and exits the program.

Maintenance Manual

This program is designed to be expandable and is written with that end in mind. Only a few of the features might be included here.

The major portion of the existing code is concerned with program initialization, command input, and parsing the command string. Function modules, except for PRINT, take up very little of the program memory. This has been deliberate. Program functions have been largely undefined for your own purposes, and the modules to implement them are the deciding factors in the completed program design.

The purpose of this manual is to explain how you can add your own program function modules to the program. All necessary information is included to let you add any function to the program. Your part in this cooperative endeavor is to decide what functions to include and then write programs to implement them.

Data Structure

The discussion of data structure will be in two sections: the structure of the command input and the structure of the ASCII files to be output by the print command. Each is treated separately.

Structure of Command Input Data. A command word is input as the first item of the command string. This is separated from the rest of the string by a space. The length of the command word is not important since the program identifies it only by the first character of the word. For this reason command words used for program function modules must be unique. None of the commands can have identical first characters. The entire command word must be entered, however, because some command words are used as file specifiers for disk input.

Up to four data items follow the command word. Each of these are preceded by a data identifier and an equal sign, and terminated by a comma. The four identifiers are S, E, D, and T. These represent in order the start of the block to be processed, the end of the block to be processed, and the destination of any output from the processing module in user memory. The final identifier, T, has no specific meaning and is used only when a fourth data item is needed by the program. The parsing routine uses these identifiers to insure that the correct data items are placed in the correct locations for use by the module. No matter what the function of the module these items are specified in this same order. The parsing routine places them in the same location no matter what command is designated for the data. It is up to the function module to load the data from these locations in order to process it correctly. You can see this clearly by examining the program listing and the program logic manual for the move and zero function modules.

Each data item is followed or terminated by a comma. Even if you are at the end of the command line, the comma must be present to enable the parser to know where the end of the data is.

If optional modifications or features are added to a function, these can be designated after the data items are entered. They are placed in a special location beginning at F088 by the parser. Indicate these in the command string by putting a slash (/) just before each option designator.

Data File Structure. As mentioned in the user's manual, the structure of data files must also be in a prespecified format in order to be displayed by the print module. The data file begins with a carriage return and is entirely in ASCII characters. Following the carriage return are the data lines. It is assumed that there are no empty spaces or blanks between any of the items. The file is assumed to be one continuous string of data from beginning to end. Each line of data begins with a line number. These start with 100 and increase in increments of 10 to a maximum of 65530, the largest number divisible by 10 contained in 16 bits in hexadecimal notation. The remainder of the line contains the contents of the line in ASCII and control codes. Each line is terminated with a carriage return.

Provisions for Expansion

The program can be expanded in two ways. You can add additional operating system commands executed by this program, or write special function modules called by the parsing routine already present. These function modules can be written as routines within the main program area to which the program transfers control when they are specified or, alternately, as separate overlay programs called and executed by the main program.

Operating System Commands. To add to the number of operating system commands executed by the program you must include them in the list of command characters. These can be found at present in locations F2A9 through F2AF. Note that only the first letter of the command is included. Therefore if two operating system commands start with the same letter they can both be executed by the program. If the starting address of this list is changed for any reason, it must be altered in line 800 of the program listing.

None of the letters in this list are used as the starting letter of a function module command word. If you have a match for any letter in this list the program goes immediately to the RETCMD routine at EEAF and ignores the remainder of the parsing routine.

Function Module Routines. Your own specially written routines require a slightly more complicated procedure because the parser must handle the data required for operation. To do this, designate how many items expected to input. Also designate whether the starting and ending data (the first two items) is in hexadecimal or decimal format. Finally, include the address of the routine or its handling routine in the jump table (F2E9 TO F31A) along with the first character of the command name.

If your routine requires no input at all, such as the present quit command, then go no farther than lines 570 and 580. Note that they contain at present a comparison with ASCII B and a return to the command prompt if the ZERO flag is set by the comparison. The first character of your command name could be substituted here and the starting address of your routine substituted in line 580. If more than one comparison is required it might be possible to patch the program, i.e., jump to another location where more memory is available, put in the necessary code and then jump back to line 590 if the tests fail.

The sequence of code in lines 610, 620, 630, and 640 provide a model for placing the required value in F04B, the storage location for the number of data items expected by the program. A single command can use the sequence in lines 610 and 620. Compare this character with the character in A and go to the value loading routine if they are the same. The routine to put the value of the correct number of items into F04B is simple. Put the desired value in A (as in line 650) and then put it in the memory location with the following line.

If several commands require the same number of items place them in a list and use STSCAN SVC to search for a match. An example of this is lines 670 through 730. These lines set up a search for a match between the character in A and the characters starting at F2B0. In this case these commands require three data items to be input. Since the zero flag is set on exit if a match is found, jump past your value loader in lines 720 and 730 if no match occurs.

These examples show how to designate the number of items expected and loaded by the program. Your next task is to determine whether the input is entirely in hexadecimal, or if the first two items will be decimal. This is handled at present in lines 1200 through 1280. Here, compare the command character with those command characters requiring decimal input in the first two locations. If there are a number of them set up a list and use STSCAN SVC again to check them. In the program as it is now the only modules using

264

decimal input are the print and hardcopy routines. This makes it simple to set up comparisons with each. If there is one of these routines the parser goes to the beginning of the decimal conversion routine at ED23. If not, continuation of the sequence puts you into the hexadecimal conversion routine.

Once these items have been taken care of there is the command interpretation to deal with. Commands are executed in one of three ways by the program. The program can simply jump to the location in memory where the module starts. A second method of execution is by using the RETCMD SVC to execute a program stored as a disk file and called as a subprogram by the main routine. The final way is to place the starting address in the jump table along with the ASCII letter designator for the module. When the LOOKUP SVC searches the table, transfer to the starting address is automatic when a jump is made to the address in the HL register on exit from the search.

These methods can be combined if desired. For example, if a function module is stored as a disk file it can be accessed from the jump table if the first character of its file name is placed in the jump table with the starting address of the RETCMD SVC routine.

The command name is placed in the command list beginning at present at F2C0 if not called from the jump table. This process can be used also in calling subprograms with the RETCMD SVC.

Finally, if your subprogram will not fit within the available memory in the main program area, you will have to locate it elsewhere and call it as a subprogram with the RETCMD SVC routine. The general memory allocations as listed on page 244 show memory from C680 to EBFF as the area for these programs. This is merely a convenience. These programs are located anywhere in available memory, but for consistency and ease they should be loaded in the same area. It is a good idea to zero this area of memory before loading any new module to avoid interference. The main program is not easily relocated. If this must be done due to memory limitations be careful to check all jumps and subroutine calls. In addition, check all references to data locations and memory work-space. You must also check references to program instructions modified by the program.

Appendix:
BASIC Comparisons

The following reproduces in its entirety an article by Terri Li entitled "Whose BASIC Does What," which appeared in the January, 1981, issue of *BYTE* magazine. This article is copyright 1981 by Byte Publications, Inc. and is reprinted by permission of Byte Publication, Inc.

*   *   *

Many articles have been written about the various new personal computers now on the market, including the ATARI 400 and 800 and the Texas Instruments (TI) 99/4, but few have tried to compare these newer units against the most popular computers.

Because of this, I have decided to do a comparison of the four most popular computers (Apple II, Commodore PET, Exidy Sorcerer, and the Radio Shack TRS-80 Model I) against the TI 99/4 and the ATARI 400 and 800. (The BASIC is the same for both ATARI 400 and 800.) To make this as fair as possible, I have compared only the computers that come with versions of BASIC supplied with the machines in ROM (read-only memory) at the time of purchase, without extended hardware (such as disk drives).

This comparison is in the form of three tables. The BASIC command, statement, or function is on the left, followed by six columns, one for each of the computers (PET, Apple II, TRS-80, ATARI, TI 99/4, Sorcerer). To the right of these columns is a brief explanation of each of these commands (since not all are self explanatory). If a particular computer interprets a BASIC command differently from the others, a notation of the difference is made.

For the Apple II computer, especially, this is true as there are two versions of BASIC that you can get with it: Integer BASIC and Applesoft. Unless otherwise stated for the Apple, the commands apply to both versions.

There are only a few additional comments that I need to make about these comparison tables.

I have not gone into a great deal of detail on the graphic capabilities of these machines, but briefly speaking, the TRS-80 has the worst point resolution, while only the Apple II, ATARI 400 and 800, and TI 99/4 have color graphics. In graphics mode, the Apple II, ATARI 400 and 800, and Sorcerer offer the most versatility, while PET is the easiest to use.

Last, the TI has the most cumbersome BASIC to use. It lacks a "free memory" command, it allows only line numbers (not statements) to be used in IF . . . THEN statements, and it does not allow the use of multiple statements per line.

As for the rest, check out the tables and decide for yourself which of the computers is best suited to your needs.

The tables also have one other use. They can assist in the translation of programs from one computer to another, since they do give comparable keywords for the different computers.

Table 1 shows the availability of BASIC system commands in six microcomputer families. In this table, and Tables 2 and 3, a check indicates the presence of a feature in a given microcomputer BASIC; a blank indicates its absence. A word or words in the table entry indicates that the feature described under the explanation column is available for a given computer using this name. These tables are not meant to be an exhaustive description of any of the six computer systems.

267

TABLE 1. AVAILABILITY OF BASIC COMMANDS IN SIX MICROCOMPUTER FAMILIES

Command	Pet	Apple	TRS-80	ATARI	TI	Sorcerer	Explanation
AUTO mm,n		~	~		NBR		Automatically numbers the lines of a program as you enter them from the keyboard, starting with line mm, using the increment n. Not available in Applesoft.
BREAK MM			~				Sets a breakpoint at line number mm; program execution will halt upon reaching this breakpoint.
CLEAR	CLR	~	~				Sets all numeric variables to zero and all string variables to null.
CLEAR N			~	~			Sets aside n bytes of memory for storage of strings; also sets numeric variables to zero and string variables to null.
CLOAD	LOAD	LOAD	~		OLD		Loads a BASIC program from cassette tape.
CLOAD?	VERIFY		~				Compares a program in memory to a program on tape; the two must match exactly.
CONTINUE	CONT	CONT	CONT	CONT		CONT	Continues execution of a program after reaching a BREAK (TI) or STOP statement (all) during program execution, or after program is halted by operator (after a Control-C, Break key, Stop key, etc.).
CSAVE	SAVE	SAVE	~		SAVE		Saves a BASIC program in memory to cassette tape.

Command						Description
DELETE MM	cursor		DEL	~		Deletes program line mm from the program. The TI uses this command to delete programs or data files from its filing system.
EDIT MM	cursor	~	cursor	cursor	cursor	Enters EDIT mode for line number mm. Lets you manipulate the characters in line number mm. The Apple, ATARI, Exidy, and Pet use on screen editing via LIST and cursor controls.
Home				cursor		Moves cursor to top line, left-most position of video, in Applesoft only. Call—976 has same function for Integer BASIC.
HIMEM		~		~	~	Sets address of highest memory address available to a BASIC program; protects data, graphics, or machine-language routines located in high memory.
LIST mm-nn	~	~	~	~	~	Lists all program lines between (and including) line numbers mm and nn. Apple Integer BASIC uses comma instead of hyphen.
LOMEM		~	~			Sets lowest address available to a BASIC program. Reset by NEW, DEL, and Control C key.
MAN		~				Apple Integer BASIC only: resets AUTO line numbering feature to manual numbering.
NEW	~	~	~	~	~	Deletes entire program from memory and resets all pointers and variables to zero and null.

Command	SYSTEM						Explanation
	PET	Apple	TRS-80	ATARI	TI	Sorcerer	
RESEQUENCE mm,nn							Renumbers program from beginning or starting with line mm incrementing in steps of nn.
RUN	?	?	?	?	?	?	Begins execution of program, starting at beginning or at line number mm.
SYSTEM	SYS	CALL-151		BYE	BYE	BYE	Puts you in monitor mode for execution of machine-language programs. ATARI and TI use BYE only to go to calculator mode from BASIC.
TROFF		NOTRACE			UNTRACE		Turns off trace features.
TRON		TRACE	?		TRACE		Tells you which line number of the program is currently being executed. Very useful in tracking down program bugs. Removes breakpoint set by the BREAK command.
UNBREAK			?		?		
(SCREEN FORMAT)	40×24	40×24	64×16	40×24	32×24	64×30	Normal screen format for text operation, number of characters per line by number of lines on screen.
(CHAR RES, M BY N)			3×2	8×8	8×8	8×8	Individual character positions on screen can be broken down into a matrix of dots, m rows of n dots per row. Not applicable to Apple II, ATARI 400/800 or the Pet.
(TOTAL PIXELS)		280 × 192	128 × 48	320 × 192	256 × 192	512 × 240	Actual number of total pixels (picture elements) that can be individually turned on and off by the program when in full graphics mode.

TABLE 2. AVAILIBILITY OF BASIC STATEMENT TYPES IN SIX MICROCOMPUTER FAMILES

Statement	PET	Apple	TRS-80	ATARI	TI	Exidy	Explanation
General							
APPEND	?					?	Allows data to be added to end of data file.
CLS	?	?	?		CALL CLEAR		Clears the video screen and returns the cursor to the top line, left-most position of the video. See also HOME.
CALL (addr)	CALL SYS	?				EN	Branches to the machine-language subroutine at the specified address addr.
CALL CHAR					?		Allows you to define a new character for the video display to be used by your program.
CALL COLOR				COLOR			Allows you to define the background color to be used for the individual characters.
CALL JOYSTK				STICK	(	?	Checks the joystick port for input.
CALL SCREEN		HCOLOR=		SETCOLOR	?		Allows you to select the background color of the video. HCOLOR=exp lets you select the color to be used in hi-res (high resolution) graphics mode in Applesoft.
CALL SOUND				SOUND	?		Lets you define the sound output to be used by your program.
CLOSE	?				?		Closes device (tape, printer, etc.) data file.

271

Statement	SYSTEM						Explanation
	PET	Apple	TRS-80	ATARI	TI	Exidy	
COLOR= n	?	?				?	Sets the color of the point for the next plot (in low resolution graphics for the Apple II).
DATA	?	?	?	?	?		Holds data for access by a READ statement.
DEF FN (name)	?	?	?		DEF		Lets you define a single-line function, called by using FN and the function name.
DEFINT			?				Defines as integer all variables beginning with specified letter, letters, or range of letters.
DEFDBL			?				Defines as double-precision floating point all variables beginning with the specified letter, letters, or range of letters.
DEFSNG			?				Defines as single-precision floating point all variables beginning with the specified letter, letters, or range of letters.
DEFSTR			?				Defines as string variables all variables beginning with the specified letter, letters, or range of letters.
DIM var(k)	?	?	?	?	?		Allocates space in memory for a variable array with as many dimensions as numbers in k, and with the specified size per dimension. Apple Integer BASIC allows one dimensional array only.

272

Command						Description
DISPLAY		~				May be used in place of PRINT, or to specify the format of data stored on tape. Display specifies ASCII format.
DRAWTO HPLOT			~			Draws a line from the last plotted point to this position. HPLOT can also plot a single point in high resolution graphics or a series of points connected in sequence.
DSP var			~	~		Displays value of the specified variable each time it changes. Available in Apple Integer BASIC only.
END	~		~	~	~	Ends execution of program and returns to command mode.
EOF			~			Writes end-of-file mark to a data file.
ERROR (mm)		~	~	~	~	Simulates the error specified by the number mm, to test ON ERROR GOTO routines.
FOR . . TO . . STEP,NEXT	~	~	~	~	~	Creates an iterative loop, with the optional step size specified. If no step size is given, a step of 1 is used. Leaving a loop before it is finished will cause problems later.
GOSUB (line),RET	~	~	~	~	~	Branches to the specified line number and continues program execution from that point until a RETURN is found. Execution then returns to the statement following the GOSUB command.
GOTO (line)	~	~	~	~	~	Branches to the specified line number.

Statement	PET	Apple	TRS-80	ATARI	TI	Exidy	Explanation
GR		~					Turns on low-resolution graphics. HGR selects page 0 of high resolution graphics, HGR2 selects page 2.
Graphics				~			Turns on graphics mode.
HLIN...AT		~			CALL HCHAR		Draws a horizontal line at the specified line number. TI lets you specify the number and type of characters in the line.
IF(exp) THEN (ln)	~	~	~	~	~	~	Tests an expression. If it is true, the statement following the THEN is executed before executing the next program line. If it is false, program execution proceeds to the next line.
IF..THEN ..ELSE			~		~		Same as previous item except execution goes to the ELSE only if the argument is false. In either case, execution continues on the next program line. TI allows only line numbers after THEN and ELSE.
IF..GOSUB ..RET	~	~	~			~	Same as IF...THEN, except a GOSUB is executed.
IF..GOTO	~	~	~			~	If the expression is true, then program execution proceeds directly to the specified line number and continues from there.
IN (port)		IN#(exp)	~			~	Goes to the specified port and gets the value there. Both the argument and the result must be in the range of 0 through 255. IN# selects specified mother-board slot for input, with 0 being the keyboard.

Command							Description
INPUT "msg" var	~	~	~	~	~	~	Goes to keyboard and awaits user input. An optional message may be printed to the video display as a prompt.
INPUT #n,var	~	RECALL	~	~	~	~ ~	Inputs data from cassette. RECALL (for Applesoft only) reads data into a single array. (Applesoft and Apple Integer BASIC have INPUT statements too.)
LET var=exp	~	~	~ ~	~ ~	~	~	Assigns the argument to the specified variable.
LPRINT							Sends value of the variable specified or a message contained within quotes to the printer. See also PRINT# for the PET and TI.
ON ERROR GOTO	ONERR	~	TRAP	~	~	~	Error trapping routine. If an error occurs within the program, then program execution goes to the specified line number and continues from there.
ON..GOSUB, RETURN	~	~	(	~	~	~	Evaluates expression; on the integer value of the expression, expr, transfers control to the expth line number after the word GOSUB. Returns to line after this line when RETURN is encountered.
ON...GOTO	~	~	~	~	~	~	Same as above except control does not return to next line.
OPEN		~		~	~ ~		Opens a device to either input or output a data file.
OPTION BASE (x)				~			Sets the lowest allowable subscript of an array, x, to either 0 or 1.

Statement	SYSTEM PET	Apple	TRS-80	ATARI	TI	Exidy	Explanation
OUT portnum, val		PR#expr	~				Sends the specified value (between 0 and 255) to the specified I/O port (between 0 and 255). PR# selects mother-board slot (0 through 7) for output where 0 = video monitor.
PADDLE		PDL		~			Gets the value of the paddle input.
PEEK	~	~	~	~	CALL GCHAR	~	Returns the value stored in the specified location. ATARI and TI are restricted to video locations only.
POINT			~	~			Checks the specified video location (graphic) and returns a 1 if it is on, returns a 0 otherwise.
POP		~	~	~			Removes the most recent addition from the stack.
POKE loc,val	~	~	~	~		~	Loads the specified value into the specified location. Both numbers are decimal and value is between 0 and 255.
PRINT"msg" or var	~	~	~	~	~	~	Sends the message within the quotes or the value of the specified variable(s) to the video display.
PRINT@			~	POSITION			Same as above except printing begins at the specified video location.
PRINT#	~	~	~ ~		~	~	Sends data to the cassette drive.
PRINT-USING			~				Prints according to the specified format.

Command							Description
PTRIG			?				Returns a 0 if the game paddle pushbutton is depressed, otherwise a 1 is returned. STRIG is used for the joystick button.
READ	?	?	?	?	?		Assigns the values stored in the data statements to the variables listed.
RECALL		?	?	?	?		Reads contents of a numeric array from cassette; available in Applesoft only.
REM	?	?	?	?	?		Remark indicator; computer does not execute anything following the REM (for the remainder of that line only).
RESET (X,Y) RESTORE	?	?	?	?	?		Turns off the graphics block at position, (x,y). Resets the data pointer to the first item in the first data line. With ATARI and TI, a line number may be specified, and the pointer will be set to the first item of data in that line.
RESUME			?	?			In Applesoft only, resumes program execution from the error routine at the specified line number.
SET (X,Y)			PLOT	PLOT HPLOT		PLOT	Turns on the graphics block (x,y). Apple Integer BASIC and Applesoft can also plot a high-resolution graphics point with HPLOT.
SPEED=exp				?			Determines speed at which characters are sent to the screen or other output device (Applesoft only).

277

Statement	PET	Apple	TRS-80	ATARI	TI	Exidy	Explanation
STOP	?	?					Halts program execution and returns to the READY prompt.
STORE		?	?	?	?	?	Writes contents of a numeric array to cassette (Applesoft only).
TAB	?	?	?				A print modifier: the variable or message is printed at the specified column.
TEXT		?			?		Converts from graphics mode to all-text mode.
UPDATE		?					Allows an opened file to be both read from tape and written to tape, changing values in the process.
VLIN...AT					CALL VCHAR		Draws a vertical line at the specified column. TI lets you specify number and type of characters in the line.
VTAB (x)		?					Moves the cursor (x) lines down from the top of the display screen.
WAIT A,B,C	?	?	?	?		?	Temporarily halts program execution until certain conditions are met.
String Functions							
ASC (string)	?	?	?	?	?	?	Returns the ASCII value of the first character of the string.
CHR$(code)	?	?	?	?	?	?	Returns a one character string defined by the value of the code (between 0 and 255). If a control code is specified, that function is executed.

Function						Description
FRE (x$)					?	Returns the amount of memory available for string variable storage.
INKEY$	GET	GET		CALL KEY	?	Scans the keyboard once and returns the character pressed. If none of the keys are pressed during the scan, returns a null.
LEFT$ (string,n)		?	?	?	?	Returns n characters from the specified string, starting at the left.
LEN String	?	?	?	?		Returns the length of the specified string.
MID$ (string,p,n)	?	?	?	SEG$		Returns a substring of length n starting at position p in the specified string; ATARI uses a subscripting procedure.
POS(str1, str2,n)				?		Returns the starting position of substring str2 inside of string str1, beginning the scan at character position n in str1.
RIGHT$ (string,n)	?	?	?	?	?	Returns n characters from the specified string, starting at the right.
STR$ (exp)	?	?	?	?	?	Converts the specified numeric expression to a string.
STRING$ (n,char)		?			?	Returns a string of length n composed of the specified character.
VAL (string)	?	?	?	(	?	Converts a string of numerals (ex "68") to its numeric value (68).
VARPTR var			ADR		?	Returns the memory address where the name, value, and pointer of variable (var) are stored.

TABLE 3. AVAILABILITY OF BASIC MATHEMATICAL AND OTHER FUNCTIONS IN SIX MICROCOMPUTER FAMILIES

Function	SYSTEM						Explanation
	PET	Apple	TRS-80	ATARI	TI	Exidy	
(precision)	9	10	6 or 16	10	14	6	The number of significant digits with which the computer operates. The TRS-80 has double-precision (16-digit) capability, but all machine supplied functions are truncated to six digits.
ABS (exp)	✓	✓	✓	✓	✓	✓	Gives the absolute value of the specified expression.
ATN (exp)	✓	✓	✓	✓	✓	✓	Gives the arctangent in radians; ATARI can be set up to use angular measures in degrees.
CINT (exp)			✓				Converts the expression into the largest integer not larger than the expression (between −32768 and 32768).
CDBL (exp)			✓				Converts the expression to double precision (16 digits).
CLOG (exp)		✓	✓	✓			Returns the base-10 (common) logarithm of the specified expression; CLOG (0) will give an error, CLOG(1) = 0.
CSNG (exp)			✓				Converts the expression to single precision (6 digits).
COS (exp)	✓	✓	✓		✓	✓	Returns the cosine of the expression, where exp is in radians.
ERL (exp)			✓				Returns the line number of the current error.

Function						Description
ERR (exp)	~	~				~	Returns a value related to the current error.
EXP (exp)	~	~	~		~	~	Returns the natural exponential.
FIX (exp)		~	~	~	~	~	Returns the integer equivalent of the expression, truncated.
FRE (exp)			~(also MEM)			~	Tells you the total number of unused and unprotected bytes in memory. MEM does not include unused string space. FRE(x$) will tell you the amount of unused string space.
INT (exp)	~	~	~	~	~	~	Returns the largest integer not greater than the expression (between —32768 and 32768).
LOG (exp)	~	~	~	~	~	~	Returns natural logarithm (base e) of the expression; the expression must be positive.
MOD (exp)	~				~		Modulo arithmetic: returns remainder after two numbers are added/subtracted, allows for some division. Available in Apple Integer BASIC only.
POS (exp)	~		~		~	~	Returns a number indicating the current position of the cursor on a line: available in Applesoft only.
RANDOMIZE			RANDOM			~	Reseeds the random-number generator.
RND (0)	~	RND	RANDOM	~	RND	RND(1) ~	Returns a pseudorandom number between .000001 and .999999; in Applesoft and TI BASIC, RND(0) returns the last random number given.

Function	PET	Apple	TRS-80	ATARI	TI	Exidy	Explanation
RND (exp)	~	~	~	~	~	~	Returns a pseudorandom number between 1 and the value of (exp). In Applesoft if exp <0 then the same value is returned each time exp is used.
SCRN (x,y)		~					Returns the color value of screen position (x,y); available in Integer BASIC only.
SGN (exp)	~	~	~	~	~	~	Returns −1 if the expression is negative, 0 if it is 0, or +1 if it is positive.
SIN (exp)	~	~	~	~	~	~	Returns the sine value of the expression; exp must be in radians.
SPC (exp)		~	~				Returns the number of skips specified in the argument. Range is between 0 and 255. SPC (0) = 256 skips.
SPC (num)				NULL			Prints the specified number of spaces.
SQR (exp)	~	~	~	~	~	~	Returns the square root of the specified expression: exp cannot be negative.
Tan (exp)	~	~	~		~	~	Returns the tangent of the expression, the expression must be in radians.
TI	~						Sets the real time clock to the value specified.
USR (x)	~	~	~			~	Passes the value X to a machine-language subroutine and executes subroutine. Address of the routine must already have been POKEd into memory.

These three operators perform given logical operations on numeric variables or expressions. (NOT works on a single number.) In most cases, these operators work bit by bit on the numeric values expressed in binary.

}

}

}

}

AND,OR,NOT

Glossary

algorithm—A step-by-step procedure that refines a task to be executed by a computer.

APL—Acronym for "a programming language;" a programming language developed in the early 1960's by Dr. Kenneth Iverson at Harvard. The basic data structure is the array. Part of the power of the language is the set of operators available for manipulating arrays.

array—A multidimensional list structure where each dimension of an element is designated by subscripts indicating its position in the whole.

ASCII code—A widely used code which represents alphanumeric characters by a single byte in memory. It is almost universally used in microcomputers.

assembler—Computer program which automatically translates assembler mnemonics into the proper instruction codes and enters them into memory.

assembly-language—The set of code words assigned to the instructions built in to a microprocessor by the manufacturer.

BASIC—One of the most popular microcomputer languages. It was developed at Dartmouth in the mid-1960's by John Kemeny and Thomas Kurtz. Designed as a teaching language, its name is an acronym for "beginners all-purpose symbolic instruction code."

binary numbers—A system of numbers based on powers of two.

BIT—A binary digit (0 or 1). The smallest basic unit of information stored in a computer.

branch—The alteration of the flow of the program process due to a test of a specified condition.

breakpoint—A temporary halt in program execution inserted by the monitor. Before proceeding it is possible to examine the contents of registers or memory locations to verify proper operation of the program.

byte—A group of eight contiguous bits in the computer memory.

case structure—A combination of several decision blocks and an equal number of process blocks. Each decision block has its corresponding process block executed if that decision is true.

circular list—A list which automatically returns to the first item at the end of the list.

COBOL—Common Business Oriented Language. Developed during the late 50's by IBM and the U.S. Government. It is the standard language for business applications.

comment—An explanatory statement appearing in the program listing to explain a particular instruction or sequence of instructions. These are ignored by the compiler, assembler, or interpreter when executing the program.

compiler—A program which translates a high-level source program into machine-language instructions.

computer programmer—A person creating a set of instructions to be executed by a computer.

CPU—Central Processing Unit, the portion of a microprocessor which interprets and executes the various instructions coded in memory.

data—Information which is operated upon by the program.

data structure—The way in which the data is organized or arranged for use by the program.

debugging—Correcting mistakes in coding and logic in a computer program.

decision—See branch

directory—A two-dimensional list in which gives location data for the second list, which in turn contains the data sought.

documentation—Any or all of a number of written descriptions and explanations concerning a computer program usually explaining its operation, its design, how to use it, and other information available from other sources.

do-until—Loop structure in which the decision comes after the process block.

do-while—Loop structure in which the decision block is executed before the process block.

drivers—Special program modules written only to produce sample data and test modules. They are not used in the final program.

flag—A specific testable bit in assembly-language programming. It can be used to activate branching instructions.

flowchart—A diagram using special symbols to show the logical relationships between various parts of a program.

FORTH—A language developed during the 60's by Charles H. Moore. It forces highly structured logical design. New functions can be created as desired and coding can be compact since functions can call themselves.

FORTRAN—The oldest of the standard programming languages. Developed during the 50's by IBM for its new computers. The name is an acronym for FORmula TRANslation, reflecting its major use as a tool in engineering and scientific research.

hand assembly—Translates assembly-language instructions into hexadecimal or binary code by looking them up in a list.

hexadecimal numbers—A system of numbers based on powers of sixteen. Two hexadecimal digits make up one byte.

high-level language—A computer language that is problem oriented rather than computer oriented as is assembly-language.

if-then-else—A combination of two process blocks and a decision block.

interpreter—A program which allows you to execute high-level instructions directly and interact with the program when necessary to make changes.

inverse—Opposite. The inverse of an expression is its opposite.

iteration—The act of repeating or doing again. In programming a sequence of code which is repeated. (see loops).

jump—An instruction which transfers control unconditionally from one location to another within a program.

linked list—A list in which the address of the **next** data item is made a part of the data in the current item.

LISP—LISt Processing language developed by John McCarthy at MIT during the late 50's and early 60's. It was developed primarily for research in artificial intelligence.

LIST—See sequential list

loops—A combination of a process block and a decision block.

maintenance manual—A manual designed for the programmer who may have to add to or modify a program at a later date.

memory map—A list of the areas of memory used by the program and the purpose served by each.

modular programming—Dividing a program into sections according to function, then subdividing each section into smaller sections until each section is small enough to easily code.

monitor program—A program which enables you to debug a machine-language program and change it where desired.

nesting—Placing a loop or subroutine entirely within another so that the inner loop will execute once for each pass through the outer loop.

nibble—A group of four bits. One half of a byte.

octal numbers—A system of numbers based on powers of eight.

PASCAL—Another teaching language developed in Europe by Niklaus Wirth. Its main advantages are its insistence on good structure before coding and the numerous coding forms available.

process—A prespecified action or sequence of actions taken upon a certain data item.

program logic manual—A manual explaining in detail the design goals of the program, what algorithms were chosen to implement them, what data structures were used and how they are manipulated by the program.

programming—The act of creating a series of instructions to be executed by a computer.

programming language—A precisely defined and completely specified set of key words recognized by a computer.

queue—A list in which the first item entered is the first to be withdrawn.

sequence—A composite of two or more process blocks.
sequential list—A form of organization in which data items are placed one after the other in designated memory locations as they are received by the program.
stack—A list in which the last item entered must be the first to be withdrawn.
structured programming—A method of program design based on the premise that any programming task can be reduced to a collection of basic concepts which fit together in very well defined ways.
subroutine—A segment of code performing a general function which is used in more than one place in a program without rewriting the segment of code.
syntax—A logical relationship which exists among all data elements.

table—A list ordered in some specific predesignated way.
topdown design—A method where the major logical blocks are written and tested using short temporary programs in place of the subprograms which should be there. Each temporary program is then expanded and tested until all are complete.
tree—A data structure used to describe complex or multiple relationships between data items.

users guide—A manual explaining how to use the program. Nothing is assumed here. The user is expected to have no understanding at all of programming or how the program might be manipulated.

variable list—A list, usually in alphabetical order, of all variables used by the program.

References

The following references range from elementary to quite advanced. Most libraries should have at least some of these titles.

GENERAL PROGRAMMING TOPICS

Chapin, Ned. *Flowcharts*. New York: Van Nostrand Reinhold Co., 1971.

Dalton, W. F. "Design Microcomputer Software Like Other Systems—Systematically." *Electronics*. January 19, 1978, pp. 97-101.

Demilo, R. A. "Hints on Test Data Selection." *Computer*. April, 1978; pp. 34-41.

Dijkstra, Edward W. *Discipline of Programming*. Englewood Cliffs, New Jersey: Prentice-Hall, Inc., 1976.

Dollhoff, T. "Microprocessor Software." *Digital Design*. February, 1977; pp. 44-51.

Halstead, Maurice H. *Elements of Software Science*. New York: Elsevier-North Holland Publishing Co., 1977.

Hughes, J. K. & Michtom, J. I. *Structured Approach to Programming*. Englewood Cliffs, New Jersey: Prentice-Hall, Inc., 1977.

Knuth, Donald E. *The Art of Computer Programming, Volume I: Fundamental Algorithms*. 1974.

——. *The Art of Computer Programming: Semi-Numerical Algorithms*, Volume II. 1981.

——. *The Art of Computer Programming, Volume III: Sorting & Searching*. 1973.

Morgan, D. E. and Taylor, D. J. "A Survey of Methods for Achieving Reliable Software." *Computer*. February, 1977; pp. 44-52.

Myers, W. "The Need for Software Engineering." *Computer*. February, 1978; pp. 12-25.

Parnas, D. L. "On The Criteria to be Used in Decomposing Systems into Modules." *Communications of the ACM*. December, 1972; pp. 1053-1058.

——. "A Technique for the Specification of Software Modules with Examples." *Communications of the ACM*. May, 1973; pp. 330-336.

Peterson, W. Wesley. *Introduction to Programming Languages*. Englewood Cliffs, New Jersey: Prentice-Hall, Inc., 1974.

Ulrickson, R. W. "Solve Software Problems Step by Step." *Electronic Design*. January 18, 1977; pp. 54-58.

——. "Software Modules are the Building Blocks." *Electronic Design*. February 1, 1977; pp. 62-66.

Van Tassel, Dennis. *Program Style, Design, Efficiency, Debugging & Testing*. Englewood Cliffs, New Jersey: Prentice-Hall, Inc., 1978.

Walsh, D. A. "Structured Testing." *Datamation*. July, 1977; pp. 111-118.

Weller, Walter J. *Assembly Level Programming for Small Computers*. Lexington, Massachusetts: Lexington Books, 1975.

Wirth, Niklaus. *Algorithms Plus Data Structure Equals Programs*. Englewood Cliffs, New Jersey: Prentice-Hall, Inc., 1975.

————. *Systematic Programming: An Introduction*. Englewood Cliffs, New Jersey: Prentice-Hall, Inc., 1973.

Yourdon, Edward U. *Techniques of Program Structure & Design*. Englewood Cliffs, New Jersey: Prentice-Hall, Inc., 1976.

LANGUAGE REFERENCES

Bowles, Ken L. *Beginner's Guide for the UCSD Pascal System*. New York: McGraw-Hill Book Co., 1980.

Couger, Dan and McFadden, Fred. *First Course in Data Processing with BASIC, COBOL, FORTRAN, RPG II*. New York: John Wiley & Sons, Inc., 1981.

Fernandez, Judi N. and Ashley, R. *Using CP/M: A Self Teaching Guide*. New York: Wiley, 1980.

Friedman, Jehosua. *Fortran IV—A Self Teaching Guide*. New York: John Wiley & Sons, Inc., 1975.

Geller, D. & Freedman, D. *Structured Programming in APL*. Englewood Cliffs, New Jersey: Winthrop Publishing Co., 1976.

Harms, Edward and Zabinski, Michael P. *Introduction to APL & Computer Programming*. New York: John Wiley & Sons, Inc., 1977.

Heiserman, David L. *Pascal*. Blue Ridge Summit, Pennsylvania: TAB Books, Inc., 1980.

————. *Programming in Basic for Personal Computers*. Englewood Cliffs, New Jersey: Prentice-Hall, Inc., 1978.

Leventhal. Lance. *Sixty-Eight Hundred Assembly Language Programming*. Berkeley. CA: Osborne/McGraw-Hill, Inc., 1978.

Loelinger, Ronald. *Threaded Interpretive Languages*. New York: McGraw-Hill Book Co., 1980.

Moore, Lawrie. *Foundations of Programming with Pascal*. New York: Wiley, 1980.

McKinley, Joe W. *Beginning Fortran*. Columbus, OH: International Scholary Book Services, Inc., 1980.

Nickerson, Robert C. *Fundamentals of Programming in BASIC*. Englewood Cliffs, New Jersey: Winthrop Publishing Co., 1981.

Peckham, Herbert. *Basic: A Hands-On Method*. New York: McGraw-Hill Book Co., 1978.

Popkin, Gary. *Introducing Structured Cobol Programming*. New York: Van Nostrand Reinhold Co., 1980.

Rector, Russell & Alexy, George. *The Eighty Eighty-Six Book*. Berkeley, CA: Osborne/McGraw-Hill, Inc., 1980.

Tracton, Ken. *Programmers Guide to LISP*. Blue Ridge Summit, Pennsylvania: TAB Books, Inc., 1979.

Wegner, P. *Programming with ADA: An Introduction by Means of Graduated Examples*. Englewood Cliffs, New Jersey: Prentice-Hall, Inc., 1980.

Weissman, Clark. *LISP One-Point-Five Primer*. Glendale, California: Dickenson Publishing Co., 1967.

Zaks, Rodnay. *Programming the Six Five Zero Two*. Berkeley, California: Sybex, Inc., 1979.

————. *Programming the Z80*. Berkeley, California: Sybex, Inc., 1979.

————. *Programming the Eighty-Eighty*. Berkeley, California: Sybex, Inc., 1979.

Software Sources

Have you ever needed a copy of a computer language for your computer but didn't know where to find it? Have you written to a supplier only to find out that he was no longer in business? These are common problems in obtaining quality software.

Usually a number of suppliers for a given item are available. Some have established reputations as reliable and stable software vendors. Among these there still may be variations in the product and price. You then have the normal problem of evaluating any prospective purchase.

One major problem is finding a list of suppliers who offer what you need. Advertisements in computer magazines are one source, of course, but they are usually filled with a number of items so that you still must search each one to see if the item you want is offered. The following list partially solves this problem.

To compile the list, I sent questionnaires to 325 software vendors known to be in business as of approximately January, 1980. Nearly one-third of those queried responded.

The inclusion of a supplier in this list does not mean that I endorse the vendor or his products. It merely reflects the fact that he furnished me with information. Those not included did not respond to the questionnaire. No significance should be attached to the fact that a particular vendor is or is not included in this list.

Software and prices change swiftly, so check with each supplier before making a purchase.

These sources are divided into three sections: Assembly Languages; High-Level Languages; Suppliers. To find a source, first determine if you are looking for an assembly language or a high-level language and turn to that section. Then find the particular language that interests you (let's say it's 6800 assembler) and, under that category, the operating system you are using, CP/M for example. After each operating system, you will find a list of vendors who offer the particular language you want for the operating system you are using. You can then find an address and telephone number for each vendor in the Suppliers section. All entries are in alphabetical order to make it easy for you to use the lists.

ASSEMBLY LANGUAGES

1802 Assembler
    CP/M   Allen Ashley
    North Star Dos   Allen Ashley
6502 Assembler
    CP/M   Digital Marketing, Ohio Scientific

CP/M-86	Digital Marketing
DOS 1.1	Computhink
MDOS II	Computhink
OS65D	Ohio Scientific
OS65U	Ohio Scientific
UCSD P-System	Softech Microsystems

6800 Assembler

CP/M	Digital Marketing, Ohio Scientific
CP/M-86	Digital Marketing
OS65D	Ohio Scientific
OS65U	Ohio Scientific
UCSD P-System	Softech Microsystems

68000 Assembler

DOS 1.1	Computhink
MDOS II	Computhink

6809 Assembler

CP/M	Digital Marketing
UCSD P-System	Softech Microsystems

8048 Assembler

CP/M	Allen Ashley
North Star DOS	Allen Ashley

8080 Assembler

CP/M	Digital Marketing, Digital Research
CP/M-86	Digital Marketing
MP/M	Digital Research
UCSD P-System	Softech Microsystems

8085 Assembler

CP/M	Digital Marketing

8086 Assembler

CP/M	Digital Marketing

9900 Assembler

UCSD P-System	Softech Microsystems

COP 400 Assembler

CP/M	Allen Ashley
North Star DOS	Allen Ashley

LSI-11/PDP-11 Assembler

UCSD P-System	Softech Microsystems

MOSTEK 3870 ASSEMBLER

CP/M	Allen Ashley
North Star DOS	Allen Ashley

S2000 ASSEMBLER

CP/M	Allen Ashley
North Star DOS	Allen Ashley

Z-8 ASSEMBLER

CP/M	Allen Ashley
North Star DOS	Allen Ashley
UCSD P-System	Softech Microsystems

Z-80 ASSEMBLER
CP/M	Digital Marketing
CP/M-86	Digital Marketing
UCSD P-System	Softech Microsystems

Z-86 ASSEMBLER
CP/M	Allen Ashley
North Star DOS	Allen Ashley

HIGH-LEVEL LANGUAGES

3D1 Graph

Apple II DOS	Sub Logic

APL

CP/M	Quasar Data Products
MP/M	Quasar Data Products

Apple Pilot

Apple DOS 3.2	Bell and Howell
Apple DOS 3.3	Bell and Howell

Basex

CP/M	Interactive Microware
Heath H-8	Interactive Microware
North Star DOS	Interactive Microware
Poly 88	Interactive Microware
SOL	Interactive Microware
Sorcerer	Interactive Microware
TRSDOS	Interactive Microware

BASIC

86 DOS	Seattle Computer Products
APPLE	Dynacomp Inc.
Apple DOS	Muse Software
Apple DOS 3.2	Bell and Howell
Apple DOS 3.3	Bell and Howell
Apple II	Hayden Book Co.
Applesoft	Andent, Inc.
ATARI	Dynacomp, Inc.
Commodore-PET	Dynacomp, Inc.
Commodore-PET 1.0	Cognitive Products
Commodore-PET 3.0	Cognitive Products
CP/A	Compumax Associates
CP/M	Compumax Associates
CP/M	Computer Pathways, Digital Marketing, Dynacomp Inc., Infosoft Systems Inc., Micro-AP, Microsoft, Ohio Scientific, Quasar Data Products, Tarbell Electronics, Westico, Inc.
CP/M 2.2	PK Systems
CP/M-86	Digital Marketing
DOS 1.1	Computhink
DOS-68	Microware
FAMOS	MVT Micro Systems
FLEX	Microware, Technical Systems Consultants

HDOS 2.0	PK Systems
I/OS	Infosoft Systems Inc.
ISIS-II	Microsoft
LDOS	Allen Gelder
M/OS-80	Infosoft Systems Inc.
MDOS	Software Dynamics
MDOS II	Computhink
Micro B12	Compumax Associates
MP/M	Quasar Data Products
MULTI/OS	Infosoft Systems Inc.
NEWDOS	Allen Gelder
North Star DOS	Allen Ashley, Dynacomp Inc.
NS BASIC Interface	Infosoft Systems Inc.
OS-9	Microware Systems Inc.
OS65D	Ohio Scientific
OS65U	Ohio Scientific
SDOS	Infosoft Systems Inc., Software Dynamics
TEKDOS	Microsoft
TRSDOS	Allen Gelder, Dynacomp Inc., Microsoft
TRSDOS Model I	Racet Computes
TRSDOS Model III	Racet Computes
Uniflex	Technical Systems Consultants
UCSD P-System	Softech Microsystems
UCSD PASCAL	Control Systems

C

(O/S not specified)	Whitesmiths Ltd.
CDOS	Infosoft Systems Inc.
CP/M	Infosoft Systems Inc., Whitesmiths Ltd.
FLEX	Technical Systems Consultants
I/OS	Infosoft Systems Inc.
IDRIS	Whitesmiths Ltd.
M/OS-80	Infosoft Systems Inc.
MULTI/OS	Infosoft Systems Inc.
NS BASIC Interface	Infosoft Systems Inc.
RSX	Whitesmiths Ltd.
RT-11	Whitesmiths Ltd.
RTE IVB	Corporate Computer Sys.
SDOS	Infosoft Systems Inc.
Uniflex	Technical Systems Consultants
UNIX	Whitesmiths Ltd.
VERSADOS	Whitesmiths Ltd.

CBASIC

CP/M	CPU International Inc.

COBOL

(O/S not specified)	Cybernetics Inc.
86-DOS	Seattle Computer Products
BLIS/COBOL	Information Processing

294

CP/M	Cybernetics Inc., Ellis Computing, Microsoft
CP/M	Ohio Scientific, Quasar Data Products, Westico
CP/M 2.2	PK Systems
HDOS 2.0	PK Systems
ISIS-II	Microsoft
M-OASIS	Cybernetics Inc.
MP/M	Quasar Data Products
OASIS	Cybernetics Inc.
OS65D	Ohio Scientific
OS65U	Ohio Scientific
RTE IVB	Corporate Computer Systems
TRS-80 Model II	Microsoft
UNIX	Cybernetics Inc.

DYNAMO

UCSD PASCAL	Pugh-Roberts Assoc.

FORTH

Apple DOS 3.1	Programma International Inc.
Apple DOS 3.2	Programma International Inc.
Apple II	Hayden Book Co., Information Unlimited
Apple II+	Information Unlimited
CP/M	Quasar Data Products
DOS 1.1	Computhink
MDOS II	Computhink
MP/M	Quasar Data Products
TRSDOS	Miller Micro Service

FORTRAN

86 DOS	Seattle Computer
Apple DOS 3.2	Bell and Howell
Apple DOS 3.3	Bell and Howell
CP/M	Microsoft, Ohio Scientific, Quasar Data Products, Westico Inc.
CP/M 2.2	PK Systems
DOS 1.1	Computhink
HDOS 2.0	PK Systems
ISIS-II	Microsoft
MDOS II	Computhink
MP/M	Quasar Data Products
OS65D	Ohio Scientific
OS65U	Ohio Scientific
TEKDOS	Microsoft
TRSDOS	Microsoft
UCSD P/System	Softech Microsystems
UCSD PASCAL	Control Systems

Infinite BASIC

TRSDOS Model I	Racet Computes
TRSDOS Model III	Racet Computes

295

LISP

Apple II	The Soft Warehouse, Microsoft, Quasar
CP/M	Data Products, Thomas W. Yonkman
DOS-68	Microware
FLEX	Microware
MP/M	Quasar Data Products
OS-9	Microware
TRSDOS	The Soft Warehouse

MARK PILOT

Apple DOS 3.2	Bell and Howell
Apple DOS 3.3	Bell and Howell

ML I

DOS 1.1	Computhink
MDOS II	Computhink

PASCAL

(O/S not given)	Whitesmiths Ltd.
86 DOS	Seattle Computer Products, Mt Micro Systems
Apple DOS 3.1	Programma International Inc.
Apple DOS 3.2	Programma International Inc.
Apple DOS 3.2	Bell and Howell
Apple Dos 3.3	Bell and Howell
CP/M	Digital Marketing, Mt Micro Systems, Microsoft, Ohio Scientific, Quasar Data Products, Westico Inc, Whitesmiths Ltd.
CP/M 2.2	PK Systems
CP/M 80	MT Micro Systems
CP/M-86	Digital Marketing, MT Micro Systems
DOS-68	Microware
FLEX	Microware, Technical Systems Cons.
HDOS 2.0	PK Systems
IAS	Oregon Software
IDRIS	Whitesmiths Ltd.
MP/M	Quasar Data Products
OS-9	Microware
OS65D	Ohio Scientific
OS65U	Ohio Scientific
PDP-11	Oregon Software
RSTS/E	Oregon Software
RSX	Oregon Software, Whitesmiths Ltd.
RT-11	Oregon Software, Whitesmiths Ltd.
Uniflex	Technical Systems Cons.
UNIX	Oregon Software, Whitesmiths Ltd.
UCSD P-System	Softech Microsystems
UCSD PASCAL	Control Systems
VERSADOS	Whitesmiths Ltd.

PEARL

CP/M	CPU International Inc., Digital Marketing,
CP/M-86	Digital Marketing

Pilot
    Apple DOS 3.1   Programma International Inc.
    Apple DOS 3.2   Programma International Inc.

PL-I
    CP/M   Digital Research, Westico Inc.
    MP/M   Digital Research

PLS
    DOS 1.1   Computhink
    MDOS II   Computhink

PRISM
    CP/M   Micro Applications Group
    CP/M-86   Micro Applications Group
    MP/M   Micro Applications Group
    ONIX   Micro Applications Group
    TRSDOS   Micro Applications Group

RPG-II
    FAMOS   MVT Micro Systems

SAL
    CDOS   Infosoft Systems Inc.
    CP/M   Infosoft Systems Inc.
    I/OS   Infosoft Systems Inc.
    M/OS-80   Infosoft Systems Inc.
    MULTI/OS   Infosoft Systems Inc.
    SDOS   Infosoft Systems Inc.

SUPER APPLE BASIC
    Apple II   Hayden Book Co.

SUPPLIERS

Allen Ashley
395 Sierra Madre Villa
Pasadena, CA 91107
(213) 793-5748

Allen Gelder
P.O. Box 11721
Main Post Office
San Francisco, CA 94101
(415) 387-3131

Andent Inc.
1000 North Avenue
Waukeegan, IL 60085

Bell and Howell
7100 North McCormick Road
Chicago, Il 60645
(312) 673-3300

Cognitive Products
Box 2592
Chapel Hill, NC 27514

Computhink
965 West Maude
Sunneyvale, CA 94086
(408) 245-4033

Compumax Associates
505 Hamilton Avenue
Palo Alto, CA 94301
(415) 321-2881

Corporate Computer Systems
675 Line Road
Aberdeen, NJ 07747
(201) 584-4422

CPU International Inc.
Box 12892
Salem, OR 97309

Cybernetics Inc.
8041 Newman Avenue
Huntington Beach, CA 92647
(714) 848-1922

Digital Marketing
2670 Cherry Lane
Walnut Creek, CA 94596
(415) 938-2880

Digital Research
Box 579
Pacific Grove, CA 93950
(408) 649-3896

Dynacomp, Inc.
1427 Monroe Avenue
Rochester, NY 14618

Ellis Computing
600 41st Avenue
San Francisco, CA 94121

Hayden Book Co.
50 Essex Street
Rochelle Park, NJ 07662
(201) 843-0550

Information Unlimited
281 Arlington Avenue
Berkley, CA 94707

Infosoft Systems Inc.
25 Sylvan Road South
Westport, CT 06880
(203) 226-8937

Interactive Microware
Box 771
State College, PA 16801
(814) 238-8294

Micro-AP
7033 Village Parkway
Dublin, CA 94566

Micro Applications Group
7300 Caldus Avenue
Van Nuys, CA 91406

Microsoft Consumer Products
400 108TH Avenue NW,
Suite 200
Bellevue, WA 98004
(206) 454-1315

Microware
5835 Grand Avenue
Des Moines, IA 50304
(515) 279-8844

Miller Microcomputer Services
61 Lake Shore Road
Natick, MA 01760
(617) 653-6136

MT Microsystems
1562 Kings Cross Drive
Cardiff, CA 92007

Muse Software
330 North Charles Street
Baltimore, MD 21201
(301) 659-7212

MVT Micro Systems
9241 Reseda Boulevard
Northridge, CA 91324
(213) 349-9076

Ohio Scientific
1333 South Chillicothe Road
Aurora, OH 44202

Oregon Software
2340 Southwest Canyon Road
Portland, OR 97201

PK Systems Inc. (Zenith)
113 North Center
Bloomington, IL 61701

Programma International Inc.
2908 North Naomi Street
Burbank, CA 91504

Pugh-Roberts Associates
5 Lee Street
Cambridge, MA 02139
(617) 864-8880

Quasar Data Products
10330 Brecksville Road
Brecksville, OH 44141
(216) 526-0838

Racet Computes
702 Palmdale
Orange, CA 92665
(714) 637-5016

Seattle Computer Products
1114 Industry Drive
Seattle, WA 98188
(206) 575-1830

Softech Microsystems
9494 Black Mountain Road
San Diego, CA 92126
(714) 578-6105

Software Dynamics
2111 West Crescent
Anaheim, CA 92804
(714) 635-4760

The Soft Warehouse
Box 11174
Honolulu, HI 96826
(808) 734-5801

Sub Logic
Box V
Savoy, IL 61874
(217) 359-8482

Technical Systems Consultants
Box 2570
West Lafayette, IN 47906
(317) 463-2502

Westico Inc.
25 Van Zant Street
Norwalk, CT 06855

Whitesmiths Ltd.
Box 1132 Ansonia Station
New York, NY 10023
(212) 799-1200

Thomas W. Yonkman
4182 Caminto Islay
San Diego, CA 92122

Index